Gender-Based Violence

Edited by Geraldine Terry with Joanna Hoare

Oxfam

First published by Oxfam GB in 2007

This edition © Oxfam GB 2007

The original source for each item in this book is provided at the end of each chapter. Original copyright information is on the Acknowledgements page (vi) which is part of the copyright notice for this book.

ISBN 978-0-85598-602-5

A catalogue record for this publication is available from the British Library.

Available from:

Bournemouth English Book Centre, PO Box 1496, Parkstone, Dorset, BH12 3YD, UK tel: +44 (0)1202 712933; fax: +44 (0)1202 712930; email: oxfam@bebc.co.uk

USA: Stylus Publishing LLC, PO Box 605, Herndon, VA 20172-0605, USA tel: +1 (0)703 661 1581; fax: +1 (0)703 661 1547; email: styluspub@aol.com

For details of local agents and representatives in other countries, consult our website: www.oxfam.org.uk/publications or contact Oxfam Publishing, Oxfam House, John Smith Drive, Cowley, Oxford, OX4 2JY, UK tel +44 (0) 1865 472255; fax (0) 1865 472393; email: publish@oxfam.org.uk

Our website contains a fully searchable database of all our titles, and facilities for secure online ordering.

Published by Oxfam GB, Oxfam House, John Smith Drive, Cowley, Oxford, OX4 2JY, UK

Printed by Information Press, Eynsham.
Inners printed on recycled paper made from 100% post-consumer waste.
Cover printed on FSC accredited 75% recycled paper.

Oxfam GB is a registered charity, no. 202 918, and is a member of Oxfam International.

Working in Gender and Development

The *Working in Gender and Development* book series brings together themed selections of the best articles from the journal *Gender & Development* and other Oxfam publications, repackaged in book form to reach a wide audience of development practitioners and policy makers, and students and academics. Titles in this series present the theory and practice of gender-oriented development in a way that records experience, describes good practice, and shares information about resources. As such, they will contribute to and review current thinking on the gender dimensions of particular development and relief issues.

Forthcoming titles include:
    HIV and AIDS
    South Asia

Acknowledgements

All materials in this book other than those listed below are copyright © Oxfam GB 2007. The following items, which have been previously published as indicated, are copyrighted as shown.

'Negotiating violence and non-violence in Cambodian marriages' (pages 56–69) by Rebecca Surtees, first published in *Gender & Development* Volume 11, Number 2, July 2003, copyright © Oxfam GB 2003.

'Social policy from the bottom up: abandoning FGC in sub-Saharan Africa' (pages 70–85 by Peter Easton, Karen Monkman, and Rebecca Miles, first published in *Development in Practice* Volume 13, Number 5, November 2003, copyright © Oxfam GB 2003.

'Reducing poverty and upholding human rights: a pragmatic approach' (pages 133–140) by Meena Poudel and Ines Smyth, first published in *Gender & Development* Volume 10, Number 1, March 2002, copyright © Oxfam GB 2002.

'A tale of two cities: shifting the paradigm of anti-trafficking programmes' (pages 141–153) by Smarajit Jana, Nandinee Bandyopadhyay, Mrinal Kanti Dutta, and Amitrajit Saha, first published in *Gender & Development* Volume 10, Number 1, March 2002, copyright © Oxfam GB 2002

Contents

List of Contributors

Nandinee Bandyopadhyay is Associate Director for PATH, India, looking after PATH's HIV programmes in India.

Susan Bird is the Regional Director of Oxfam America for Central America, Mexico, and the Caribbean, based in El Salvador. She holds a master's degree in Intercultural Management and Sustainable Development.

Sarah Chynoweth is the Reproductive Health Program Manager at the Women's Commission for Refugee Women and Children. She works to improve the lives and defend the rights of refugee and internally displaced women, children, and youth and works to ensure that their voices are heard from the community level to the highest councils of governments and international organisations.

Rutilio Delgado is the Coordinator of the Cooperative Games and Education for Peace Program, and member of the Masculinities Team of Centro Bartolomé de las Casas.

Mrinal Kanti Dutta is Programme Director at Durbar.

Peter Easton is Associate Professor in the Graduate Program in Socio-Cultural and International Development Education at Florida State University. He has worked for many years in adult and community education in Africa and in the evaluation of development programmes.

Chitra Gopalakrishnan is a development consultant who assists with all the communication initiatives of the 'We Can' campaign.

Ceri Hayes is Senior Programmes & Policy Manager at WOMANKIND Worldwide. WOMANKIND Worldwide is a UK-based international women's human rights and development organisation, established in 1989, which works with partner organisations around the world to promote women's rights and tackle gender inequality.

Joanna Hoare was Acting Editor on *Gender & Development* journal between July 2006 and June 2007. She has an MSc in Gender and Development from the London School of Economics and Political Science, and has a particular interest in issues around gender, citizenship, and conflict in the former Soviet Union.

Sara Humphreys is a visiting lecturer at the University of Sussex, UK. Previously, she has worked in Botswana, Ecuador, and Namibia as a teacher and teacher educator. Her research interests are in gender and school processes and qualitative research methods.

Kaori Izumi is the HIV and Rural Development Officer at the Food and Agriculture Organisation (FAO), Rome. Her work includes research, programming, and policy advice on the issues of land reform, land tenure, HIV and AIDS, and women's and children's property rights and livelihoods. She is a member of the Global Coalition on AIDS and Women established by UNAIDS and partners, under which FAO and the International Centre for Research on Women co-convened the Global Coalition on AIDS and Women's Property Rights.

Smarajit Jana is currently working as an adviser to National AIDS Control Programme in India and is the Chief Adviser for Durbar.

Jackie Kirk is a specialist in education in emergencies and reconstruction, with a particular focus on gender and teachers. She works part-time as an adviser to the International Rescue Committee and is a research associate/consultant with the McGill Centre for Research and Teaching on Women, working on a number of research, writing, and other projects related to gender, education, conflict, and peacebuilding. Jackie convenes the Gender Task Team of the Inter-Agency Network for Education in Emergencies.

Fiona Leach is senior lecturer in international education at the University of Sussex, UK. She has worked in the field of education and development for many years, and before becoming an academic was a teacher and education adviser in Africa. She has carried out several studies on gender violence in African schools. She is the author of *Practising Gender Analysis in Education* (Oxfam 2003).

Mandy Macdonald is an independent research and editorial consultant specialising in gender issues, and a member of the Management Committee of the Central America Women's Network (CAWN).

Larry Madrigal is the Director of Centro Bartolomé de las Casas and co-facilitator and researcher, in the Masculinities Programme, specialising in religion and gender. He has a master's degree in theology and is a holistic therapist.

Mona Mehta is Oxfam GB's Global Adviser on violence against women. She is based in Delhi.

Rebecca Miles is Associate Professor in the Department of Urban and Regional Planning and the Center for Demography and Population Health at Florida State University. Her interests include the effects of the social environment on health and safety, and gender planning for development and health.

Karen Monkman is Associate Professor in the Educational Policy Studies and Research Department at DePaul University. Her interests include non-formal education, gender and empowerment, and grassroots social change.

John Bayron Ochoa is a Development Worker for Gender and Masculinities of the Progressio Programme El Salvador. He is a social worker and a master's degree candidate in social research.

Erin Patrick is a consultant with the Women's Commission for Refugee Women and Children where she works exclusively on firewood collection and sexual violence in displaced settings. She is the author of *Beyond Firewood: Fuel alternatives and protection strategies for displaced women and girls* (Women's Commission for Refugee Women and Children 2006).

Julieanne Porter was the Acting Assistant *Editor for Gender & Development* journal between February 2006 and September 2007. She has a BA (Hons) in History and Women's Studies from La Trobe University, Melbourne, and is an active campaigner on development issues.

Meena Poudel is a Nepalese sociologist, currently researching experiences of trafficked women for her PhD at the School of Sociology, Newcastle University.

Marina Prieto-Carrón is a lecturer/researcher at the University of Bristol and a member of the Management Committee of the Central America Women's Network (CAWN).

Amitrajit Saha is Associate Director for PATH, India, looking after PATH's Sexual and Reproductive Health programmes in India.

Ines Smyth is a Global Gender Adviser at Oxfam GB, currently on sabbatical as a Gender Specialist at the Asian Development Bank, Manila until early 2008.

Rebecca Surtees is an anthropologist and researcher at the Nexus Institute in Vienna. She has experience both as a researcher and in the implementation of development programmes in South-East Europe, West Africa, and South-East Asia. This has included working on gender issues and human rights with the United Nations in East Timor and Kosovo, with NGOs and international organisations in Canada, Indonesia, and South-East Europe, and as a researcher in Cambodia, West Africa, and South-East Europe. Her main areas of research have included human trafficking, prostitution, gender-based violence, and development issues.

Walberto Tejeda is the Co-ordinator and Researcher of the Masculinities Programme of Centro Bartolomé de las Casas. He holds a degree in philosophy and is a holistic therapist. His field of research is intersectionality of methodologies and integrated development.

Marilyn Thomson is an independent gender consultant and visiting fellow at City University and a member of the Management Committee of the Central America Women's Network (CAWN).

Introduction

Geraldine Terry

Overview

This collection of articles on gender-based violence (GBV) is aimed at development and humanitarian practitioners, policy makers, and academics. This readership includes gender specialists, non-gender specialists who are nevertheless interested in how GBV impinges on their work, and academics and graduate students concerned with GBV as a rights and development issue. Most of the articles originally appeared in the journal *Gender & Development*. The exception is the article by Easton *et al.*, which first appeared in the journal *Development and Practice*.

This book brings together some of the most interesting and innovative work being done to tackle GBV in various sectors, world regions, and socio-political contexts. Although most of the articles are concerned with development rather than humanitarian settings, two of them (the first by Chynoweth and Patrick, the second by Kirk), look at post-conflict situations. Taken as a whole, the articles cover a wide range of manifestations of GBV. These include femicide or the murder of women because they are women, domestic and sexual violence, female genital mutilation or cutting (FGM/FGC), the sexual exploitation of girls at school, and trafficking for prostitution. The localities covered are in South and East Asia, sub-Saharan Africa, and Central America.

The book begins with Ceri Hayes' useful overview of various anti-GBV interventions being implemented by women's organisations supported by UK-based WOMANKIND Worldwide. Chapters 2–4 document manifest-ations of gender-based violence occurring in specific contexts that have not up to now received sufficient attention: property grabbing in Southern and East Africa; femicide in Central America; and sexual attacks on women and girls during firewood collection outside displaced people's camps. These chapters also provide examples of how women's organisations, government bodies, and development aid agencies are responding.

Chapters 5–8 present specific anti-GBV initiatives designed to reduce violence against women and girls in diverse development situations:

tackling domestic violence in Cambodia; community initiatives to end FGM/FGC in West Africa; working with men in El Salvador; and an ambitious regional campaign to end violence against women in South Asia.

In Chapter 9 Fiona Leach and Sara Humphreys argue for an understanding of GBV that goes beyond violence against women, taking as their focus sexual harassment and violence in schools in the global South. Their chapter is complemented by Kirk's exposition in Chapter 10 of a specific strategy designed to prevent the sexual exploitation of girls at school: the employment of female Classroom Assistants in humanitarian camps in West Africa.

Chapters 11 and 12 are both concerned with responses to the trafficking of women in South Asia, but present different perspectives. Poudel and Smyth are concerned in Chapter 11 with the denial of human rights which they see as intrinsic to trafficking; they provide an overview of how one international NGO, Oxfam, understands and responds to the phenomenon. In Chapter 12 Jana *et al.* focus on the agency of individual trafficked women.

Type the words 'gender-based violence' into an Internet search engine, and you will bring up a plethora of policy papers and other documents from United Nations (UN) agencies, multilateral and bilateral aid organisations, and NGOs working in development, as well as women's organisations. This wealth of material testifies to the achievement of women's human-rights activists in getting the issue recognised by the international development community, in particular during the 1990s. Thanks to them, GBV is now acknowledged as a critical human-rights and development issue, as well as a serious public-health concern.

However, as many of the UN documents themselves make clear, GBV is still woven into the texture of millions of women's daily lives, all over the world. In many countries, there is little or no political will to address manifestations of GBV despite, or perhaps because of, its prevalence. Deep-seated and pervasive attitudes that condone or encourage GBV constitute another, linked, factor that perpetuates indifference and inaction. These obstacles to change are mentioned in many of the chapters here. Several point out the necessity of working on both national, political levels and on personal levels in order to end the GBV pandemic.

Definitions

The terms GBV and violence against women (VAW) are often interchanged, but they are not synonymous. The Declaration on the Elimination of Violence against Women (1993), defines VAW as a sub-category of GBV: 'Any act of gender-based violence that results in, or is likely to result in, physical, sexual or psychological harm or suffering to women, including threats of such acts, coercion or arbitrary deprivations of liberty, whether occurring in public or private life'.[1] So, as well as VAW, GBV encompasses, for instance, male violence against gay men, the involvement of women in the phenomenon of property grabbing (see Chapter 2), and harsh beatings of male pupils by male teachers, also mentioned in this volume as a 'performance of aggressive masculinity' (see Chapter 9).

There are problems with the term GBV, both in itself and in the way it is used by the international development community. As Leach and Humphreys point out, it implies that there are some types of violence that are *not* rooted in gendered power relations, whereas they argue that all violence is, in fact, gendered. They go so far as to call for a reconsideration of the 'female victim/male villain' dichotomy. While it is necessary to be precise in the way terms are used, and avoid a short-hand elision of 'GBV' and 'VAW', it is also important not to obscure the reality that, as Hayes points out in her article, women and girls constitute the vast majority of GBV victims, and men the majority of perpetrators. Other objections to the term GBV are that it means little to non-gender specialists and that it is a dry, technical term for a phenomenon that violates basic human rights, causing vast pain, suffering, and humiliation. Apart from Chapter 9, all the chapters focus on VAW rather than other aspects of GBV. However, the term GBV is used throughout, in keeping with common practice.

Forms of GBV

GBV occurs in all societies and at all stages of a woman's life-cycle. For instance, it can occur before a girl is even born, as with sex-selective abortion in northern India, and continue to menace women in old age, as with elder abuse in industrialised countries and so-called 'witch-hunts' in some rural areas in India. Some types of GBV, for instance sexual violence and domestic violence, occur in all cultures, although they are more common in some societies than in others, and are also differentiated by the extent to which societies punish or condone them. Other manifestations, such as dowry murder, are specific to particular cultures. Some forms change or die out over time. The harmful traditional practice of binding of Chinese women's feet has long been a thing of the past, while a new form of violence, property grabbing, seems to have risen up recently, or at least increased in frequency, in Southern and East Africa, linked to the HIV and AIDS epidemic (Chapter 2). Within the same location and time-period, women may experience GBV in different ways, depending on: their income and who controls it; social status; occupation; ethnicity; religion; and sexuality.

Because of its nature, GBV is hard to research; it is often enacted away from the public eye, and women who experience it may be afraid to speak out, or may accept it as a 'normal' part of life. Considering its apparent scale, there have been relatively few studies that attempt to measure the prevalence of different types of GBV in societies. One of the most authoritative recent studies, by the World Health Organization, concerns physical and sexual violence against women by their male 'intimate partners'. Researchers spoke to over 24,000 women at 15 sites in 10 countries. Depending on the location, between 15–71 per cent of the women interviewed said they had experienced this type of violence, which indicates that the problem is widespread.[2] However, this is only one of the types of GBV that women experience.

During violent conflicts, women and men experience violence in different ways, because of their gender. During recent conflicts in Bosnia, Liberia, the Democratic Republic of Congo, northern Uganda, Burundi, Darfur in Sudan, and elsewhere, rape has been used systematically as a weapon of war. In humanitarian contexts, such as displaced people's camps, women and girls are especially vulnerable to GBV. For instance, a recent survey found that at least six out of ten women in northern Uganda's largest camp for displaced people had been sexually and physically assaulted, threatened, and humiliated by men in the camp.[3] In non-conflict emergencies, such as after the 2004 tsunami, women are also vulnerable to GBV and coercion. For instance, Oxfam partner organisations noticed high levels of domestic violence in post-tsunami camps in Sri Lanka. Because more women than men were killed by the tsunami in some affected areas, there is now a gender imbalance within some of the affected populations, with anecdotal evidence that young women are being coerced into marriages with older men whose wives were drowned.[4]

A human-rights, public-health, and development issue

GBV arises from and maintains power imbalances between women and men, both as groups and as individuals. Some men use violence to compel or constrain women at personal, household, community, and state levels, and as a tactic during armed conflicts. Since the international community 'named' VAW in the early 1990s, a lot has been written about it as a human-rights violation, a large-scale public-health problem, and a development concern. As well as being an important human-rights violation itself, it also prevents women from realising their other rights, be they economic, social, cultural, civil, and/or political. Chapter 2 on property grabbing presents a good example of how GBV can be used quite deliberately to deny women their economic rights, for instance.

The World Health Organization recognises GBV as an important public-health issue. As well as being a direct cause of injury, ill-health, and death, it affects women's health indirectly too, through unwanted pregnancies and their attendant health risks, mental illness, sexually transmitted diseases, and HIV and AIDS. The HIV and AIDS epidemic in sub-Saharan Africa is closely linked to domestic and sexual violence in the region. Women and girls are particularly vulnerable to HIV and AIDS. This is due not only to their physiology but also to economic, social, and cultural inequalities that place them in a subordinate position *vis-à-vis* men regarding decisions about sexual relations. GBV enforces these inequalities. In Zambia, for example, sexual violence and coercion is an important factor in the high rate of HIV infection among girls and young women (Human Rights Watch 2002).[5]

From an international development viewpoint, GBV threatens the achievement of objectives such as the Millennium Development Goals. Its prevalence is fundamentally at odds with MDG 3: promote gender equality and empower women. With reference to South Asia, Oxfam claims that VAW 'explains the uniformly poor gender-related development indices in crucial sectors like health, nutrition, education, political participation, and employment'.[6] It is a significant cause of individual women's poverty, and poverty in general, in the global South. This is clear if we use UNDP's concept of 'human poverty'; a state where 'opportunities and choices most basic to human development are denied – to lead a long, healthy, creative life and to enjoy a decent standard of living, freedom, dignity, self-respect and the respect of others'.[7] For many women, GBV prevents or undermines all these desirable outcomes. GBV and women's individual material poverty can interact in a vicious circle. At the household level, GBV can constrain women's choices, limit their productivity, and prevent them from bargaining effectively with their husbands or partners, which in turn exacerbates their vulnerability. As for beyond the household, many women find it unsafe to work in the fields, sell food in the market, or carry out any economic activity outside the house, due to the threat of GBV. In his book, *Development as Freedom*, Amartya Sen argues that 'there is nothing more important in the political economy of development than the adequate recognition of women's participation and political, economic, and social leadership'.[8] By limiting women's choices, GBV exerts a powerful drag on positive social change for whole societies. Taking a different, non-instrumental line, Yakin Ertürk, the UN Special Rapporteur, argues that in societies where it is prevalent, GBV is in itself an indicator of blocked development, because it 'can only be sustained within a repressive and unjust cultural, social and political environment.'[9]

Milestones in international agreements

The Declaration on the Elimination of Violence against Women (1993) addresses the abuse of women at home, in the community, and by the state. According to the Declaration, states have a duty to prevent, investigate, and punish acts of violence against women. The Declaration lists three broad types of VAW, including VAW within the family, violence occurring within the general community, and lastly violence perpetrated or condoned by the state, wherever it occurs. The Declaration came after years of campaigning by women's NGOs all over the world. It was, and is, a significant milestone, because it makes it clear that VAW, including domestic violence, is a public human-rights concern. The Beijing Platform for Action was developed two years later, at the Fourth World Conference on Women. It declared that 'governments are now obligated to respond to women's demands to be free from violence, to take steps to prevent violence, and to adopt measures to punish perpetrators when women's human rights are violated' (Beijing Platform for Action 1995).[10]

Other agreements and developments in international jurisprudence have addressed GBV in conflict and humanitarian contexts. For instance, UN Security Council Resolution 1325 (2000) spells out what needs to be done to improve protection of women in conflict zones, as well as ensure their participation in peace-building.[11] Another important recent event was the establishment of the International Criminal Court (ICC) in 2003. The Rome Statute, which legally established the ICC, defined atrocities such as rape during armed conflict as a weapon of war and a gender-based crime for the first time.

Though they may seem very remote from ordinary women's lives, these are all important achievements that should not be taken for granted. In the eyes of many women's human-rights activists, an international legislative and policy framework is the necessary first step in achieving gender justice. However, although it is now over a decade since the Declaration on the Elimination of Violence against Women, huge challenges remain for its consistent and effective implementation. Many states have reneged on their commitments under the Beijing Platform for Action to support women in realising their full range of rights, including their right to be free from GBV. Such a holistic approach would be a powerful strategy for reducing GBV, but it needs firm political will on the part of governments, a major shift in the development paradigm, and a substantial reallocation of public resources.

In the absence of adequate international and governmental responses to GBV, many women's civil-society organisations have had to step in. The type of initiatives they implement can be broadly divided into first, providing services to women and girls who experience GBV, and second, carrying out activities designed to prevent or reduce GBV. Service provision includes shelters, counselling, and legal advice. Prevention and reduction strategies include calling on governments to put suitable legislation in place, or strengthen existing national legislation; and raising people's awareness of, and changing their attitudes to, GBV – for instance through public education campaigns. Many women's NGOs use a holistic analysis and a multi-dimensional approach, assisting women to realise their full range of rights, in particular economic rights, as a way of reducing their vulnerability.

There are also a few men's NGOs trying to tackle GBV, in particular domestic and sexual violence. Their strategy is usually one of raising men's awareness of GBV as a social justice issue, and encouraging them to question their own attitudes and behaviour. Probably the best-known example is the White Ribbon Campaign, a Canadian public education campaign which has spread to several other countries. Chapter 7 describes a community-level project that works with men in El Salvador, using experiential methods to reflect on the dominant cultural model of *machismo* and how it has influenced their own lives and relationships.

Themes arising from the articles

Political will, legislation, and attitude change

Governments and institutions such as aid agencies often lack the will to address GBV, even where laws, codes of practice and so on are in place. This is because it is tied up with gendered power relations that are deeply entrenched in cultures. Most of the work described in this volume has been carried out against a backdrop of official indifference to, failure to act against, or even collusion in, GBV. For instance, Chynoweth and Patrick write in Chapter 4 that the vulnerability of women in displaced people's camps has long been recognised, but even so the humanitarian community has not adequately addressed it. In Chapter 3 Prieto-Carrón *et al.* argue that governmental institutions in Central America, such as the courts and police, have created an enabling environment for the large-scale murder of women by ignoring GBV or even colluding with the perpetrators. Chapters 11 and 12 on trafficking in South Asia indict official rescue and rehabilitation processes for coercing women and denying them choices, and show how corrupt police and immigration officials are themselves involved in violating trafficked women's rights, including the right to be free from GBV.

This lack of political and institutional will to end GBV is sustained by public attitudes. In many societies, GBV is seen as part and parcel of life, and there is little or no pressure on governments to address it. For instance, in Chapter 7 on working with men, Bird *et al.* point out that, in Central America, most people do not see GBV as a serious problem, despite its high prevalence and the particular shocking phenomenon of femicide in the region (see also Chapter 3). Mehta and Gopalakrishnan describe the 'We Can' campaign in Chapter 8, and take the view that laws, policies, and programmes against GBV, although necessary, will have little impact unless individuals change their attitudes and stand up against GBV. Bird *et al.* echo this in Chapter 7; they maintain that only when individual men start to take responsibility for VAW, find non-violent outlets for their emotions, and regard themselves as change agents, will social transformation follow. Without this, they claim, legislation and criminal justice are unlikely to be effective.

In relation to FGM/FGC, Easton *et al.* take a different view on the matter of legislation in Chapter 6. Rather than arguing that legislation and policies need to go hand in hand with changes in attitudes, they maintain that there is a tension between national legislation and community action against GBV. In fact, they posit legislation and 'community empowerment' as mutually exclusive strategies. This raises the questions: who constitutes the community, and how does 'community empowerment' mesh with the empowerment of individual women? At the same time, the authors state that attention to women's human rights is the best setting for communities choosing to abandon FGM/FGC. Their position on the question of anti-GBV legislation may arise from the specific Senegalese context of the initiatives they document. This is a country with several distinct ethnic groups, not all of whom practise FGM/FGC to the same extent. In such a situation, national legislation against the practice might be seen as an attack on the culture of one particular ethnic group by others, as such to be fiercely resisted. Mehta and Gopalakrishnan (Chapter 8) agree with Easton *et al.* that real and lasting change must come from individuals acting in the context of a supportive social environment, and that community action is crucial. They turn their spotlight on the individual change agents who build that critical mass, and the necessity to transform power relations in order to achieve real impact.

Building on, and challenging, local cultures

Like Easton *et al.*, Surtees (Chapter 5) documents how a rights-based approach to GBV needs to be culturally negotiated at local levels. Both chapters show the importance of invoking, and building on, those aspects of local cultures that support positive change. In the context of Cambodia, Surtees highlights how a women's organisation has adapted the official marriage-reconciliation procedure, creating a new process that safeguards women who experience domestic violence, and gives them the space to choose whether or not to stay in the marriage. However, as both these chapters make clear, there is also a need to challenge prevailing cultural norms. This point comes up again in Kirk's chapter on the strategy of using female Classroom Assistants (CAs) to respond to teachers' sexual exploitation of girl pupils, a problem that is not restricted to humanitarian settings (Chapter 10). The presence of the CAs in schools, and in particular the fact that they are in charge of giving pupils their exam grades, has created a safer learning environment for girls. However, the strategies that the CAs use to protect the girl pupils are socially conservative; according to Kirk, their strictures to girls 'reflect rather than challenge prevailing gender attitudes'. She writes that what is needed is the empowerment of women and girls, so that they feel they have the same rights as boys. On an immediate and practical level, she suggests gender training for teachers and CAs, improving CAs' access to continued education, and creating links between the CAs and women's groups in the community.

Addressing men's involvement

Gender analysis is concerned with the relations between women and men, both as individuals and groups: not women in isolation. Men's roles, responsibilities, attitudes, and behaviour need to be brought into work on GBV, although it is important to note that this has to be done within a political framework, taking account of gendered power relations. Chapter 7 focuses on men's involvement in curbing GBV (Bird *et al.*), and this theme is also touched on by Easton *et al.* (Chapter 6), Chynoweth and Patrick (Chapter 4), and Surtees (Chapter 5). According to Chynoweth and Patrick, 'programmes that do not engage men and boys run the risk of fostering resistance'. Bird *et al.* go further and argue that without working with men, lasting change will be elusive, but they insist that projects that try to raise men's self-awareness must never divert energy and resources from women's empowerment initiatives, advising that men's anti-GBV projects should maintain continuous feedback links with women's organisations as a corrective mechanism.

It is important to avoid the trap of thinking that all men are violent by nature. As Bird *et al.* point out, men are not born violent; the authors point instead to the way culturally dominant ideas and beliefs set out what is acceptable and shape men's behaviour. They see GBV's cultural roots as providing hope, because this means models of masculinity that encourage GBV, such as *machismo* in Central America, can evolve. As children, many men in the region have been victims or witnesses of GBV; they can be forces for change. The awareness in Chapter 4 that some men are GBV survivors resonates with Leach's and Humphreys' observations that some boys suffer GBV in schools (Chapter 9).

On the question of male agency in curbing GBV, Bird *et al.* describe how the *Centro Bartolemé de las Casas* uses two strategies to encourage this: the formation of critical thinking, and leadership development. This may be a useful dichotomy for agencies planning similar initiatives. Much of the 'working with men' literature is based on projects in Central and Latin America. However, similar initiatives from outside that region are mentioned in this volume, such as the activities of the Integrated Tribal Women's Welfare Society, which conducts gender training and counselling for men, and has achieved reduced violence against women (see Chapter 1).

Supporting individual women's agency

Several of the contributors to this collection are concerned with the issue of supporting the agency of women who experience GBV, rather than regarding these women as 'victims'. This comes across very clearly in Chapter 12 (Jana *et al.*). The authors argue that women are trafficked in the first place due to a combination of individual choices, and that trafficked women must participate in efforts to prevent it and mitigate its negative impacts. Surtees, in her analysis of the work of the Cambodian Women's

Crisis Centre, shows how the organisation enables women to exercise choice in their response to domestic violence. Easton *et al.* (Chapter 6) show how a small group of villagers, mainly women, started a community movement against FGM/FGC, and how an individual female 'cutter' took the challenge to neighbouring villages. On a bigger scale, the 'We Can' campaign has set out to involve 5 million women and men as 'Change Makers'. Chapter 8 (Mehta and Gopalakrishnan) shows how the Change Makers, many of whom have themselves experienced GBV, are taking action in their own households and communities, by talking to people, sending postcards to friends, lobbying village councils, and so on. They hope that such a 'people to people' approach will build a critical mass for change throughout South Asia, and help to reduce alarmingly high levels of GBV.

A holistic framework implies a multi-dimensional approach

As well as interventions that directly and specifically address GBV, there is a need for a holistic approach using multi-dimensional strategies that address the root causes of women's vulnerability, as well as its impact. Indeed, many GBV specialists would argue that this is the only approach that can bring about a significant and sustainable impact. As Hayes points out in Chapter 1, women's ability to live free from violence is linked to their economic rights. She mentions the Kembatta Women's Self-Help Centre, which is providing vocational training, credit and income-generation schemes to help women affected by forced marriage and FGM/FGC to become economically self-reliant. In Chapter 4 on reducing women's vulnerability to GBV during firewood collection, Chynoweth and Patrick also discuss the importance of creating an enabling economic environment. Displaced women need to be able to work in order to generate some income, so allowing them to do this, and creating opportunities for them to generate income, is just as important as measures that address GBV more directly, such as patrolling firewood collection areas. Income-generation projects, as well as helping women to become less vulnerable to GBV, can also function as entry-points for addressing it. This is useful because, by its nature, GBV is often difficult to raise head-on, and such projects can create safe spaces for women. For instance, Hayes mentions the knitting workshops run by Peruvian NGO DEMUS, which allowed women, for the first time, to discuss their experiences of sexual violence during the civil war there, as well as making goods to sell.

In relation to trafficking, Jana *et al.* (Chapter 12) point out that many poor South Asian women are vulnerable partly because they lack labour rights and are deprived of education and information. Using the example of relief to flood victims in Bangladesh, Poudel and Smyth briefly indicate how anti-GBV measures can be integrated into assistance during emergencies. The programme they mention included measures to prevent the trafficking of adolescent girls by raising awareness of the risks involved, as well as helping to meet households' economic needs.

The diversity of the chapters here attests to the myriad forms and contexts of GBV, its pervasiveness, and the many creative ways that women, and men, are challenging it in development and humanitarian contexts. Despite their dissimilarities, generic patterns and causal factors emerge. The chapters should help development practitioners and policy makers in several ways. First, they situate anti-GBV interventions in a broad analytical framework, which understands GBV as a phenomenon that both arises from and perpetuates gender inequalities. Second, they provide examples of successful strategies and activities which, while not completely transferable, can be adapted and tested elsewhere. Third, they alert mainstream development and humanitarian practitioners whose objectives do not focus on GBV to the ways it may be impacting on the women and girls they are assisting, so that they can take this into account in their planning and implementation. Finally, the resources section at the end of this book presents a valuable selection of reports, publications, and organisational websites that can be drawn on to promote enhanced understanding of GBV, and the sharing of experiences.

Notes

1   http://www.un.org/documents/ga/res/48/a48r104.htm.

2   World Health Organization (2005) *Multi-country Study on Women's Health and Domestic Violence against Women,* available at: http://www.who.int/gender/violence/who_multicountry_study/summary_report/en/index.html.

3   *Uganda: Rape Rampant in Largest Northern IDP Camp,* Reuters Foundation, 17 June 2005, available at: http://www.alertnet.org/thenews/newsdesk.

4   Oxfam (2005) *The Tsunami's Impact on Women,* available at: http://www.oxfam.org.uk/what_we_do/issues/conflict_disasters/bn_tsunami_women.htm?searchterm=women+tsunami.

5   Human Rights Watch (2002) *Suffering in Silence: The Links between Human Rights Abuses and HIV Transmission to Girls in Zambia,* available at: http://www.hrw.org/reports/2003/zambia>/.

6   Oxfam International (2004) 'Towards Ending Violence against Women in South Asia', Oxfam Briefing Paper No. 66, p 1.

7   United Nations Development Programme (1997) *Human Development Report,* New York: Oxford University Press, p 15.

8   A. Sen (1999) *Development as Freedom,* Oxford: Oxford University Press, p 103.

9   United Nations Economic and Social Council Commission on Human Rights (2003) *Towards an effective implementation of international norms to end violence against women,* paragraph 57.

10   http://www.un.org/womenwatch/daw/beijing/platform/plat1.htm.

11   http://www.un.org/events/res_1325e.pdf.

1 Tackling violence against women: a worldwide approach

Ceri Hayes

Introduction

The impact of violence against women (VAW) is now well-documented. It denies women their most basic human rights, such as the right to health, and is a major threat to the social and economic development of communities and whole countries. In development terms, it directly endangers the achievement of the Millennium Development Goals related to gender equality and women's empowerment, poverty reduction, infant and maternal health and mortality, educational attainment, and combating HIV and AIDS.

But despite recognition within the development community of the urgent need to tackle violence against women, millions of women around the world continue to suffer violence in the home and in the community, with devastating physical, emotional, and psychological effects.[1]

Advocates for women's rights have campaigned hard over the years to bring the issue of violence against women to the world's attention. As a result of their efforts, a number of states have taken significant steps at the national level towards the eradication of violence against women. However, these steps have primarily focused on improving laws relating to violence against women. Far less has been done to enforce legislation and to tackle the underlying causes of the problem – the imbalance of power between women and men and the way in which gender roles are articulated at all levels of society.

This chapter discusses some of the strategies WOMANKIND Worldwide and its partner organisations have used to tackle violence against women, within a broader framework of challenging inequality and unequal power relations between women and men.

WOMANKIND's approach

WOMANKIND (WK) works in partnership with organisations around the world to tackle violence against women through a range of initiatives and interventions, from prevention work in schools in the UK to integrated community responses challenging the practice of female genital mutilation in Ethiopia.

Our work recognises that violence is a universal phenomenon, but that women in general, and some distinct groups of women, may be particularly vulnerable to violence, such as women living in poverty, widows, indigenous women, disabled women, women in detention, women in situations of armed conflict, and women living in rural or remote communities.

Our focus is on tackling violence against *women*, since we recognise that while men and boys may be the target of gender-based violence and women may also be the perpetrators of gender-based violence, women constitute the vast majority of victims of gender-based violence and men the majority of perpetrators. However, our work is also based on an understanding that women and men must work together and involve the wider community in order to bring about lasting change in the attitudes and behaviours which perpetuate all forms of gender-based violence.

The principles and standards set out in international human-rights instruments, in particular the UN Convention for the Elimination of Discrimination against Women (CEDAW) and the Beijing Platform for Action (BPFA) provide a global framework for this work that cuts across cultural, religious, and national limitations. But at the same time, partners are careful to adopt a culturally sensitive approach to ensure interventions are 'owned' by the local community, thus contributing to their sustainability.

This chapter reflects on the lessons learnt from our work around the world and highlights the challenges and opportunities posed by the multiple strategies WK and its partners are employing to tackle different forms of violence against women in a range of contexts.

Using a rights lens

As an organisation working to promote women's rights and gender equality, in addition to fighting poverty, WK is particularly interested in the intersection between violence against women and other women's human rights. In our experience, a rights-based analysis can help to provide an understanding of the often complex linkages between women's experience of violence and the denial of their social, economic, political, and legal rights. By highlighting the indivisibility and interconnected nature of the full spectrum of women's human rights as set out in international human-rights treaties, we are able to look at all the factors impacting on women's lives and to respond accordingly.

For instance, many of WOMANKIND's programmes to tackle violence against women are complemented by work to challenge women's exclusion from public life and increase their participation in decision-making processes at all levels. This has been shown to decrease their vulnerability to violence by helping them find support and solutions to the problem, such as legal protection, counselling, and advice. More broadly, it also helps women to challenge existing power structures, and enables them to have more of a say in the laws, policies, institutions, and structures which govern their lives.

Women's ability to live lives free of violence may also be constrained by the denial of their *economic* rights in the same way that lack of economic empowerment may make them more susceptible to violence. Thus, a number of our partners working to tackle VAW are also implementing women's economic empowerment programmes, using these as an entry point to wider community outreach work. Where they lack the capacity to implement these programmes, they work closely with other organisations that have this as their focus to ensure the women have access to a range of services.

In Ethiopia, for instance, the Kembatta Women's Self-Help Centre[2] complements its services for women affected by female genial mutilation (FGM) and early and forced marriage by providing vocational training and credit and income-generating schemes to enable women to become economically self-sufficient. Their work also focuses on environmental restoration and land productivity to promote sustainable livelihoods.

A rights lens is also helpful when addressing the intersection between HIV and AIDS and VAW. HIV and AIDS has worsened the context in which the social and economic marginalisation of women and the assertion of some dominant forms of masculinity combine to make women increasingly subject to oppressive social structures and violence, yet this dimension of the pandemic is often ignored. International human-rights instruments, such as CEDAW and the International Covenant on Economic, Social & Cultural Rights contain useful provisions which are relevant to the protection of women's rights in the context of preventing and responding to HIV and AIDS, such as ending discrimination against women in the field of health care and eliminating harmful stereotypes and practices, which may compound women's vulnerability to HIV infection.

The Musasa project in Zimbabwe[3] works to better understand the link between VAW and HIV and AIDS and to respond with appropriate services. By encouraging organisations working on HIV and AIDS to adopt a gendered analysis to their work, they are working to promote an under-standing of the linkage between HIV and AIDS and VAW. For instance, Musasa has developed HIV and gender-based violence policies for hard-to-reach groups like Zimbabwe's closed and male-dominated four-million-strong Apostolic Church. While HIV and AIDS health and protection issues are easily understood, Musasa ensures that this is underpinned by strong messages about a women's right to live free from violence and sexual abuse.

Education and prevention

Public awareness-raising campaigns and education initiatives in schools are increasingly being used to challenge the stereotypical perceptions of male and female sexuality and status that underlie gender-specific discrimination and violence. However, it is clear that most interventions still have a focus on responding to the effects of violence against women, rather than tackling its root causes. A number of WOMANKIND's partners have chosen to adopt a more holistic approach to tackling VAW.

In Zimbabwe, the Musasa project began by offering shelter, counselling, and legal services to survivors of domestic violence, but soon realised that it also needed to combine this work with awareness-raising and prevention initiatives if it was to bring about lasting change. To date, much of its prevention work has focused on young people in tertiary education. This has involved training young women and men to act as peer educators who can in turn educate their peers to resolve conflict in relationships in non-violent ways. The organisation is now working with the Ministry of Education to introduce discussion of domestic and gender-based violence into the school curriculum to reach primary and secondary school children and young people. An ongoing challenge that the organisation faces in the delivery of this work is ensuring that a gendered understanding of violence and domestic violence remains a core part of all training materials and delivery.

In the UK, WOMANKIND's *Challenging Violence, Changing Lives* programme for secondary school students and their teachers has developed a number of tools to raise awareness and transform the attitudes of young people to stop violence against women, including lesson plans, a Stop Sexual Bullying campaign and an interactive website called *Respect4Us*.[4] However, it has proved an uphill struggle to get prevention work onto the education agenda, because there is a perception that the UK has 'done' gender equality; other equalities issues such as disability and sexual orientation are now seen as more pressing.

WK has also joined forces with a number of other UK women's rights organisations to demand that the government devise and implement an integrated, cross-departmental VAW strategy. The End Violence against Women Coalition Campaign (EVAWCC),[5] which was launched in November 2005, calls for a comprehensive and integrated approach to tackling VAW and greater awareness-raising of the true levels of VAW and its impact on individuals, families, and communities.

Working with men and boys

Our experience shows that it is important to ensure that most components of work to tackle violence against women are firmly rooted in women's experiences and building the capacity of women, but that men and boys are also key actors in efforts to tackle the problem. There is now recognition that beyond the issue of direct physical or emotional violence there is the need for all men to 'speak out' against violence, and for women and men to work together to challenge existing definitions of masculinity that provide the foundation for violence.

In the UK, WK's schools work has benefited enormously from the input, experience, and support of Michael Kaufman, one of the originators of the Canadian White Ribbon Campaign,[6] which has become a global expression of support for women living with men's violence. We have adopted and adapted the campaign for use in schools in England and Wales, shifting away from the Canadian focus on men speaking out about men's violence against women to a UK focus on men and women speaking about all forms of violence against women. This has enabled the organisation to address areas where women are also the perpetrators of violence against other women – from areas such as forced marriage to sexual bullying and name calling. This approach also ensures that we are not handing over responsibility for violence against women to men to solve, which could reinforce stereotypes that portray women as hapless victims. Rather we see the issue as one to be tackled jointly.

This is a view shared by our partners. In India, WK's partner the Integrated Tribal Women's Welfare Society (ITWWS) works with Irula communities in Chennai who are on the bottom rung of the caste system, to tackle violence against women and increase their participation in *panchayats*, the lowest level of local-government structures. ITWWS recognises that the prevailing patriarchal social system in India is largely to blame for problems of domestic violence in the community and is also one of the biggest obstacles to women's participation in politics.

For this reason, they have made counselling sessions and gender-training programmes for men an integral part of their programme in order to create the space for men to talk about the problems and pressures they face and to help them change their behaviour and approach to relationships. The impact of the work has been measured by the reduction in the levels of violence towards women; men increasingly encouraging their wives to participate in community groups and local politics; and improved attitudes towards girl children.

Integrated community approaches

Many of the programmes WOMANKIND supports function on multiple levels and with a range of different actors. Co-ordination between these different actors is extremely important. There are a number of examples of 'best practice' in this area, but it is clear that much more needs to be done to encourage a more integrated approach between different stakeholders if interventions to tackle violence against women are to succeed.

The Gender Advocacy Programme (GAP) in South Africa[7] has established a Domestic Violence Task Team as part of its work to tackle domestic violence in the Saldanha Bay municipality of the Western Cape. When the project was established in 2004, its first campaign posters were torn down overnight, such was the sensitivity surrounding this issue in the community. But in just two years, the project team has built strong relationships with government departments and service providers including schools, health-care workers, and the police, NGOs, community-based organisations (CBOs), and community members to improve services and treatment for survivors of domestic violence. A key achievement has been the establishment of a Protocol detailing the quality and scope of services that survivors of domestic violence should be able to access throughout the reporting process. This was drafted jointly by a range of service providers, and members of four community initiatives providing support to survivors. The reluctance of health workers to report or testify in domestic violence cases remains a key challenge. Many of the health workers have themselves experienced violent relationships, so GAP is now working to support them individually, which will in turn, it is hoped, improve their professional responses.

In Ghana, the Nkyinkyim project[8] has a strong focus on working with traditional and religious leaders and engaging the whole community in its efforts to tackle the pervasive problem of domestic violence. The project, which was developed in response to country-wide research indicating a high prevalence of domestic violence, has adopted a unique response to the problem in rural areas where women's access to services such as legal support and health care can be very limited. Partner organisations support the community to establish COMBATS or Community-Based Action Teams, which are responsible for raising awareness about the issue of domestic violence, as well as working with traditional and religious leaders to establish a system of locally appropriate sanctions, such as public 'naming and shaming,' against perpetrators.

The support provided by the COMBATS has helped to overcome women's reluctance to report incidences of violence to state agencies for fear of shaming their village. Their voluntary status also allows individual cases to be resolved without any cost implication for the woman. This approach has fostered a sense of 'ownership' of the project among the whole community that has resulted in not only the incidence of violence against women decreasing, but also a reduction in other types of intra-familial violence.

Culturally appropriate responses

Given that power relations which subordinate women may manifest themselves in very different ways depending on the context, it is clear that a one-size-fits-all approach to tackling VAW is unlikely to succeed.

This is a particularly important factor to consider when tackling violence against women in conflict or post-conflict situations, where the influence of different dimensions of gender, class, and ethnic discrimination and their intersection may be even more complex. Other factors such as the historical context of the conflict, the complicity of state and non-state actors in acts of violence and displacement, and the impunity of the justice system all need to be taken into account when designing responses and interventions. As a result, countries emerging from conflict have seen the growth of a variety of locally specific, alternative, and often informal approaches to tackling the legacy and ongoing incidence of violence.

WOMANKIND's partner in Peru, DEMUS (Estudio para la Defensa y los derechos de la Mujer)[9] has become a pioneer in facilitating the recovery and rehabilitation of rape victims, through its recent pilot project in the remote region of Manta. This project uses innovative and sensitive techniques to explore the causes and impact of sexual violence against women before, during, and after the civil war. In the rural indigenous community of Manta, there was no tradition or concept of counselling as it is understood in the North, so DEMUS organised knitting workshops for the women that allowed them, on the one hand, to make goods to sell and bring in an income, but also served as a pretext for getting the women together to talk and start coming to terms with the past.

Cultural norms and traditions are also an important consideration when tailoring interventions. In Afghanistan strict societal codes are invoked in the name of tradition and religion to justify the denial of women's most basic human rights. Levels of violence against women are extremely high and more than eight out of ten acts of VAW are committed by a male family member such as a husband, father-in-law, son, or cousin (UNIFEM 2006).

In this context, WOMANKIND's partner, the Afghan Women's Education Centre (AWEC)[10] is slowly working to overcome resistance to women's rights by integrating training on the role of human rights within Islam into their work. By exploring different teachings of the Koran they are able to counter harmful interpretations and demonstrate that the promotion of women's rights can be a positive force for change, rather than a concept that is at odds with Islam. They also meet regularly with the principal decision-makers in the community, such as the district officers, elders, and Mullahs to create trust and increase acceptance of their work. After initial resistance, this approach has started to yield results, with women and men observing reduced levels of violence in the last year. Partners report that change has come about because women now feel more supported and they enjoy increased levels of self-esteem and confidence, enabling them to speak out and report incidents of violence to the *shuras*[11] for arbitration.

As these examples demonstrate, types of violence and responses may be regionally or culturally specific, but underlying these differences is a common cause – the perpetuation of women's subordination by men.

For this reason, it can be extremely valuable to share lessons and approaches transnationally. The exchange of knowledge, learning and experience, with our partners and other organisations, has enabled WK to strengthen the impact of our policy work and programmes considerably. For instance, in 2003 we invited partners from Zimbabwe, Ghana, and South Africa to the UK to participate in an exchange with a focus on legislative responses to domestic violence. Their visit was timed to coincide with a UK sector consultation on domestic violence legislation as part of preparations for a national Domestic Violence Bill, and was an important opportunity for the UK sector to learn from the experiences of domestic violence programmes in Africa.

Access to justice

Despite their obligations under international and national laws, states are still failing to protect women and many cases of violence continue to be widely tolerated and go unpunished by authorities. In many countries, the justice system merely perpetuates not only the systemic inequalities between women and men in wider society, but also inequalities with regard to class, ethnicity, and race. A ground-breaking study by WHO in 2006 found that violence against women is worse in Peru than in countries with lower economic development such as Ethiopia, Bangladesh, and Namibia and stated that a corrupt legal system was partly to blame, with just a tiny proportion of those men responsible for sexual violence being sentenced (Garcia-Moreno et al. 2006).

The failure of the justice system to bring perpetrators to justice prompted WK partner organisations DEMUS in Peru and Coordinadora de la Mujer in Bolivia to present cases at a series of national and regional tribunals, organised by a coalition of women's organisations with the aim of highlighting violations of women's economic, social, and cultural rights and exploring whether such cases could be litigated. Most of the cases have involved incidences of violence against women, including forced sterilisation of women, rape, and femicide.[12] The tribunals have provided activists with a platform from which to demand an end to impunity, and their efforts have led to a number of rulings in favour of survivors of violence in national and regional courts.[13]

In many countries where WK works, prevailing social, cultural, and traditional norms often pose an additional barrier to the effective implementation of national and international laws aimed at tackling violence against women. Culture is often used as a defence for the perpetuation of harmful traditional practices such as FGM and early and forced marriages, and women who reject these practices are accused of bringing dishonour to the family and community. They also lose their social and economic status in society, unless they follow what is seen as their socially prescribed role.

WK's partners in Ethiopia, Sudan, Kenya, Somalia, Somaliland, and Egypt are tackling these deeply held beliefs through a combination of formal and informal education that teaches communities about the harmful effects of FGM, at the same time as providing vocational training and income-generating schemes to ensure that rejection of these traditions does not result in financial hardship.

Media and campaigns

Campaigning remains one of the most effective ways of breaking the silence surrounding violence against women, and activists have developed a diverse and often innovative range of approaches for raising awareness of the issue of VAW and for bringing about changes in attitudes, policies, and practices. The International *16 Days of Activism* campaign[14] is an excellent example of the vibrancy of the women's movement and its determination to speak out against VAW and raise visibility of the issue.

Increasingly too, it is not just women who are speaking out. In South Africa, the Gender Advocacy Project's soccer tournament has become an annual event aimed at raising awareness amongst men of the effects of domestic violence on women, children, and the whole community. The event, which draws a big crowd of people, is attended by a variety of local male role models who speak out against domestic violence and challenge men attending the soccer matches to become advocates of non-violence.

Many organisations have also started to incorporate work with the media into their efforts to tackle violence against women, in recognition of its enormous influence on the way our 'gendered' roles, characteristics, and behaviour develop. Rape Crisis Cape Town (RCCT),[15] WK's partner in South Africa, use a 'Speak Out' model to demystify the rape-reporting process – from police, to clinic, to court – and show the positive futures that rape survivors have been able to build for themselves, thus encouraging other women to report their experiences. RCCT has created 'Speak Out' guidelines for journalists on factors to consider when interviewing a survivor of violence. This is already helping to counter media myths and stereotypes around rape in South Africa.

Monitoring and evaluating the impact of interventions

While interventions and responses to violence against women are now wide-ranging and diverse, there is still relatively little factual evidence available to demonstrate the impact of these initiatives. This is in large part due to the fact that tackling violence against women requires changes in values, attitudes, and behavioural norms, which can be difficult to quantify or measure over the short term.

Given that the long-term impact of interventions may not be perceptible within several years (the duration of most grants), many donors have been reluctant to fund this work in the past. It is, of course, understandable that donors want to see concrete outcomes as a result of their funding, but it is important that Northern-based NGOs like WK play a role in advocating for improved funding structures to better support work to tackle violence against women.

Many organisations are also working to address the need to redefine and develop new and alternative evaluation methods. In Peru, our partners have developed a set of Minimum Standards on Violence Against Women, based on a combination of rights set out in national, regional, and international legal instruments, to guide their work and to provide a baseline against which progress can be tracked. The monitoring and implementation of these standards is still at the pilot stage, but it is hoped they will prove extremely useful for monitoring at the local level.

WK has also been devising ways of strengthening the monitoring and evaluation of campaign activities during the 16 Days of Activism. In the past, we have provided small grants to African women's organisations to support their campaign activities during the annual campaign, but we have come to realise many organisations working on VAW have a limited capacity to undertake monitoring and evaluation of the impact of these initiatives.

With this in mind, and based on the findings of research undertaken in 2005, WK is now supporting work to strengthen the monitoring and evaluation of 16 Days campaign activities. The learning from these activities will be disseminated in 2007 to increase knowledge and understanding amongst activists of what makes for a successful campaign to tackle violence against women.

Policy and influencing work

The landmark recognition of violence against women as a human-rights abuse at the 1993 Vienna Conference on Human Rights[16] established unequivocally that states are responsible for the prevention of violence against women and for bringing perpetrators to justice, whether these acts are committed in the private or public arena. Subsequent international and regional declarations and texts have further elaborated the responsibility of states to develop policies and programmes aimed at eradicating violence against women and to provide adequate resources to achieve this aim.

This work has provided women's human-rights activists with a series of standards against which to hold their governments to account and challenge the policies and practices of a range of actors including the UN, regional development bodies, and international financial institutions.

WK and its partners seek to ensure the implementation of these standards in a number of ways. At the international level, we make use of a number of different UN mechanisms to lobby governments to fulfil their promises to eliminate violence against women. For instance, in October 2005, WK and partner organisations made a submission to the UN Secretary-General's Study on All Forms of Violence Against Women, setting out key issues requiring the urgent attention of governments and calling for a global plan to tackle VAW. We have used CEDAW Shadow Reports as an opportunity to highlight government inaction, and examples of best practice for combating and eliminating VAW.[17] And, in September 2005, we joined forces with other women's organisations around the world to urge world leaders meeting at the World Summit to address the omission of VAW from the Millennium Development Goals (MDGs). This action on the part of women's organisations resulted in the expansion of MDG 3 on gender equality and women's empowerment beyond its limited focus on primary education.

At the national and local level, WOMANKIND has been active in the UK End Violence Against Women Coalition Campaign's attempts to influence policy change. This has included the use of a system of grading to measure the performance of different government departments on a range of issues related to VAW. The Coalition's initial 'Making the Grade' report created quite a stir in government circles, and the plan is to publish a new report each year for the life of the campaign, inviting government departments to let us know each year what they have done to improve on the previous year's performance.

Conclusion

Given the scale and complex nature of violence against women, it is very difficult to make a claim that an example of 'best practice' is universally applicable. However, our experience suggests that the prevalence of violence against women can only be reduced through a combination of sustained, strategic, and comprehensive measures to address both the short-term requirements of individual survivors, such as health care and bringing the perpetrators to justice, and the longer-term cultural and attitudinal changes required to challenge the acceptance of violence against women.

Using a human-rights framework can help us to better understand and address the causes and consequences of the problem. It also acts as a reminder that VAW is a pandemic that threatens the fulfilment of government commitments in other areas of human rights and international development and therefore requires all development actors to play their part in finding a solution. This involves states and civil society working together with communities to find local solutions to VAW. It also requires political will and significant increases in the resources available to respond to the pandemic and to support the women's organisations already engaged in tackling this problem.

Acknowledgement

This article is an edited abstract from the new WOMANKIND report 'Tackling Violence against Women...A Worldwide Approach'. For a free copy contact ceri@womankind.org.uk or go to http://www.womankind.org.uk.

References

Garcia-Moreno, C., H. Jansen, M. Ellsberg, L. Heise, and C. Watts (2006) *WHO Multi-Country Study on Women's Health and Domestic Violence Against Women*, New York: WHO.

Sen, P. C. Humphreys, and L. Kelly (2003) 'Violence Against Women in the UK', CEDAW Thematic Shadow Report London: WOMANKIND.

UNFPA (2000) *The State of World Population 2000: Ending Violence Against Women & Girls*, New York: UNFPA.

UNIFEM (2006) *Uncounted & Discounted: A Secondary Data Research Project on Violence Against Women in Afghanistan*, New York: UNIFEM, available at http://afghanistan.unifem.org/PDF_Documents/Uncounted%20_Discounted.pdf (last accessed 2 April 2007).

Notes

1 Around the world, at least one in every three women has been beaten, coerced into sex, or abused in some other way — most often by someone she knows, including by her husband or another male family member (UNFPA 2000).

2 See http://www.womankind.org.uk/ethiopia.html for further information.

3 See http://www.womankind.org.uk/our-partners-zimbabwe.html for further information (last accessed 17 January 2007).

4 See http://www.womankind.org.uk/uk-schools.html (last accessed 17 January 2007).

5 See http://www.womankind.org.uk/uk-schools.html (last accessed 17 January 2007).

6 The White Ribbon campaign is a Canadian campaign devoted to educating men about the effects and consequences of violence against women http://www.whiteribbon.ca (last accessed 17 January 2007).

7 See http://www.gender.co.za/ (last accessed 17 January 2007).

8 See http://www.womankind.org.uk/our-programme-ghana.html (last accessed April 2007).

9 See http://www.demus.org.pe/ (last accessed 17 January 2007).

10 See http://www.awec.info (last accessed 17 January 2007).

11 Informal consultation forums active in discussing and seeking solutions to conflict at the family and local level.

12 Femicide is the mass killing of women because they are women. The term was coined in response to the murders of hundreds of women in the city of Juarez in Mexico.

13 For example, Karen Llontoy, a Peruvian woman, won the right to have an abortion, despite being denied access to the procedure. The ruling was the first of its kind by the UN Human Rights Committee and was a great victory for DEMUS and its partners in Peru.

14 See http://www.cwgl.rutgers.edu/16days/home.html for further information (last accessed 2 April 2007).

15 See http://www.rapecrisis.org.za/ (last accessed 2 April 2007).

16 The World Conference on Human Rights was held in Vienna on 25 June 1993.

17 WOMANKIND produced a CEDAW Thematic Shadow Report on Violence Against Women in the UK in 2003 (Sen *et al.* 2003). In 1998 our partner Masimanyane Women's Support Centre also produced an NGO Shadow Report to CEDAW with a focus on violence against women.

2 Gender-based violence and property grabbing in Africa: a denial of women's liberty and security

Kaori Izumi[1]

Introduction

Defining gender-based violence

Gender-based violence refers to violence that targets individuals or groups on the basis of their gender. The United Nations' Office of the High Commissioner for Human Rights' Committee on the Elimination of Discrimination against Women defines gender-based violence against women as 'violence that is directed against a woman because she is a woman or that affects women disproportionately', in its General Recommendation 19. This includes acts that inflict physical, mental or sexual harm or suffering, the threat of such acts, coercion, and other deprivations of liberty (UN Office for Coordination of Humanitarian Affairs 2004).

Gender-based violence against women goes beyond immediate physical damage to the victim. Psychological damage, and the threat of further violence, erodes a woman's self-esteem, inhibiting her ability to defend herself or take action against her abuser. It also represents a violation of her human rights, as detailed in the Universal Declaration of Human Rights (1948), which at article 3 states: 'Everyone has the right to life, liberty and security of person', and at article 5 reads, 'No one shall be subjected to torture or to cruel, inhuman or degrading treatment or punishment.'

Property grabbing as a form of gender-based violence

Property grabbing, whereby an individual is forcibly evicted from her home by other family members, traditional leaders or neighbours, and is often unable to take her possessions with her, is occurring today throughout Southern and East Africa. Although property grabbing occurs in many different forms, empirical evidence collected demonstrates that it is affecting women disproportionately, with many women being forced from their homes on the death of their husbands, and having to move from rural areas to urban slums and informal settlements in cities.[2] As such, it represents a form of gender-based violence in itself, as well as often being accompanied by other acts of extreme violence against women, including physical abuse, harassment, and intimidation, in violation of women's human rights. Customary law and practices governing women's inheritance and property rights, women's vulnerable socio-economic and political status, gendered power relations, and the new dimension brought in by HIV and AIDS, are further weakening the property rights of women who are already vulnerable.

It is also important to note that while property grabbing constitutes gender-based violence against women, this does not mean that perpetrators are always men. For instance in matrilineal societies in the northern part of Namibia and in Zambia, sisters-in-law are said to be the main perpetrators, although in the event, it may be male relatives who physically remove property from widows and force them out of their homes (Izumi 2003).[3] As the NGO Women and Law in Southern Africa in Zambia put it 'today's grabber is tomorrow's victim'.

Since 2000 I have travelled extensively in Southern and East Africa and met many women and children who have lost land, property, and livelihoods. Most of them were HIV positive widows, but others included married or divorced women who had escaped domestic violence, and girls engaging in sex work in order to raise school fees for their younger siblings. Their properties had been taken by their close relatives, by brothers and parents-in-law, uncles and aunts, grandparents. What struck me was not only the brutality of their experiences of being evicted and losing their property, and the destitution that had followed, but also the resilience of these women and children, who were determined to struggle for their survival with dignity, providing support to other women and children in similar situations. The meetings with these women and children motivated me to organise national and regional workshops in South Africa, Zimbabwe, Namibia, and Zambia, where some of them told their stories. As a result of these journeys and workshops, several reports and books have been published in the hope that the issue of HIV and AIDS and women's property rights will be taken up by aid agencies as an emergency that requires urgent interventions.[4] These women's stories also form the basis of this article.

HIV and AIDS and property grabbing

According to the 2004 United Nations Programme on HIV/AIDS (UNAIDS) Global Report, in sub-Saharan Africa at the end of 2003, 25 million people were estimated to be living with HIV, and a further 12.1 million children had been orphaned after losing their parents to AIDS-related illnesses. AIDS is a disease that creates orphans and widows, and it is anticipated that more land and property disputes will occur between wives of polygamous husbands, between widows or orphans and family members of the deceased, between siblings, and between widows and their children, as more men die of HIV and AIDS-related illnesses.

The nature of HIV and AIDS as a disease often puts women whose husbands have died of AIDS-related illnesses in a vulnerable situation in terms of negotiation over inheritance, due to the stigma attached to the disease. Husbands often accuse their wives of infecting them, although often it is women who are infected by their husbands, many of whom become infected as a result of extramarital sexual relations. In fact, married women are far more vulnerable to infection than unmarried women, given the lack of control that they often have over sexual contact and the use of contraception. After the husband's death, his family may continue to blame the widow for his illness and death. And even where there is no evidence that a husband has died of an AIDS-related illness, his relatives may still accuse the widow of being HIV positive, and use this as justification to evict her and take her property.

In addition to the stigma associated with the disease, women who have lost their husbands to AIDS-related diseases are vulnerable for other reasons. Economically, many widows have often exhausted their financial resources by the time their husbands die, in order to pay hospital fees and funeral costs. And as many widows who lose their husbands to AIDS-related diseases are HIV positive themselves, their own health has often started to deteriorate by the time their husbands die. So when widows do manage to challenge property grabbing in the courts, relatives may deliberately delay court cases in the hope that the HIV positive widow will die of an AIDS-related disease before the judge reaches a decision. The stigma attached to HIV and AIDS means that other members of a widow's social network who in 'normal' circumstances would have defended and supported her will not do so, for fear of being seen to help a 'witch' who has killed her husband.

Thus, stigma, poverty, deteriorating health, lack of support, physical and mental harassment, and humiliation by in-laws all together put pressure on widows who are already in a situation of extreme distress, sometimes leading to premature deaths.

Women's property rights: the erosion of customary norms and practice

Many of the women affected by property grabbing are themselves sick and impoverished, and their land and possessions may amount to little more than a tiny shack or cooking pot. But evidence suggests that the family members carrying out property grabbing are often wealthy. In Zimbabwe for instance, in 80 per cent of all the property-grabbing cases brought to the office of the Master of the High Court, those trying to evict women from their homes are middle-class, relatively wealthy family members who already own their own properties.[5] This implies that poverty alone cannot explain why property grabbing occurs. Some argue that family support systems and customary practices that used to provide social safety nets for widows and orphans have gradually weakened. They cite as reasons the larger social, economic, and political developments that have occurred as countries in this region have become more urbanised and industrialised, and more focused on nuclear families and individual economic advancement (Rose forthcoming).

Women in Southern and East Africa have never enjoyed the same statutory rights to property as men, but under customary laws and practices they have had limited rights to use and benefit from property belonging to their male family members. For instance, while a widow had no formal inheritance rights, she could remain in her family homestead, and continue farming and grazing livestock after her husband's death for the remainder of her life, in her capacity as guardian of their children. Widows could also depend on the protection of their sons, once they grew up. But these practices have gradually been eroded, and increasing numbers of widows are facing evictions and property grabbing after their husbands die.

The problem is significantly affecting young widows who do not have children, and who are likely to form new relationships with other men when their husbands die. These young widows are often forced to return to their natal homes, while older widows are in a stronger position to stay in the marital home because of their well-established social networks and relations (Aliber *et al.* 2004). Widows without sons also tend to be more vulnerable to eviction and dispossession, compared with those who do have male children.

Statutory legal reform — is it the answer?

Rural women largely depend on customary law and practice for their inheritance and property rights. Where statutory laws regarding property rights do exist, some wealthy women living in urban areas have been able to acquire property in their own right. But in cases like these, women enjoying independent property rights are often considered by men to be a threat to social stability. Along with control of women's sexuality and economic activities, control over women's right to own property is an important aspect of male dominance over women in this context.

Legal reform does not necessarily improve the situation if there are no enforcement mechanisms, and if legal assistance and support services are not affordable or accessible for women (Englert forthcoming). For instance, in Zambia the Intestate Successsion Act of 1989 (Government of Zambia 1989)[6] gave surviving spouses the right to inherit 20 per cent of their husband's or wife's property on their death. However, a group of widows in Monze district commented that their children were dying as a result of this law, as angry relatives of their late husbands were using witchcraft to harm them.[7] This confirms the complexity of the issue, and the sensitivities surrounding it, which cannot be resolved simply by legal reform.

Moreover, HIV positive widows sometimes refrain from reporting cases of property grabbing to the police because of the stigma of their HIV positive status. They may also be wary of damaging relations with the in-laws who have taken their property, for fear that after they have died, the in-laws will then not be prepared to look after their children (Izumi 2006b).

Empirical evidence

Interviews conducted between 2001 and 2006 with women who have been victims of property grabbing, and discussions with groups providing support to them, confirmed that property grabbing and forced evictions from marital homes is a new form of gendered violence against women, denying them their human rights to access to shelter, livelihoods, and property, and most fundamentally a life with self-esteem as a human being.[8] In this section, some individual cases of property grabbing from women are presented. They come from a collection of testimonies published in *Reclaiming our lives – HIV and AIDS, women's land and property rights and livelihoods in Southern and East Africa* (Izumi 2006a).

Cecilia Gunda, Zimbabwe

Cecilia Gunda, a 57-year-old widow, died on 30 December 2005 after being stabbed by her stepson at the home she had shared with her husband. Her murder followed a High Court judgement making her the rightful heir to the matrimonial home. Her stepson was arrested and remanded in prison, but was recently released on bail, pending trial (Izumi 2006c).

Marvis Hadziucheri, Zimbabwe

Marvis Hadziucheri had been married for 28 years when her husband died in 2004. After the funeral, his relatives came to her village. They exhumed his grave, demolished her house and burned her granary, taking all the harvested grain from the farm, as well as the livestock and farming tools. Marvis was left with the clothes she wore. She took the case to the High Court and won, but her husband's relatives went on to appeal the case (Izumi 2006a). Marvis is still awaiting the outcome of the appeal.

Theresa Chilala, Zambia

Theresa Chilala is a 78-year-old widow. After her husband's funeral in 1990, one of her brothers-in-law collected everything from her house, including the oxen, ploughs, household goods, over 30 cows, and iron-roofing sheets. Another brother-in-law then wanted her to marry him and when she refused, he began to bury dead relatives in front of her house, to try and force her from her land. The first grave was dug in 1994. Theresa took the case to the land tribunal, but lost, and was ordered to pay 50 million kwacha (equivalent to $12,000 at the time of the interview in 2005) to the brother-in-law. However, he continued to bury dead relatives on the land. In total, 17 graves had been dug by the time the last burial was made on 6 June 2005 (Izumi 2006a; 2006c; FAOSAFR 2005). In 2006 the Royal Foundation of Zambia, an organisation of chiefs, intervened and held a meeting with all the parties, at which the brother-in-law promised not to dig any further graves.

Edvina Kyoheirwe, Uganda

When Edvina Kyoheirwe's husband was diagnosed HIV positive, he blamed Edvina and became violent towards her, threatening to kill her. She was forced to close her successful business and farm, and fled the marital home with her youngest son to escape further violence. She now lives as a squatter in Kampala, and has formed a small group of women living with HIV, all of whom had been evicted from their rural homes when their husband died of AIDS-related illnesses (Izumi 2006a; FAOSAFR 2005).

Flavia Kyomukama, Uganda

Flavia Kyomukama is HIV positive. Deteriorating health meant she was forced to stop working, at which point her husband began to abuse her physically and verbally. He then decided to divorce her. The couple had accumulated considerable family property, but she lost everything, right down to her school certificates. Her husband also took the children, and would not let Flavia contact them. She went to court to try and get custody of the children, but ended up abandoning the case as the stress that it was causing her was making her health even worse. Some years later, her 14-year-old son fell sick and tested HIV positive. He then moved to his mother's house, and refused to return to his father. Flavia's husband recently sued Flavia, blaming her for not sending their son to school in the period when he was ill (Izumi 2006a; FAOSAFR 2005).

Anna Ndonge, Kenya

Anna's husband died of an AIDS-related disease. When she also fell ill, Anna was abandoned by her mother-in-law without food and care for two weeks. Her mother came from Mathare slum in Nairobi to pick her up, but her husband's relatives would not let them take anything away with them, not even clothes for Anna and her children. Anna worked as a home-based carer in Mathare until her death in March 2004 (Izumi 2006a).

Alice Karoki, Kenya

Alice Karoki's husband died of an AIDS-related illness in 1999, and Alice also tested HIV positive. Her husband's family took possession of the house they owned in Nyanza, a rural area of Kenya, and removed possessions from the home where they lived in Mathare slum. Each time Alice tried to start a new life from scratch, her deceased husband's family followed her and took her property. She sought help from an assistant chief, who was then murdered. Some of her husband's relatives were arrested in connection with the crime, and in the course of the investigation it was revealed that the assistant chief was handling several cases of property grabbing from widows in the community. Eventually, Alice made contact with the Mathare Home Based Care Group, who provided her with the material and psychosocial support that she needed to be able to start a new life with her two children. Today, she is a co-ordinator of the HIV and AIDS Support Group of Mathare Home Based Care Group, which provides care and support to HIV- and AIDS-affected people in the community (Izumi 2006a).

Responses to property grabbing

Despite the lack of legal support and formal protection, many women who have been victims of property grabbing are standing up for their rights, with support from groups at the community level. The judiciary and police are also responding with new initiatives to support the fight against property grabbing. In this section, I present some of the inspiring initiatives undertaken by individual women, local communities, and the police.

A woman fights back — Beatrice Wanjiru Muguiyi, Kenya

Beatrice Wanjiru Muguiyi lost her son to an AIDS-related illness. Her husband told her that he had lost his only heir and had been left with five prostitutes, meaning his wife and four daughters. Beatrice and her four daughters were evicted from their home, and her husband married another woman who had four grown-up sons and two daughters. Beatrice took the case to court, but made little progress. So she decided to take things into her own hands. On 8 July 2005 she returned to the home she had shared with her husband, and where he was now living with his second wife and stepchildren, and refused to leave again. She made it clear to her husband that the home was rightfully hers and she had come back. Eventually, he relented, and she got her home back (Izumi 2006a).

Community Watch Dog — GrootsKenya

As a part of Women Land Link Africa project (WLLA), GrootsKenya (a grassroots NGO engaged in community development) initiated a Community Watch Dog project to document cases of property grabbing, and to sensitise communities on women's property rights during their visits to rural areas.[9] In one case, the group successfully negotiated with relatives who had evicted an HIV positive widow, managed to secure a plot of land for her, and mobilised the community to build her a shelter. They also provided support to a local chief who was helping victims of property grabbing, and facilitated peer-learning among other local chiefs.

Negotiating land with chiefs for HIV positive women's groups — SWAPOL, Swaziland

Swazi Positive Living (SWAPOL) was established in 2001 by five HIV positive women, who had faced hostility from their in-laws as a result of their HIV status. The group's aim is to sensitise families and communities about issues relating to HIV and AIDS. In Swaziland women are legally considered to be minors, who do not have the right to own property. As a result of this, many of SWAPOL's members were evicted from marital homes and lost their property when their husbands died. In 2001, SWAPOL began negotiating with chiefs for a piece of land for their group members to grow food. After long negotiations, a female chief who was herself looking after an orphaned child eventually agreed to provide some land for SWAPOL members to use; she then persuaded chiefs from other areas to allocate land to be used by SWAPOL.

Today SWAPOL has 13 farming plots where women grow maize and vegetables. Some of their produce is used to feed orphans in their communities at neighbouring care points, where orphans and other vulnerable children receive meals twice a day (Izumi 2006a).

The Victim Support Unit — Zambia

The Victim Support Unit (VSU) was established in Zambia in 1994 during the Zambia Police Service Reform Programme. The Police Amendment Act No. 14 legalised the VSU and empowered the Unit to intervene to recover grabbed property. In recent years, the VSU has had some success, with 228 convictions out of 734 reported cases in 2003 (up from 57 out of 909 reported cases in 2001). Although there are many more cases that go unreported, this nevertheless represents significant progress. A challenge facing the unit is to strengthen their capacity with improved financial and technical expertise (Izumi 2006a; FAOSAFR 2005).

Memory Book project

Memory Book is a simple means of keeping families and their assets together, assuring surviving relatives of sustainable livelihoods in the future. The project teaches parenting and communication skills, talks about the process of disclosing HIV status by parents to children, and children to parents, helps families prepare for eventual separation in the event of death, and explores ways for parents and children to handle death when it comes. It also helps families plan for the future. This includes writing wills to secure the children's property rights. It is a simple way of showing family and children the facts about their property before parents die, and of helping to protect children from property grabbing (Izumi 2006a).

Conclusion

In Southern and East Africa today, property grabbing has become a major form of gender-based violence in the context of HIV and AIDS. Property grabbing denies women their rights to decent shelter, livelihoods, and lives with self-esteem. In some cases, women have literally lost their lives defending their right to property. By contrast, owning their own property, and being secure in the knowledge that their right to that property cannot be challenged, gives women security, peace of mind, independence, and freedom. It gives women the power to control and to be in charge of their own lives.

The section above detailed some local responses to property grabbing, but what should be done at the national, regional, and international levels to protect women from property grabbing, and to stop relatives forcibly taking property from women?

Property grabbing should be criminalised with enforceable punishments, and this should be accompanied by large-scale public campaigns to raise awareness of the issue, and to inform people that it is an illegal act. The judiciary and police need to be trained on international standards, conventions on women's rights, and the third Millennium Development Goal, which promotes gender equality and the empowerment of women. More financial resources and technical expertise should be directed to the judiciary and police, to allow them to intervene more effectively in cases of property grabbing. Information about inheritance and property rights should be included in the school curriculum so that children are educated on these rights at a younger age (Izumi 2006d). Community sensitisation is important, especially of key actors such as local chiefs, as chiefs are often the first to hear about cases of property grabbing. But most importantly, women themselves should be made aware of their rights and how to defend them. For this to happen, affordable and accessible legal and police support systems should be established.

Two positive recent developments have been the inclusion of articles relating to the right of women to own property and housing, and to inherit property, in the Revised Draft Outcome Document of the High Level Plenary Meeting of the United Nations' General Assembly of September 2005,[10] and in the Protocol to the African Charter on Human and People's Rights on the Rights of Women in Africa,[11] which came into force in November 2006.

Para 58 of the Revised Draft Outcome Document states:

> *the full and effective implementation of the Beijing Declaration and Platform for Action is essential to achieving the internationally agreed development goals, including those contained in the Millennium Declaration; and to promote gender equality and to eliminate pervasive gender discrimination (among others) by;*

*Guaranteeing the right of women to property, housing and inheritance laws
and ensuring secure tenure of property and housing to women;*

*Ensuring equal access to women to productive assets and resources,
including land, credit and technology;*

Meanwhile, article 20 of the Protocol to the African Charter on Human and
People's Rights on the Rights of Women in Africa protects widows' human
rights, and article 21 enshrines the right of women to inherit property
(African Commission on Human and Peoples' Rights 2003).

Despite the devastation that they have faced, there is resilience among
the survivors of property grabbing, and there are inspiring initiatives by
support groups which are trying to assist these women. There is a need to
break the vicious cycle of poverty, HIV and AIDS, and property grabbing, if
women and their children are to be able to live with peace of mind.
Although property grabbing has gained attention from aid agencies,
effective responses have generally not been forthcoming. The time has come
for donors, national governments, NGOs, and UN agencies to give their
commitment and immediate action to end property grabbing, so that
women and children can live free from worry.

This article was originally published in Gender & Development, *volume 15,
number 1, March 2007.*

References

African Commission on Human and Peoples' Rights (2003) 'Protocol to the African
Charter on Human and Peoples' Rights on the Rights of Women in Africa', available
at http://www.achpr.org/english/_info/women_en.html (last accessed 30 March
2007).

Aliber, Michael, Cherryl Walker, Mumbi Machera, Paul Kamau, Charles Omondi
and Karuti Kanyinga (2004) *The Impact of HIV/AIDS on Land Rights – Case Studies
from Kenya*, Cape Town: HSRC Press.

Englert, Birgit, Elizabeth Daley (eds.) (forthcoming) *Women's Rights to Land in
Eastern Africa in the Era of Privatization*, Oxford: James Currey (under review).

FAO Sub-Regional Office for Southern and East Africa (FAOSAFR) (2005) 'Property
and a Piece of Land Give Women Peace of Mind – Report on National Workshop on
HIV and AIDS, Women's Property Rights and Livelihoods in Zimbabwe', Harare:
FAOSAFR, 1–2 December 2004.

Government of Zambia (1989) 'Intestate Succession Act 1989' (No. 5 of 1989), 14 May
1989, available at http://www.ncbi.nlm.nih.gov/entrez/query.fcgi?cmd=Retrieve
&db=PubMed&list_uids=12344543&dopt=Abstract (last accessed 30 March 2007).

Izumi, K. (2003) 'Property Stripping in Namibia', Harare: FAO.

Izumi, K. (ed.) (2006a) *Reclaiming our Lives – HIV and AIDS, Women's Land and
Property Rights and Livelihoods in Southern and East Africa – Narratives and Responses*,
Cape Town: HSRC Press.

Izumi, K. (ed.) (2006b) *The Land and Property Rights of Women and Orphans in the Context of HIV and AIDS – Case Studies from Zimbabwe*, Cape Town: HSRC Press.

Izumi, K. (ed.) (2006c) 'Report of the National Conference: Women's Property Rights and Livelihoods in the Context of HIV and AIDS', report prepared for the FAO Sub-Regional Office for Southern and East Africa, Lusaka, Zambia, 25–27 January 2006.

Izumi, K. (ed.) (2006d) 'Report of the Regional Workshop on HIV and AIDS and Children's Property Rights and Livelihoods in Southern and East Africa', report prepared for FAOSAFR (7–8 March).

Rose, L. (2006) *Children's Property Rights and Inheritance Rights and their Livelihoods: The Context of HIV and AIDS in Southern and East Africa*, Livelihood Support Programme (LSP), FAO, Rome.

Universal Declaration of Human Rights (1948) available at http://www.un.org/Overview/rights.html (last accessed 30 March 2007).

UN Office for Coordination of Humanitarian Affairs (2004) 'Our Bodies – Their Battle Ground: Gender-based Violence in Conflict Zones' – IRIN Web Special on violence against women and girls during and after conflict. Definitions of sexual and gender-based violence, available at http://www.irinnews.org/webspecials/ gbv/print/p-Definitions.asp (last accessed 30 March 2007).

Notes

1 Disclaimer: The article does not necessarily represent the views of the Food and Agriculture Organisation of the United Nations (FAO) and the author is solely responsible for all views expressed in this article. The author would like to thank Robin Palmer, Oxfam GB, for his comments on earlier drafts of this article.

2 For instance, there are many women who live in Mathare, the second biggest slum in Nairobi with a population of slightly less than one million people, not because they were born or married in Mathare, but because they have been forced out of their marital homes in rural areas (Esther Mwauru-Muiru, Co-ordinator of GrootsKenya, quoted in Izumi 2006a, 21).

3 This is partly explained by the practice of the matrilineal inheritance system, in which children inherit property from their mother's brother.

4 A joint regional workshop on women's land rights was organised by FAO and Oxfam GB in Pretoria in 2003, and national workshops were held in Zimbabwe in 2004, in Namibia in 2005, and in Zambia in 2006. A regional workshop on HIV and AIDS and children's property rights and livelihoods was also held in 2006. For more information, please see:
http://www.oxfam.org.uk/what_we_do/issues/livelihoods/landrights/ downloads/eBook_reclaiming_our_lives.pdf (accessed 27 November 2006).

http://www.oxfam.org.uk/what_we_do/issues/livelihoods/landrights/ downloads/eBook_land_&_property_rights_of_women_&_orphans_in_ zimbabwe.pdf (accessed 27 November 2006).

http://www.oxfam.org.uk/what_we_do/issues/livelihoods/landrights/ downloads/namibia_womens_land.doc (accessed 27 November 2006).

http://www.oxfam.org.uk/what_we_do/issues/livelihoods/landrights/downloads/zimbabwe_workshop_report_hivaids_womens_property_rights_and_livelihoods.pdf (accessed 27 November 2006).

5 Personal communication with Master of High Court in Zimbabwe, Mr Nyatanga, 2005.

6 'Part 1, number 2, states that this Act applies only to those to whom customary law would have applied if the Act were not in existence and that the Act has no bearing on land held under customary law, family property, or chieftainship property. Part 1, number 3, defines the various terms used in the Act. Intestate succession rights are laid out in Part 2 and hold that the property of the deceased is to be divided with 20% assigned to surviving spouse(s) (distributed according to duration of marriage and other factors); 20% to the parents of the deceased; 50% to the children to be distributed proportionately and according to educational needs; and 10% to other dependents in equal shares. The law makes provisions for the distribution of the various shares if there are no survivors in that category. If no spouse, children, parents, or dependents survive, the estate is distributed to near relatives. If there are no near relatives, the estates devolved upon the state. In the case of a monogamous marriage, a surviving spouse or child shall receive equally and absolutely the personal chattels of the intestate. If the estate contains a house, the surviving spouse(s) and child(ren) shall receive title to that house as tenants in common. The surviving spouse(s) shall have a life interest in the house until the spouse remarries. Widows and children are entitled to the homestead property of the intestate and equal shares in the common property of the intestate. If the estate does not exceed a designated amount, the entire estate will devolve upon the surviving spouse or child or both or if there is no spouse or child, upon the parents. The court may appoint an administrator of the estate and guardians of minors' (Government of Zambia 1989).

7 Communication with a widows' group in Monze, July 2004.

8 Interviews with individual women took place in Kenya, Uganda, Zambia, Zimbabwe, and Namibia. I also spoke to women NGO leaders from Rwanda, South Africa, Swaziland, and Tanzania.

9 WLLA is a joint project initiated by the Centre on Housing Rights and Evictions (COHRE), Huairou Commission, FAO, and the United Nations Human Settlement Programme in 2005 with the objective of linking grassroots women with NGOs, community-based groups, academia, and donors who are supporting women's secure land, property, and housing rights http://www.wllaweb.org (accessed 27 November 2006).

10 Draft resolution referred to the High-level Plenary Meting of the General Assembly by the General Assembly at its fifty-ninth session, 2005 World Summit Outcome, adopted on 16 September 2005, United Nations.

11 For a list of countries that have ratified the Protocol, please see http://www.africaunion.org/root/au/Documents/Treaties/List/Protocol%20on%20the%20Rights%20of%20Women.pdf (last checked by the author 4 October 2006).

3 No more killings! Women respond to femicides in Central America

Marina Prieto-Carrón, Marilyn Thomson,
and Mandy Macdonald

Introduction

The first cases of what has become known in Mexico and Central America as femicide (*femicidio* or *feminicidio* in Spanish)[1] emerged in 1993 in Ciudad Juárez on the Mexico–US border, when reports began to appear in the media of the discovery of the mutilated bodies of raped and murdered women on waste ground outside the city (Garwood 2002; Ertürk 2005). Femicide is now reaching alarming proportions across Central America (Clulow 2005; Thomson 2006). In Guatemala, for example, over 2,200 women have been reported murdered since 2001 (Amnesty International USA 2006). In fact, feminist researchers carrying out a regional study to compare trends in the different countries have found that in Guatemala, El Salvador, Honduras, Nicaragua, and Costa Rica, taken together, at least 1000 women die each year as a result of femicide or other forms of gender-based violence (Puntos de Encuentro 2006).

Mexican and Central American women's organisations use *femicidio* as a legal and political term to refer to the murder of women killed *because they are women*. This is not a new phenomenon, but it is one which has seen a dramatic increase in recent years. The killings are carried out deliberately with extreme cruelty. Frequently, particularly in Nicaragua, they are carried out by partners or relatives of the victim, but in a high proportion of cases the murderers seem to be men connected with criminal activities. As such, they represent a new group of perpetrators not previously known for killing women, or at least not known for killing women in these proportions, or with these motives. Women's mutilated corpses, left in public places, are being used as a weapon to spread terror amongst women; in this sense, and because the murders are committed with such brutality, femicide can be seen as a hate crime against women (Kennedy 2006).

The extent to which these crimes represent acts of hatred towards women can be seen in the descriptions provided by organisations working around femicide. A relatives' and survivors' association in Guatemala

(Sobrevivientes n.d.) reports the violent murder of Maria Isabel Veliz Franco, who was found dead in December 2001. Maria Isabel, a 15-year-old student who worked in a shop, was raped and tortured; her body was found in a bag, tied with barbed wire, her face disfigured and her nails torn out. Similar crimes are also reported elsewhere in the region. For example, in Honduras, women's naked, tortured bodies were found with their legs open as a demonstration of male power; and two young women were found dead with a message to the former presidential candidate written on their bodies, warning him off his campaign against criminal gangs (known as *maras* or *pandillas*) (Kennedy 2005a).

In this article we suggest that femicide is an extreme form of the gender-based violence (GBV) that many women suffer at home, in the workplace, in the community, and in their relations with the state; violence that is intrinsically linked to deeply entrenched gender inequality and discrimination, economic disempowerment, and aggressive or *machismo* masculinity. Femicide represents a backlash against women who are empowered, for instance by wage employment, and have moved away from traditional female roles. These are deaths that cause no political stir and no stutter in the rhythm of the region's neo-liberal economy because, overwhelmingly, state authorities fail to investigate them, and the perpetrators go unpunished.

This article is based mainly on secondary sources from the region, but also reflects what the authors have learned from Central American feminists and women's organisations over several years of work with the London-based Central America Women's Network (CAWN), and with the Centre for Women's Studies in Honduras (CEM-H).[2] Central American women's organisations are active around femicide and GBV in general, and we acknowledge a debt in this article to their energetic research and advocacy. We write in the hope of helping to transmit their voices to a wider English-speaking audience.[3]

Although we focus here on the killing of women, we recognise that men are also killed violently in Central America. However, these murders do not usually have a gender-specific motive. Men who do not conform to the *machista* stereotype (the overtly masculine identity defined by Latin American culture), for instance homosexual men or transsexuals, are at risk of gender-based violence (Amnesty International USA 2003), but on the whole men are not killed because they are men and gender inequality does not underpin their murders (Aguilar 2005; Monárrez-Fragoso 2002).

Femicide — anatomy of a gender crime
Who are the victims?

Guatemala has the highest number of femicides in Central America and Mexico, but increasing numbers of women are also being killed in Honduras, El Salvador, and Costa Rica. Victims come from a range of social and economic backgrounds, which vary from country to country, as do the circumstances in which they are killed. In Costa Rica, for instance, migrant women are especially targeted, while the number of femicides is lower in Nicaragua, where they are linked specifically to domestic violence.[4] Many of the murdered women are from the most marginalised sectors of society, and it has become common for the media to present them as prostitutes, *maquila* (factory) workers,[5] and members of *maras*. Indeed, young, poor women working on the margins of legality are in a very vulnerable situation and are more likely to be attacked. According to the most up-to-date figures held by CEM-H, among the women murdered in Honduras many of the victims of femicide live in densely populated areas and are poor (Martínez 2006a).

One group of victims which has received much academic attention, particularly in Ciudad Juárez, Mexico (see for example Garwood 2002), and to a lesser extent in Central America, is that of women *maquila* workers. Large multinational companies recruit young women to work in manufacturing and assembly-line production of commodities such as garments and electronic goods, ostensibly because of their 'nimble fingers' and aptitude for the work, but also because they are cheap and supposedly docile workers (Elson and Pearson 1981). Several factors put women *maquila* workers at high risk of violent assault: they are often migrants, and the nature of their work often obliges them to do overtime, which often means walking long distances at night, even if they are scared to do so (Mónarrez-Fragoso 2002). They are more vulnerable if they are heads of households, as they are often forced to work longer hours to support their families. Raquel, a Nicaraguan *maquila* worker, explained how 'some women workers have to walk through dangerous areas. There have been rapes and assaults. It is dangerous'. Another worker, Elsa, said she preferred not to do any overtime and lose valuable income rather than risk her life, because she would have to walk home late at night on her own (both quoted in Prieto-Carrón 2006, 4–5).

However, many victims across the region do not conform to this stereotype of the *maquila* worker. Eighty-five per cent of the women killed in Mexico are not *maquila* workers (Lagarde 2006), while 45 per cent of the victims in Guatemala are housewives (Aguilar 2005). In Honduras, CEM-H reports that many victims are housewives and students.

Who are the killers?

Violence in the region has been exacerbated by decades of savage conflict and organised crime, and more recently by trafficking in drugs and people, and a general lawlessness that has followed the formal cessation of the civil wars.[6] There is a culture of violence connected to drug traffickers and other criminal gangs (Bähr Caballeros 2004) and public institutions prefer to attribute femicides to this, rather than seeing them as an expression of male hostility to women. In this way the state's actions (or inaction) favour the escalation of femicide.

Women's organisations and feminist advocates disagree with the official interpretation of the causes of these crimes. Giovanna Lemus, director of the End Violence against Women Network (Red de la no Violencia Contra la Mujer) in Guatemala, argues that 'whoever is killing, it needs to be investigated, because it is clear that not only the *maras* are responsible for these killings' (cited in URNG 2005, 76). In 2003, of the 383 women killed in Guatemala, only six murders could be attributed to street gangs (Amnesty International 2005a). Attempts by the authorities and the media to blame the gangs for the murders obscure the structural and root causes of femicide, which are inherent in GBV in the region.

Women are not necessarily killed by strangers in public places. Aguilar (2005) argues that women suffering domestic violence or trying to leave their violent partners are at significant risk. Similarly, Almachiara D'Angelo points out that 'domestic violence cannot be separated from femicides, especially in Nicaragua, where women are killed by their husbands and partners. In this sense, femicide can be considered as an extreme form of domestic violence that kills women' (quoted in Prieto-Carrón 2006, 4–5). Other studies in the region show that a high percentage – more than 60 per cent – of femicides are committed by an intimate partner or male family member, and occur in the victim's own home (Carcedo and Sagot 2001; Martínez 2006b). Furthermore, there are cases where the perpetrator was not known to the victim but the crime was 'masterminded' by the partner or ex-partner, who contracted members of the police or paramilitary forces to carry it out (Puntos de Encuentro 2006). Sometimes women are killed 'as an act of revenge against a close male relative of the women, related to drugs, gang warfare or networks involved in traffic and sexual exploitation' (Martínez 2006b). The killings have a motive, they are planned, and the perpetrators are known to their victims (Sobrevivientes n.d.).

Femicide and gender discrimination

Many feminist organisations and defenders of women's rights in Mexico and Central America argue that women are killed because they are women and that GBV is at the root of the problem (see for example Las Dignas 2004). They contend that femicides are the 'tip of the iceberg' (Lagarde 2006, 3) of cycles of gender-based aggression that patriarchal societies impose on women in the private and public spheres, and in different and often combined forms (physical, psychological, sexual, and economic). This analysis includes the less widely recognised categories of 'institutional' and 'symbolic' violence within the nexus of discrimination and violence, giving a more comprehensive framework for the gender analysis of the social, political, economic, and cultural aspects of femicide.

Inequality, poverty, and violence

There is an increasing body of literature showing the links between poverty, gender inequality, and violence against women (Pickup *et al.* 2001; Kennedy 2005b). In Latin America, studies show an increase in domestic violence in low-income neighbourhoods (Chant 1997) that has worsened during the region's economic crisis. Women from poor and marginalised communities are often constrained by traditional attitudes that subordinate them within the family and limit their mobility. Lack of qualifications and skills restricts the type of work they are able to do and therefore the income they are able to contribute to the household. In addition, these studies show that in poor households where the male partner cannot find work, unemployed men feel that their status in the household and the community is undermined; this may lead to the use of violence against their spouses to impose their authority (Pickup *et al.* 2001).

The neo-liberal economic model itself propitiates gender violence by impoverishing and disempowering women (Olivera 2006). Most jobs available to women – for instance factory jobs in the *maquila* industries – are low-paid and exploitative. The privatisation of public services, which both takes away women's jobs in the public sector and increases the cost of services to the consumer, has driven many women into informal and unprotected forms of labour, as street vendors, domestic servants, prostitutes, and even 'mules' transporting drugs inside their bodies, in which violence practically comes with the job. Young women in poor urban areas may join criminal gangs in the search for some kind of meaning in their disenfranchised lives (Bähr Caballeros 2004).[7] Migration also exposes women to violence: young women who leave rural homes (where they may already have experienced violence) for a job in the city are often exposed to fresh dangers, while women left behind in both rural and urban areas when male workers migrate often find themselves as overburdened and vulnerable heads of households.

Backlash against women

The increase in the number of femicides can also be linked to women's empowerment. Some feminist and women's organisations consider that femicides are a backlash against women who have stepped outside the 'safe' domestic sphere to earn an independent living (Aguilar 2005; Gargallo 2005; Monárrez-Fragoso 2002). Although the *maquila* sector is notorious for violating labour rights, some feminists have pointed to the liberating and positive aspects of this kind of employment for many women around the world (Férnandez-Kelly 1983; Lim 1997; Rosa 1994; Ver Beek 2001). Despite their very limited options in an unequal globalised economy, *maquila* workers are empowering themselves by securing employment outside the home. But for this, they are then labelled by society as 'sexual subjects lacking value, worth and respectability as a result of their structural position in the global economy', and therefore 'worthless, temporary and disposable' (Garwood 2002, 20). As a result, their violent deaths are regarded by the authorities as not worth investigation.

These crimes against women have created an environment of fear in which many women are afraid to leave their homes. Consequently, those in power, both in the household and in state institutions, can exert greater control over women's behaviour and mobility. In this respect, violence and the fear of violence are a form of social control used to terrify women and prevent them from participating in the public sphere, considered the male domain. As perpetrators generally go unpunished, the subordination of women in this way and the gender inequality that it underpins are legitimised. As Suyapa Martínez from CEM-H notes, femicides are: 'a reaction against women's empowerment: [men are saying,] "I'm denying you a public space, I'm denying you freedom, the right to go out and have fun, to have a personal life"' (Martínez 2006a).

A continuum of violence

As mentioned above, femicides are the culmination of a continuum of violence in cultures where less extreme acts of violence against women are considered socially acceptable by both men and women. Research shows that femicide victims are in some cases already 'survivors of domestic violence': for example, 60 per cent of women in Mexico who were murdered by their partners or their partners' accomplices had previously reported domestic violence to public authorities who did not respond (Lagarde 2006). The testimonies below illustrate how women survive 'lesser' acts of violence in their everyday lives, as some men use violence to impose their will in situations that could potentially escalate into more extreme forms of attack:

He wanted me to give him a son and it took me too long... to become pregnant... He would tell me, 'Son of a bitch, you're no good for shit, not even to have children.' (Woman from Costa Rica, Sagot 2005, 1301)

He struck me again on my temple and almost strangled me. It took me two months to recover, to be able to swallow again. (Woman from Honduras, Sagot 2005, 1300).

The socio-cultural environment in which 'everyday acts of violence' are possible is one in which femicide is also possible. *Machista* cultural attitudes are reinforced in newspapers, commercials, songs, and soap operas, which reproduce myths justifying violence against women, such as 'women like to be beaten', 'she provoked him', and 'he was drunk or under the influence of drugs' (URNG 2005, 49–54).

The state's response

Governments in the region are allowing men to get away with murder. This was highlighted by Yakin Ertürk, the UN Special Rapporteur on Violence against Women, in the report of her mission to Guatemala in 2004. The murders continue because national justice and public-order systems ignore them. Impunity facilitates further murders and, in a cultural climate where violence is commonplace, men kill women because they can.

In Mexico and across Central America, public institutions from social services to the courts ignore, discount, belittle, and cover up femicide, sometimes colluding with perpetrators, creating an enabling environment for its growth. In Guatemala, for instance, 70 per cent of murders of women were not investigated and no arrests were made in 97 per cent of cases (Amnesty International USA 2006). In the case of Maria Isabel Veliz Franco, mentioned above, it is claimed that forensic evidence (the perpetrator's hair and semen) found in her body was not examined for DNA analysis (Sobrevivientes n.d.). In Guatemala, according to the Human Rights Commission Report of 2003 (Procuradería de Derechos Humanos), in 82 per cent of cases of femicide, no suspect has been identified, and more than 70 per cent of the cases have not been investigated at all (URNG 2005). The police and the judicial system lack interest and political will, and there is no funding available to investigate these crimes.

State justice systems ignore legislation

All the countries in the region have ratified the Convention on the Elimination of All Forms of Discrimination Against Women (CEDAW) and are signatories to other international and regional agreements that protect women against violence. These include the Inter-American Convention to Prevent, Sanction and Eradicate Violence against Women (Convention of Belém do Pará), approved and widely ratified in 1995. However, none of these countries has reformed its national legislation to make it coherent with these international commitments, or drawn up regulations and provided funding to implement either the international agreements or existing national policies against GBV. In addition to the lack of policy and mechanisms to address gender-based violence in general, no Central American government has responded adequately to these horrific murders. Officials persist in their claims that they are spontaneous or accidental acts and do not take appropriate actions to investigate them (Kennedy, quoted in Gargallo 2005). They also dismiss claims that these murders have anything to do with unequal gender relations, but it can be argued that the failure of state authorities to investigate violent crimes against women is itself evidence of gender discrimination, and of discrimination on the basis of class and ethnicity, as victims are often poor, indigenous, or migrant women. As Marcela Lagarde has noted, 'it's necessary to change the living conditions of women, to change the relations of supremacy of men and the patriarchal content of laws... it's a substantive problem for democratic governance' (cited in Portugal 2005).

Crimes go unreported

Under-reporting of femicides contributes to impunity. Researchers from several Latin American organisations preparing a report on femicide for the Inter-American Human Rights Commission found that:

> the states do not have an official system for compiling information which would permit us to know the precise magnitude of the problem so as to make an adequate response ... Moreover, where official figures do exist, they are always found [to be lower than] the figures coming from NGOs, showing a tendency by the governments to downplay the problem. In general, the information systems do not disaggregate data by sex, age or ethnicity. Neither do they make it possible to establish any kind of relation between victim and perpetrator. Every country has different indicators for organizing the data relating to the murders of women ... even within the countries information systems are [not consistent]. (Feminicidio en América Latina 2006, 5–6)

Femicides are made invisible when records of deaths are not sex-disaggregated (Martínez 2006a; see also CLADEM 2001). The above-cited report also reveals that information about femicides is mostly recorded and disseminated by relatives of the victims and civil-society organisations (Feminicidio en América Latina 2006). The research for this article confirms significant gaps in the data available and their reliability.

Service providers facilitate impunity

Insensitive, prejudiced, and inadequate responses by service providers also play a big part in the patriarchal social nexus that facilitates femicide by 'normalising' violence against women, particularly domestic violence, as not being serious or a real danger to women. A Nicaraguan woman reported that 'the doctor did not ask me anything, he just said, "You seem very sad, what you need is a lot of vitamins"; while a woman from Costa Rica said, 'I used to tell the doctor, "Don't prescribe me any more pills, I am not crazy! I am hurt, but not crazy!"' (Sagot 2005, 1305). In Honduras, a physician argued that 'the demand is very high; we don't have time to talk with the patients. We only look at the medical problem' (Sagot 2005).

A legal service provider from Nicaragua said:

> All in all, it's a very painful experience. Many times women go to the police in tears, and the police tell them not to be irresponsible and waste their time with that kind of complaint... They tell them, 'tonight your man is going to be between your legs again'. (Sagot 2005, 1307)

Research documenting the testimonies of mothers of femicide victims illustrates the contempt and lack of sensitivity towards the victim and her family. As the mother of Maria Isabel Veliz Franco reported: 'When they gave me her body, I was on the floor, crying, and still they were telling me not to exaggerate' (Amnesty International 2005b). According to the Guatemalan Women's Group (Grupo Guatemalteco de Mujeres), which keeps records and supports victims' relatives, poverty and racial discrimination are key barriers for individual women and families, preventing many from seeking access to justice (Lemus 2006). Families often abandon legal procedures because they receive death threats or become disillusioned when they receive no response from the authorities. People do not trust the system or the bureaucracy, they fear reprisals, and they often cannot afford to pursue their cases.

The failure of service providers to treat victims and their relatives with respect, and to take their experiences seriously, represents a form of institutional violence, compounding the violence exercised by the state in allowing femicide to be committed with impunity.

Challenging state impunity at the international level

Women's organisations are beginning to see some successes in their campaigns to challenge impunity in cases of femicide. In recent years, human-rights organisations such as Amnesty International, the International Federation of Human Rights, the Centre for Justice and International Law, and the UN Special Rapporteur on Violence against Women have undertaken official missions, produced research reports, and supported women's organisations' struggle for justice. Women politicians in Central America, in collaboration with women's organisations, have spoken out at international hearings. For example, a Guatemalan congresswoman, Alba Maldonado, has spoken at several international meetings, including at the European Parliament:

> I have taken up this issue of feminicidios as a priority… because the State has abandoned its social responsibility and insecurity, violence and femicide have been unleashed. I have no doubt where the responsibility lies: I affirm it both outside and inside Guatemala.
> (Maldonado 2006)

At a hearing at the European Parliament in April 2006, there was a call for the EU to take action, for example by making the provision of aid to countries in this region conditional on national governments strengthening their efforts to stop violence against women (Thomson 2006).

The response of women's organisations

Under incredibly difficult circumstances, with minimal resources, and often against considerable odds, women and women's organisations in Central America and Mexico are responding to gender violence with a variety of strategies (Aguilar 2005). In this section we outline some of these activities.

Organising across the region

Since the early 1990s, when the scale of the murders in Ciudad Juárez became apparent, women's organisations have come together to protest against systematic gender violence and demand justice. In 2001, a three-year, continent-wide campaign began, co-ordinated by the Latin American and Caribbean Feminist Network against Domestic and Sexual Violence (part of ISIS International)[8] with the slogan 'For women's lives: not one more death' (*Por la Vida de las Mujeres, Ni una Muerte Más*). Large numbers of women participated in demonstrations and marches on the International Day to End Violence Against Women (25 November) and on International Women's Day (8 March), and the campaign succeeded in mobilising women's organisations, collectives, and NGOs throughout Latin America. When Central American women's organisations met in Guatemala in December 2004 for the second Central American Feminist Meeting,[9] they recognised that femicide had become a region-wide tragedy and that none of their governments was addressing it seriously. They decided to form the Central American Feminist Network against Violence against Women (*Red Feminista Centroamericana contra la violencia hacia la mujer*, hereafter referred to as the *Red Feminista*)[10] and issued a public statement which argued that 'there is a context favourable to violence against women and resistance by the state to protecting [women's] rights to live a life free from violence', condemned femicide as 'a brutal form of violence against women,' and criticised 'the high level of impunity and corruption in the justice systems' (Puntos de Encuentro 2006, 74).

At the grassroots

In Mexico and in Guatemala, relatives of femicide victims were instrumental in getting the issue on to the public agenda. Without funding or experience in fighting for justice, the mothers of the young victims have confronted the police and the judicial system, at great personal cost. Self-help organisations have now been formed to denounce impunity, generate income, support the orphaned children of the murdered women, and cover legal and other costs, which remain a great challenge for family members (Lemus 2006).

Women's organisations in the region are also working more generally on gender-based violence. This includes projects offering support to women survivors with help lines, counselling, and psychological therapy. Some organisations work in the poorest communities training community leaders to contribute to the prevention of violence, and to promote equitable gender relations in their communities. Others are also working to prevent violence against women and girls through workshops with the wider community, particularly working with young men to explore alternative, non-violent masculinities.[11]

CEM-H is one of these organisations, implementing a project in some of the most marginalised communities in Honduras, offering emotional and legal support to women affected by violence, as well as providing resources and tools, and training legal monitors (*promotoras*) to help women learn about their rights as women.

Research and advocacy

There is little data on femicides in Central America (Aguilar 2005), as pioneering research by CEFEMINA in Costa Rica found (Carcedo and Sagot 2001), so research and information gathering has become a priority for women's organisations. In 2005 the *Red Feminista* set up a research group to monitor the situation in Honduras, El Salvador, Nicaragua, Guatemala, and Costa Rica.[3,10] Their aim is to generate research findings to be used to create public awareness and advocate for official action to prevent and punish violent crimes against women.

This research will inform regional advocacy initiatives at the highest possible levels, and campaigning to raise public awareness. Women's organisations see the legal framework as one of their greatest challenges. They want to change penal codes so that femicide is recognised as a distinct crime separate from homicide, because very often data are not disaggregated and it is difficult to analyse the gendered nature of the murder of women. The *Red Feminista* is working closely with a network of women lawyers linked to the International Centre for Justice and International Law based in Washington, and with other international organisations, to take their advocacy to the highest levels possible. They also want the police to keep accurate, sex-disaggregated, up-to-date records; failures in this respect are a key factor in impunity. As Suyapa Martínez from CEM-H argued in a recent interview with CAWN:

> *in Honduras we have several key challenges. We want the State to take preventative measures. We don't just want them to put more police on the streets, we also want integrated public policies. We want to go into these cases in greater depth and to transcend the national level and denounce them internationally. It's important to carry out campaigns regionally and internationally – these crimes are happening throughout the world. It's important that women raise their voices to denounce them and demand an end to femicide.* (Martínez 2006b)

Conclusion

Women's organisations, and feminist researchers and politicians, believe that femicide, like all gender-based violence, requires attention at all levels of society and government, including the judiciary, the police force, and relevant public service providers. As we have argued in this article, femicide in Central America and Mexico is an expression of gender discrimination and unequal power relations between men and women, operating in both the private and public spheres. While the murder, torture, and mutilation of individual women by individual male aggressors makes gender discrimination starkly visible, institutionalised discrimination is evident in the failure of governments both to investigate these murders in particular and to protect the rights of women in general. This is not only a social problem but also one of security. The state and its institutions, by lacking the political will to confront femicide, have in effect stimulated its reproduction.

The efforts of women's organisations must be supported at all levels. International support is needed, through different networks and collaborations, such as the project between CAWN in London and CEM-H in Honduras. Women's organisations are closer to the women victims of violence and to their realities. As we have outlined in this article, together with feminist advocates, they have developed a framework of analysis that locates femicides as part of a continuum of gender-based violence in all aspects of women's lives, the most extreme manifestation of many other kinds of violence that women suffer.

International donors need to take a position on gender-based violence, because it exists in all the social processes that their programmes are trying to address. A greater distribution of funds towards programmes promoting gender equality would be a starting point. With regard to Central America, pressure is needed to stop the impunity of governments. For example, co-operation treaties between the European Union and the countries in this region should include the condition that governments take action to solve crimes against women. As long as the international community ignores violence against women in Central America, there is little hope of stopping the killing of women. Women in Central America deserve our international support.

This article was originally published in Gender & Development, *volume 15, number 1, March 2007.*

References

Aguilar, A. L. (2005) 'Femicidio...la pena capital por ser mujer', Guatemala 14 July 2005, available at http://www.isis.cl/Feminicidio/doc/doc/1311lapena.doc (last accessed 14 August 2006).

Amnesty International (2005a) 'Guatemala memorandum to the Government of Guatemala: Amnesty International's concerns regarding the current human rights situation', 20 April 2005, available at http://web.amnesty.org/library/pdf/AMR340142005ENGLISH/$File/ AMR3401405.pdf (last accessed 23 October 2006).

Amnesty International (2005b) 'Guatemala: no protection, no justice: killings of women and girls – facts and figures', media briefing, News Service No 146 , 9 June 2005, available at http://web.amnesty.org/library/Index/ENGAMR340252005?open&of= ENG-2M2 (last accessed 14 August 2006).

Amnesty International USA (2003) 'Transgender activist faces death threats as murder toll in Honduras' LGBT community soars', press release, 10 September 2003, available at http://www.amnestyusa.org/outfront/document.do?id=AC144AAF65D F7E3385256D9D0061590C (last accessed 29 July 2006).

Amnesty International USA (2006) 'Murders of women in Guatemala increasingly frequent in 2006, new Amnesty International Report finds', press release, 18 July 2006, available at http://www.amnestyusa.org/women/document.do?id=ENGUSA200607 18001 (last accessed 29 July 2006).

Bähr Caballeros, K. (2004) *Violencia Contra las Mujeres y Seguridad en Honduras: Un Estudio Exploratorio*, Tegucigalpa: PNUD.

Berkowitz, A. D. (2004) 'Working With Men to Prevent Violence Against Women: An Overview (Part 1)', Pennsylvania: National Resource Center on Domestic Violence, available at http://www.vawnet.org/DomesticViolence/Research/VAWnetDocs/ AR_MenPreventVAW1.pdf (last accessed 23 October 2006).

Carcedo, A. and M. Sagot (2001) *Femicidio en Costa Rica: Cuando la Violencia contra las Mujeres Mata*, San José: OPS/INAMU.

Chant, S. (1997) *Women-Headed Households: Diversity and Dynamics in the Developing World*, London: Macmillan Press.

CLADEM (Latin American and Caribbean Committee for the Defence of the Rights of Women) Nicaragua & National Feminist Committee (2001) 'Alternative report to the Government of Nicaragua's 4th and 5th Reports to the CEDAW', Managua, July, available at http://www.cladem.org/english/regional/monitoreo_convenios/cedaw nicaraguai.asp (last accessed 26 July 2006).

Clulow, M. (2005) *Women as Citizens, Participation for Women's Rights in Central America*, London: One World Action, April 2005. Also available online at http://owa.netxtra.net/_uploads/documents/Final.english.short.women ascitizens.pdf (last accessed 26 July 2006).

Elson, D. and R. Pearson (1981) 'Nimble fingers make cheap workers: an analysis of women's employment in third world export manufacturing', *Feminist Review* 7 (Spring): 87–107.

Ertürk, Y. (2005) 'Integration of the Human Rights of Women and the Gender Perspective: Violence Against Women, report of the special rapporteur on violence against women its causes and consequences', Addendum: Mission to Guatemala, E/CN.4/2005/72/Add.3, 10 February 2005, UN Commission on Human Rights.

Feminicidio en América Latina (2006) 'Documento Elaborado con Motivo de la Audiencia sobre "Feminicidio en América Latina" ante la Comisión Interamericana de Derechos Humanos', available at http://www.isis.cl/Feminicidio/doc/doc/Informe%20Audiencia%20CIDH.doc (last accessed 2 August 2006).

Fernández-Kelly, P. (1983) *For We Are Sold, I and My People: Women and Industry in Mexico's Frontier*, Albany: State University of New York Press.

Gargallo, F. (2005) 'El feminicidio en la República Maquiladora' Suplemento masiosare, *La Jornada*, México D.F., 17 de julio de 2005, available at http://www.jornada.unam.mx/2005/jul05/050717/mas-cara.html (last accessed 2nd August 2006).

Garwood, S. (2002) 'Working to death: gender, labour, and violence in Ciudad Juárez, Mexico', *Peace, Conflict and Development*, available at http://www.peacestudiesjournal.org.uk/docs/working2.pdf (last accessed 11 December 2006).

Kennedy, M. (2005a) 'The Feminisation of Poverty, and the Impact of Globalisation on Women', paper presented at the School for Policy Studies, University of Bristol, 11 April 2005.

Kennedy, M. (2005b) 'Desigualdad de Género en Honduras: El Impacto de la Pobreza y la Violencia en las Mujeres', presentation by CEM-H, Tegucigalpa, August 2005.

Kennedy, M. (2006) correspondence with co-author.

Lagarde y de los Ríos, M. (2006) 'Feminicidio' paper presented at Universidad de Oviedo, 12 January 2006, available at http://www.ciudaddemujeres.com/articulos/article.php3?id_article=77 (last accessed 2 August 2006).

Las Dignas (2004) 'La Violencia Contra las Mujeres en el 2003 a Través de la Prensa', January 2004, San Salvador, available at http://www.isis.cl/femicidio/fdocument.html, (last accessed 2 August 2006).

Lemus, G. (2006), presentation at the EU Parliamentary Hearing, sub committee for Human Rights on Femicides in Mexico and Central America, Brussels, 19 April 2006.

Lim, L. (1997) 'Capitalism, imperialism and patriarchy: the dilemma of third-world women workers in multinational factories', in N. Visvanathan *et al.* (eds.) (1997).

Maldonado, A. (2006) 'No Más Horror en Guatemala', paper presented at the EU Parliamentary Hearing, sub committee for Human Rights on Femicides in Mexico and Central America, Brussels, 19 April 2006.

Martínez, S. (2006a) 'Femicides in Honduras', presentation at a meeting of the Central American Women's Network, CAWN, London, 1 July 2006.

Martínez, S. (2006b) Co-author interview with Suyapa Martínez, Centro de Estudios de la Mujer Hondureña, London, July 2006.

Monárrez-Fragoso, J. (2002) 'Serial sexual femicide in Ciudad Juárez: 1993–2001', *Debate Feminista* 13 (25) April.

Morales Gamboa, A. (2002) 'Situación de los Trabajadores Migrantes en América Central', Geneva: ILO, available at http://www.ilo.org/public/english/protection/migrant/download/imp/imp53s.pdf (last accessed 26 July 2006).

Olivera, M. (2006) 'Violence against women and Mexico's structural crisis', *Latin American Perspectives* 33(2): 104–14.

Pickup, F., S. Williams, and C. Sweetman (2001) *Ending Violence against Women: a Challenge for Development and Humanitarian Work*, Oxford: Oxfam.

Portugal, A. M. (2005) 'El Feminicidio a la OEA', 26 January 2005, available at http://www.mujereshoy.com/secciones/3523.shtml (last accessed 2 November 2006).

Prieto-Carrón, M. (2006) 'Gender-Based Violence in the Lives of Nicaraguan Women Maquila Workers', Newsletter No 21, Autumn 2006, London, CAWN.

Puntos de Encuentro (2006) 'Lo que cocinamos: II Encuentro Feminista Centroamericano', *La Boletina* No 64, p 74. Also available online at http://www.puntos.org.ni/boletina, last accessed 20 November 2006.

Radford, J. and D. Russell (1992) *Femicide: The Politics of Woman Killing*, Buckingham: Open University Press.

Rosa, K. (1994) 'The conditions and organisational activities of women in free trade zones – Malaysia, Philippines and Sri Lanka, 1970–1990', in Rowbotham and Mitter (eds.) (1994).

Rowbotham, S. and S. Mitter (eds.) (1994) *Dignity and Daily Bread*, London: Routledge.

Sagot, M. (2005) 'The critical path of women affected by family violence in Latin America: case studies from 10 countries', *Violence Against Women* 11(10): 1292–318.

Sobrevivientes (Familiares y Mujeres Sobrevivientes de la Violencia) (n.d.), available at http://www.Sobrevivientes.org/doc (last accessed 2 August 2006).

Thomson, M. (2006) 'Challenging violence against women and girls', *Central America Report* (CAR) Spring 2006, London.

URNG, Unidad Revolucionaria Nacional Guatemaleca (2005) 'Feminicidio en Guatemala: Crímenes Contra la Humanidad', Unidad: November 2005, available at http://www.congreso.gob.gt/uploadimg/documentos/n1652.pdf (last accessed 2 November 2006).

Ver Beek, K. A. (2001) 'Maquiladoras: exploitation or emancipation? An overview of the situation of maquiladora workers in Honduras', *World Development* 29(9): 1553–567.

Visvanathan, N., L. Duggan, L. Nisonoff, and N. Wiegersma (eds.) (1997) *The Women, Gender and Development Reader*, London: Zed Books.

Welsh, P. (2001) *Men aren't from Mars: Unlearning Machismo in Nicaragua*, London: CIIR.

Notes

1 The English term 'femicide' was first popularised by the academics Jill Radford and Diane Russell (1992) in their book *Femicide: The Politics of Woman Killing*. They argue that society is organised to make violence part of all relations, reinforced by cultures that legitimise violence against women.

2 CAWN is a UK-based organisation that works to increase awareness in the UK and Europe of violations of women's human rights in Central America and which supports the work of women's organisations to end discrimination against women in the region. CAWN produces a regular newsletter and bulletins, organises conferences and speaker tours and carries out research on women's rights in Central America (www.cawn.org). In 2006, CAWN embarked on a five-year project with CEM-H, focusing on GBV (www.cemh.org.hn), with the financial support of the Big Lottery Fund.

3 The Central American Feminist Network against Violence against Women (Red Feminista Centroamericana contra la Violencia hacia las Mujeres), supported by UNIFEM and founded in February 2005, is undertaking a regional study on femicide. Although this was not available at the time of writing, very valuable research from women's organisations and women's advocates is already accessible and we have referred to it as widely as possible.

4 The fact that in Nicaragua there is less violence related to organised crime, drugs, and prostitution than in other Central American countries needs to be researched. A factor could be the greater social consciousness in the population and the impressive community organising, as a legacy of the Sandinista Revolution (1979–1990).

5 *Maquilas,* or *maquiladoras,* are factories in Mexico and Central America manufacturing textiles and garments and producing assembly-line electronics and other goods for export. They may be located in free-trade zones or outside them, but all benefit from the same special export regimes and tax advantages.

6 For example, Guatemala suffered 36 years of civil war, during which rape and murder of women were widespread, particularly of Mayan women in rural areas. But the signing of the Peace Accord in 1996 has not ended the violence against women (or men and children). Similarly in El Salvador, a civil war in the 1980s between the Farabundo Martí Liberation Front (FMLN) and the incumbent government lasted for over 13 years, while the Nicaraguan *contras* fought a war against the left-wing Sandinista revolution in Nicaragua, supported by the USA.

7 A significant proportion of female workers in Central America also migrate (see for example Morales Gamboa 2002).

8 One outcome was the setting up of a data bank by ISIS International with research findings and documentation on the anti-violence movement. This is an important resource available online for all women's organisations. See: www.isis.cl/Feminicidio/index.htm (last checked by authors 2 August 2006).

9 II Encuentro de la Red Feminista Centroamericana contra la Violencia hacia las Mujeres. This was a specifically Central American conference, not the Latin-America-wide Encuentro Feminista that has been held since 1981. For information on the Central American conference see *La Boletina* (2006 64: 75) which can be accessed at www.puntos.org.ni/boletina (last checked by authors 20 November 2006).

10 The network members working on this research are: the Women's Studies Centre – Honduras (CEM-H); the Feminist Collective for Local Development (Colectivo Feminista de Desarrollo Local) El Salvador, the Guatemalan Women's Group , CEFEMINA in Costa Rica and Almachiara D'Angelo, an independent researcher in Nicaragua.

11 Men can also be allies in the struggle against gender-based violence, by not personally engaging in violence, by intervening against the violence of other men, and by addressing the root causes of violence (see for example Berkowitz 2004). Pioneering work with men to combat gender violence has been carried out, for instance, in Nicaragua, by CANTERA, an NGO that runs popular education training courses on masculinity, and the Nicaraguan Association of Men against Violence (Welsh 2001).

4 Sexual violence during firewood collection: income-generation as protection in displaced settings

Sarah K. Chynoweth with Erin M. Patrick[1]

Introduction

Sexual violence towards women and girls is often widespread during conflict and displacement, and studies suggest that sexual violence rates may increase in post-conflict settings (Vlachova and Biason 2005). During displacement, women and girls are targeted for sexual violence when they leave the confines of their camp or settlement to forage for firewood[2] in order to cook food for their families or to sell what they gather for profit. Although this problem has been a long-standing concern, it has not been adequately addressed by the humanitarian community.

Emergency response and development actors have recognised improved overall co-ordination and the development of a common strategy as two ways to help protect women and girls from the onset of a conflict right through to the post-conflict phase. This chapter outlines the problem of violence during firewood collection and highlights some solutions that humanitarian actors can implement throughout the stages of a conflict, as identified in the recent Women's Commission for Refugee Women and Children (Women's Commission) global study, 'Beyond Firewood: Fuel alternatives and protection strategies for displaced women and girls' (2006b), conducted from 2005 to 2006. The chapter will specifically explore the critical need for income-generation activities and how such activities can help bridge the gap between relief and development, given the complex and long-term nature of modern conflict.

Sexual violence in conflict

Suggestions that rape is relatively new as weapon of war are fallacious. Sexual violence, specifically rape, has been part of war and conflict throughout human history (Durham and Gurd 2005). Rape in war has taken on several different forms. Before the fall of the Roman Empire, for example, in ancient Greece and Egypt, acts of rape during conflict were considered 'rewards' for the victors and conquered women were often deemed 'spoils of war' (Robinson 2002). Opportunistic rape – which is perpetrated by anyone acting with impunity in the climate of lawlessness that accompanies armed conflict – has and continues to be prevalent in conflict settings. Modern warfare, on the other hand, has seen an increase in rape as a tactic or weapon of war: rape is systematically and deliberately used to intimidate and traumatise a population, in which case the perpetrators are enemy combatants. This type of sexual violence may also be used as a strategy of genocide or ethnic cleansing by using rape to impregnate women with 'the child of the enemy' (Ward 2002).

Although data on sexual violence in conflict-affected settings is scarce, systematic, organised rape during conflict appears to have greatly escalated since the First World War (Ward and Marsh 2006), during which German troops used rape to terrorise local populations in the invasion of Belgium (Zuckerman 2004). Historians estimate that over two million women were raped by soldiers of the Russian Army at the end of the Second World War, and many were raped multiple times, with some women reporting 60 or 70 different attacks (Hitchcock 2004; Mark 2005). Rape was used as a tactic in the Japanese invasion of China during the Second World War (Chang 1997) and the Bangladesh war of liberation from Pakistan in 1971 (Thomas and Ralph 1994). The American military in the Vietnam War also made rape a 'standard operating procedure aimed at terrorizing the population into submission' (Eisen-Bergman 1975, 69).

However, sexual violence in war and conflict did not receive much international attention and publicity until the Balkan Wars in the 1990s. An unknown number of people were raped during this decade-long conflict in which 'rape camps' were established to torture and impregnate women and girls, many of whom were forced to continue their pregnancy until delivery (Helsinki Watch 1992). Systematic rape of up to 500,000 women and girls during the Rwandan genocide (UNHCHR 1996), including the mutilation of their breasts and genitalia, received some media attention only after the slaughter ended (Human Rights Watch 1996), and rape in the current conflict in Darfur, Sudan has sparked interest in certain journalists who attempt to raise awareness on the issue. But prior to this, numerous campaigns of mass rape and sexual torture in recent conflicts went virtually unnoticed, such as those in Bangladesh, Cambodia, Cyprus, Democratic Republic of Congo, Haiti, Liberia, Somalia, and Uganda (UNICEF 1996).

Sexual violence during fuel/firewood collection

While rape and sexual violence are now recognised as weapons of war during conflict and have started to receive attention in the international media, less attention has been paid to the ongoing vulnerability of women and girls in camp settings. This is particularly the case regarding sexual violence experienced by women and girls when they collect firewood. Although the United Nations (UN), through the World Food Programme (WFP), is mandated to provide food during a complex humanitarian emergency, no UN agency is specifically mandated to provide fuel to cook the food. The food distributed by WFP, such as beans or whole grains, often cannot be eaten uncooked – and no humanitarian agency considers cooking fuel its responsibility, even less so a protection concern. As a result, refugee and internally displaced women and girls must leave the relative safety of their camp or settlement to forage for firewood to cook food for their families or to sell for income. Millions of women and girls knowingly risk rape and other forms of sexual assault by trekking up to ten hours a day, several times a week in search of fuel. Perpetrators may be others who have been displaced by the conflict or disaster; members of other clans, villages, religious groups, or ethnic groups; military personnel; rebel forces; humanitarian workers from UN or international agencies; members of the host population; or family members. The burden of gathering firewood falls upon women and girls not only because cooking-related activities are considered 'women's work', but also because of a commonly held belief that men and boys would be killed if they were the ones to leave the security of the camp in search of firewood, whereas women and girls are 'only' risking rape (Women's Commission for Refugee Women and Children 2006d).

In Burundian refugee camps in Tanzania, one study reported that the majority of rapes among refugee women and girls occur outside of the camp perimeter while they are gathering firewood (Southern Africa Documentation and Cooperation Centre 2002). According to an early study, approximately 90 per cent of rapes among Somali refugees living in Dadaab and Kakuma camps in Kenya occurred when gathering firewood (Olila *et al.* 1998). Somali women and girls walked up to ten kilometers in the semi-arid landscape, during which warring clans targeted them for rape. These rapes often involved multiple perpetrators and were accompanied by additional violence such as stabbing or beatings. Further, given that the tradition of infibulation, the most severe form of female genital mutilation/cutting in which a girl's labia are sewn shut, is prevalent among these refugees, excruciating pain and long-term medical complications as a result of rape were commonplace (Fitzgerald 1998). The medical implications may have been particularly serious for this group of women, but in all instances, rape has a great number of long- and short-term medical, psychosocial, and economic consequences. Although too complex to address fully in this chapter, some consequences may include unwanted pregnancy, transmission of HIV or other sexually transmitted infections, loss of livelihood, community ostracisation, divorce, attempted suicide, or even murder by the survivor's family members who may feel she has disgraced or dishonoured their family (Médecins Sans Frontières 2004).

Adolescents

Adolescent girls are particularly vulnerable in conflict-affected settings and their particular needs are often neglected or overlooked by relief agencies due to their age and lack of social status. Like all young people, refugee and internally displaced adolescent girls have special needs during their years of development. However, due to forced displacement from their homes, exposure to violence, acute poverty, and separation from their families and communities, displaced adolescent girls face additional difficulties. They often lack sufficient education, health care, protection, livelihood opportunities, recreational activities, and friendship and family support. Furthermore, displaced adolescents may begin sexual relations at an earlier age and take more sexual risks, such as having sexual intercourse without using a condom. They are more vulnerable to sexual abuse and exploitation in the absence of traditional socio-cultural constraints. Indeed, according to the Christian Children's Fund, firewood collection in refugee camps and settlements is typically assigned to girls, rather than adult women, placing them at extreme risk of violence (Christian Children's Fund 2006).

Some *ad hoc* efforts by the humanitarian community to address this complex issue have been undertaken. For example, the use of parabolic solar cookers and distribution of kerosene in Bhutanese refugee camps in Nepal have relatively successfully reduced the need for women and girls to leave the camp in search of firewood. Fuel-efficient stove programmes in Darfur and eastern Chad have also significantly reduced the total amount of firewood needed for cooking in some settings. Other initiatives have not been as successful: in one instance, UNHCR provided firewood to Congolese refugees in Burundi, but girls still ventured out for firewood because the distributed wood was too large to split (UNHCR 2004).

Solutions

Although the international community has long been aware of the risks related to firewood collection, at the time of writing, co-ordinated, effective strategies are not in place to address the issue. From 2005 to 2006, the Women's Commission conducted a global study to assess protection strategies in the context of firewood collection and to develop recommendations for humanitarian actors in all phases of a complex emergency. Five strategies were identified which, when adequately and systematically implemented in consultation with displaced women and girls, could effectively reduce the physical threat to, and vulnerability of, the displaced population.

First, providing fuel directly to displaced people can reduce if not eliminate the need for women and girls to venture outside of the camp or settlement to forage for firewood. Although direct provision of fuel is expensive and cannot be sustained over the long term, it is an effective protection strategy that should be considered in the early days of a crisis.

Second, national and international security forces should provide transportation to firewood-collection sites or routinely patrol the collection routes in the emergency phase as well. It is essential that female members of security forces consistently participate in the patrols, and that frequent consultations are held with displaced women and girls regarding their concerns and needs. Third, humanitarian agencies should promote fuel-efficient technologies, including food-preparation techniques and fuel-efficient stoves, and alternative fuels, such as briquettes or ethanol-based fuels, to lessen the need for firewood. It is essential to determine the appropriateness of each alternative fuel or fuel-efficient technology in context, and a number of factors, including the local environment, weather patterns, and local cooking customs need to be taken into consideration in order to be effective. Fourth, although all humanitarian actors should share responsibility for a multi-sectoral, holistic intervention, these solutions must be co-ordinated by a single body with responsibility for the synchronisation of fuel-related initiatives, including identifying all alternative fuels and fuel technologies available for use in camp settings.[3]

Finally, to be effective, the strategies outlined above must be coupled with income-generation activities, and it is on this topic that we will focus in the remainder of this chapter. Often, displaced women and girls collect firewood not only for cooking, but to sell in order to generate income. Given the scarce resources and extremely limited economic opportunities in displaced settings, many families rely on this income for survival. No fuel alternatives or improved cooking technologies will significantly reduce the number and frequency of women and girls collecting firewood outside camps without alternative income-generation activities in place. In addition, providing income-generation activities to women and girls can help protect them from other forms of sexual abuse and exploitation, such as trafficking and transactional sex.

Income-generation activities

Income-generation activities are essential to any fuel strategy. A report by Community, Habitat and Finance (CHF) International/University of California-Berkeley on the effectiveness of fuel-efficient stoves in reducing firewood collection among internally displaced people in Darfur demonstrated the importance of coupling income-generation activities with other fuel strategies. Although one type of fuel-efficient stove (the 'Tara' stove) reduced firewood consumption up to 50 per cent and is easily and inexpensively produced locally, women and girls are still forced to rely on wood for income generation and will continue to put themselves at risk to gather it. Indeed, when a group of internally displaced women was asked, 'If you obtained an FES [fuel-efficient stove], what would you do with the time you save using the FES?' approximately half of the respondents said they would use the increased available time to collect wood for income purposes (Galitsky *et al.* 2006).

Legal issues

Despite the fact that numerous international legal instruments preserve the right of refugees to work in their host country, including the International Covenant on Economic, Social and Cultural Rights, the Convention on the Status of Refugees and the Universal Declaration of Human Rights, many countries that host refugees have explicit policies in place that prevent refugees from engaging in any activity outside of the camp that could generate income. However, refugees may be able to engage in paid work or produce goods for sale inside the camp, as translators or health-care workers for aid organisations, for example, or by producing and selling food, soap, or other goods. Internally displaced populations, on the other hand, are more likely to be allowed to work outside of the camp confines as there are seldom restrictions on their freedom of movement.

In some countries paid work and income-generation activities are not allowed even within the camp. For example, the government of Thailand has only recently rescinded its 22-year-old policy restricting refugees' freedom of movement. This confined refugees to camps with no legal right to work, including undertaking income-generation activities within the camp. Bhutanese refugees in Nepal continue to be prohibited from selling goods within the camps, primarily due to complaints from local vendors whose businesses were undercut by the competition. In protracted situations like these, women and girls will remain dependent and at risk unless direct advocacy by the UN, local and international NGOs, and others to host-country policy-makers is undertaken. The focus of such advocacy efforts needs to be on the realisation of rights for refugees and the creation of an enabling economic environment so that they may legally work and generate income.

Market survey

Where displaced populations are allowed to engage in income-generation activities, it is imperative that a market survey is developed to guide the establishment of any income-generation activity. A market survey can determine the demand for skills in the local market, whether the requisite raw materials are available, and if there is any local competition, as well as provide insight into the sustainability of the proposed activity. It is essential that any income-generation activity undertaken will generate at least as much, if not more profit than that earned by gathering and selling firewood.

Active engagement with the women and girls themselves is also necessary for the success of the income-generation project. Agencies should develop a 'culture of inquiry' where lessons learned, good practices, and other information can be pulled together and analysed in an effort to design and develop an effective strategy (Longley and Maxwell 2003, 22). Women and girls should be asked what type of work they want to do, what skills they perceive as particularly valuable, and to determine the constraints on their ability to participate in any given activity (for example, the need to care for children or disapproval from male family members). Focus groups, structured interviews, and informal consultations can be held to solicit direct input. When women and girls are consulted and engaged in programme design, their existing skills can be developed and they can help lead and manage income-generation initiatives directly. Neglecting to consult women and girls may hamper the success of the project. International relief agencies, for example, may erroneously base their skills-trainings and livelihood projects on Western gender stereotypes: women and girls may be trained in sewing, although it is traditionally men who sew for profit in many less-developed countries, such as in India and Ethiopia, and men may be recruited into agricultural activities, which are traditionally considered women's work (UNESCO 2006).

Fostering an active dialogue with the displaced community through a 'culture of inquiry' can also flesh out cultural traditions that may have an impact on determining the appropriateness of different income-generation activities. Top-down initiatives may not resonate with the population or may be prohibited due to cultural traditions. One humanitarian agency in Darfur, for example, distributed egg-laying chickens among displaced women as an income-generation activity in an effort to prevent them from leaving the camp in search of firewood for income purposes. It was only after the organisation had invested in chickens, wire, and feed that staff learned that Darfuri women do not 'touch' eggs or chicken after reaching puberty (Women's Commission for Refugee Women and Children 2006e).

Income-generation activities proposed should match local market needs with existing skills and seek to further develop available skill sets. As with all skill development, it is important to start with, and build on, those skills and experiences already existing in the target population, including non-monetised skills such as caring for children, cooking, cleaning, and harvesting. Most women possess numerous skills for work that they have undertaken but for which they have never earned income. These skill sets are often transferable in employment settings and for income-generation activities.

Finally, the stage of the conflict must also be taken into consideration. If repatriation or return is forthcoming, extending the market survey to include the market needs of the destination community or region is extremely valuable. Even if repatriation or return is not imminent, it is advantageous to develop a long-term livelihoods strategy that incorporates a broader range of skills that would be useful in areas of return. For example, over one million people displaced by the 20-year conflict in southern Sudan have voluntarily returned home as of August 2006 (Internal Displacement Monitoring Center 2006). Due to lack of appropriate livelihood or income-generation skills learned while in displacement, few returnees have entrepreneurial experience, and the local markets are dominated by foreigners, for example, by Ugandans, Kenyans, and further north by northern Sudanese. Indeed, many returnees are unaccompanied women with children who have resorted to collecting firewood to sell in the markets because they do not have other viable skills for earning an income. They subsist on a hand-to-mouth existence with few, if any, plans or strategies for their long-term economic livelihood (Women's Commission for Refugee Women and Children 2006e).

Working with girls

In situations of conflict, the dearth of youth-friendly services is a significant barrier to ensuring girls' right to a healthy, safe, and productive life. It is important to recognise that adolescent girls can and should be a part of the solution in addressing this gap. Young people in general, and adolescent girls in particular, have a very limited voice in their communities. Although displaced girls are often identified as a high-risk group that requires special assistance and protection, it is imperative to realise that they should not be defined solely by their perceived vulnerability, as they also have skills, knowledge, experience, and the ability to identify and realise solutions. Their participation in the assessment, design, and implementation of training and education programmes should be incorporated into relief efforts, as adolescent girls are creative, energetic, and important agents for constructive change within their communities. They need to be provided with training and education opportunities that do not simply prevent them from foraging for firewood but prepare them for adulthood – an adulthood that comes with economic choices and opportunities.

Male involvement

Relief agencies that establish income-generation initiatives targeted towards women and girls may neglect the roles and needs of men and boys, which can undermine the initiative as well as increase the risk of gender-based violence against women. Normal social structures, including gender roles, are disrupted during the course of displacement. Men's traditional roles as the sole provider for and protector of their family, roles which are common in many societies, often change dramatically in the context of displacement. Alternately, the change in social fabric may create new opportunities for women such as participation in leadership and decision-making, and changes in the traditional gendered division of labour. Given this potentially radical shift in social norms, compounded by the multi-faceted loss experienced as a result of displacement, programmes that do not engage men and boys run the risk of fostering male resistance, and may even cause rates of domestic and other forms of gender-based violence against women to increase, as men feel emasculated and frustrated at their own lack of livelihood opportunities (Women's Commission for Refugee

Women and Children 2005). Moreover, if men do not accept altered gender roles, women may be forced back into conventional labour roles upon return or repatriation. All income-generation activities for women and girls should actively engage men, either by providing a distinct role within the initiative, or establishing a separate income-generation project specifically for interested men. Income-generation activities targeting women should not add to the often undue responsibility of household tasks women shoulder. Instead, such activities need to facilitate a more equitable distribution of labour, including that undertaken by men.

Overall protection

Safe and sustainable opportunities for displaced women and girls to earn income do not just serve as a tool of protection in the context of firewood collection, but also more generally. During displacement, women and girls often become economically dependent on aid organisations and on men, increasing their vulnerability to exploitation and abuse. Skill trainings and income-generation activities increase women's economic self-sufficiency and sense of self-worth, which simultaneously reduces their risk of sexual exploitation, including trafficking. Further, when women are not economically vulnerable, they can more easily remove themselves from abusive or exploitative situations when they have the means to financially support themselves and their family.

When women are excluded from participating in economic life, they may suffer marginalisation, oppression, and discrimination. Women and girls who experience inequality and social exclusion are less likely to challenge hostile legal and social systems that fail to protect their rights, thereby further heightening their vulnerability (Women's Commission for Refugee Women and Children 2006c). Engaging in income-generation activities gives women and girls a sense of economic empowerment, builds social capital, and can help combat marginalisation through their active participation in the labour market. Conversely, women and girls who are not able to earn an income are more likely to put themselves at risk by collecting firewood to sell, or engaging in sex work or illegal work, all of which increase their vulnerability to violence and exploitation. Transactional or survival sex is also a common economic coping strategy used by displaced women and girls when the only thing they have to sell or exchange for goods is their bodies. A recent report on Burmese refugees in Thailand noted that 'traffickers take advantage of the lack of viable income-generation options for refugees in the camps' (Women's Commission for Refugee Women and Children 2006a, 34).

Although income-generation activities may protect women from gender-based violence, they may also be beneficial to women who have survived sexual assault, abuse, or exploitation by helping to improve self-esteem and self-confidence. For example, the establishment of women's centres in camps or settlements that offer skills-building and literacy classes as well as income-generation projects may aid the recovery of gender-based violence survivors as well as benefit all women who access the services (UNHCR 2003).

Repatriation and return

Income-generation activities are not only an important protection mechanism, but vital in the development of self-reliance, which is critical for the rebuilding of families, communities, and nations upon return home or resettlement to another country. Given that 68 per cent of all refugees are now displaced, on average, for 17 years (US Committee for Refugees and Immigrants 2005), developing sustainable, relevant, and culturally appropriate income-generation activities is essential to successful reintegration of displaced populations into communities of origin, if and when they finally return. Indeed, refugees and internally displaced persons often identify livelihoods, including income-generation activities, as one of their most pressing needs (Women's Commission for Refugee Women and Children 2001; Women's Commission for Refugee Women and Children 2000).

Income-generation activities can also promote and maintain a culture and its customs. For example, ethnic Karen refugees who have fled Myanmar and now live in camps in Thailand learn traditional loom weaving, sewing, embroidery, and the use of natural dyes which enables them not only to produce a profit to assist themselves and their families, but also to raise awareness of Karen culture by selling their products in the local community and abroad (Karen Women's Organization 2006). Income-generation activities are only one of the many interventions that facilitate sustainable solutions and are vital for refugees' successful repatriation and reintegration. These kinds of activities, however, are some of the most critical since they reduce women and girls' vulnerability to sexual violence, abuse, and exploitation and provide women and girls with choices and opportunities.

Conclusion

Sexual violence during firewood collection in conflict-affected settings is rampant, as are other forms of sexual abuse and exploitation. However, it is a problem that the international community can mitigate. Direct provision of fuel, patrolling of firewood collection routes or transportation to collection sites, and the promotion of alternative fuels and fuel-efficient technologies, when coupled with income-generation activities, are strategies that can help reduce sexual violence in displaced settings. To ensure these strategies are effective, it is essential that they are implemented in a co-ordinated manner in collaboration with displaced women and girls. Moreover, income-generation activities can also help bridge the gap between relief and development efforts and prepare women and girls for a role in the eventual reconstruction and peace-building in their home countries and communities.

In the context of complex humanitarian emergencies, the line between emergency response and development blurs and the concept of a linear transition from humanitarian to development-led response is contestable. Although the emergency phase may last only a few months, the post-emergency stage can deteriorate back into an acute phase if the conflict resumes. In chronic emergency settings, certain areas may stay in an acute phase while others move towards the post-emergency phase. Restoring stability in crises is a complex and unpredictable process: a coherent, multi-faceted strategy is essential to a successful and sustainable transition. Income-generation activities, when designed and implemented effectively and in collaboration with the displaced population, can contribute to a successful durable solution for displaced women and girls while simultaneously protecting them from sexual violence.

References

Chang, I. (1997) *The Rape of Nanking: The Forgotten Holocaust of World War II*, New York: Basic Books.

Christian Children's Fund (2006) 'Life Is Harsh for Children in Chad Refugee Camps', available at http://interaction.org/newswire/detail.php?id=5041 (last accessed 19 December 2006).

Durham, H. and T. Gurd (2005) *Listening to the Silences: Women and War*, Leiden, The Netherlands: Koninklijke Brill.

Eisen-Bergman, A. (1975) *Women of Vietnam*, San Francisco: Peoples Press.

Fitzgerald, M. (1998) 'Firewood, Violence against Women and Hard Choices in Kenya', Refugees International, available at http://www.refugeesinternational.org/files/9305_file_060198_Kenya.pdf?PHPSESSID=5c...fliegen%3C/a (last accessed 2 April 2007).

Galitsky, C., A. Gadgil, M. Jacobs, and Y. Lee (2006) 'Fuel Efficient Stoves for Darfur Camps of Internally Displaced Persons Report of Field Trip to North and South Darfur, Nov. 16–Dec.17, 2005', CHF International and Lawrence Berkeley National Laboratory.

Helsinki Watch (1992) *War Crimes in Bosnia-Herzegovina*, New York: Helsinki Watch.

Hitchcock, W. (2004) *The Struggle for Europe: The Turbulent History of a Divided Continent, 1945 to the Present*, New York: First Anchor Books.

Human Rights Watch (1996) *Shattered Lives: Sexual Violence During the Rwandan Genocide and its Aftermath*, New York: Human Rights Watch.

Internal Displacement Monitoring Center (2006) 'Sudan: Slow Return to the South while Darfur Crisis Continues Unabated. A profile of the internal displacement crisis, August 2006', available at http://www.internal-displacement.org/8025708F004CE90B/(httpCountries)/F3D3CAA7CBEBE276802570A7004B87E4?OpenDocument (last accessed 2 April 2007).

International Labour Office (2003) 'Reintegrating Refugees and IDPS', Geneva: International Labour Office.

Karen Women's Organization (2006) *KWO 2005 Annual Report*, Mae Sot, Thailand: Karen Women's Organization.

Longley, C. and D. Maxwell (2003) 'Working Paper 182: Livelihoods, Chronic Conflict and Humanitarian Response: A Synthesis of Current Practice June 2003', London: Overseas Development Institute.

Mark, J. (2005) 'Remembering rape: divided social memory and the Red Army in Hungary 1944–1945', *Past & Present* 188: 133–61.

Médecins Sans Frontières (2004) 'Consequences of Rape: Women and Girls are Scarred', available at http://www.msf.org/msfinternational/invoke.cfm?objectid =E16B6E3F-4E4E-4D13-BFE78E2539E6EAFD&component=toolkit.article&method =full_html (last accessed 2 April 2007).

Olila, S., S. Igras, and B. Monahan (1998) *Assessment Report: Issues and Responses to Sexual Violence, Dadaab Refugee Camps, Kenya, 16-23 October*, Nairobi, Kenya and Atlanta, USA: CARE.

Rehn, E. and E. Johnson Sirleaf (2002) *Women War Peace: The Independent Experts' Assessment on the Impact of Armed Conflict on Women and Women's Role in Peace-building*, Progress of the World's Women 2002, New York: UNIFEM.

Robinson, B. (2002) 'Rape of Women During Wartime: Before, During, and Since World War II', available at http://www.religioustolerance.org/war_rape.htm (last accessed 2 April 2007).

Southern Africa Documentation and Cooperation Centre (2002) 'Focus on Sexual Violence among Burundi Refugees', available at http://www.sadocc.at/news2002/ 2002-153.shtml (last accessed 2 April 2007).

Thomas, D. and R. Ralph (1994) 'Rape in war: challenging the tradition of impunity', *SAIS Review* 1: 82–99.

UNESCO (2006) *Guidebook for Planning Education in Emergencies*, Paris: International Institute for Educational Planning.

UNHCHR (1996) 'Report on the Situation of Human Rights in Rwanda submitted by Mr. René Degni-Segui, Special Rapporteur of the Commission on Human Rights', Commission on Human Rights.

UNHCR (2004) 'UNHCR, Refugees Work Together to Prevent Rape', UNHCR News, available at http://www.unhcr.org/cgi-bin/texis/vtx/news/opendoc.htm?tbl =NEWS&page=home&id=40697ab57 (last accessed 2 April 2007).

UNHCR (2003) *Sexual and Gender-based Violence against Refugees, Returnees and Internally Displaced Persons: Guidelines for Prevention and Response*, Geneva: UNHCR.

UNICEF (1996) *State of the World's Children*, New York: UNICEF.

US Committee for Refugees and Immigrants (2005) *World Refugee Survey 2005. Warehousing: Inventory of Refugee Rights*, Washington DC: US Committee for Refugees and Immigrants.

Vlachova, M. and L. Biason (eds.) (2005) *Women in an Insecure World*, Geneva: Geneva Centre for the Democratic Control of Armed Forces.

Ward, J. (2002) *If Not Now, When? Addressing Gender-Based Violence in Refugee, Internally Displaced, and Post-Conflict Settings*, New York: RHRC Consortium.

Ward, J. and M. Marsh (2006) 'Sexual Violence Against Women and Girls in War and Its Aftermath: Realities, Responses, and Required Resources', a briefing paper prepared for the Symposium on Sexual Violence in Conflict and Beyond, Brussels, Belgium, 21–23 June 2006.

Women's Commission for Refugee Women and Children (2006a) *Abuse Without End: Burmese Refugee Women and Children at Risk of Trafficking*, New York: Women's Commission for Refugee Women and Children.

Women's Commission for Refugee Women and Children (2006b), *Beyond Firewood: Fuel Alternatives and Protection Strategies for Displaced Women and Girls*, New York: Women's Commission for Refugee Women and Children.

Women's Commission for Refugee Women and Children (2006c) *Displaced Women and Girls at Risk: Risk Factors, Protection Solutions and Resource Tools*, New York: Women's Commission for Refugee Women and Children.

Women's Commission for Refugee Women and Children (2006d), *Minimum Initial Services Package (MISP) for Reproductive Health in Crisis Situations: A Distance Learning Module*, New York: Women's Commission for Refugee Women and Children.

Women's Commission for Refugee Women and Children (2006e) 'Reproductive Health Program Trip Report to Darfur, Sudan April 2006', not published.

Women's Commission for Refugee Women and Children (2006f) 'South Sudan Education and Livelihoods Trip Report', not published.

Women's Commission for Refugee Women and Children (2005) *Masculinities: Male Roles and Male Involvement in the Promotion of Gender Equality. A Resource Packet*, New York: Women's Commission for Refugee Women and Children.

Women's Commission for Refugee Women and Children (2001) *Against All Odds: Surviving the War on Adolescents: Promoting the Protection and Capacity of Ugandan and Sudanese Adolescents in Northern Uganda*, New York: Women's Commission for Refugee Women and Children.

Women's Commission for Refugee Women and Children (2000) *Making the Choice for a Better Life: Promoting the Protection and Capacity of Kosovo's Youth*, New York: Women's Commission for Refugee Women and Children.

Zuckerman, L. (2004) *The Rape of Belgium: The Untold Story of World War I*, New York: New York University Press.

Notes

1 This article is made possible by the generous support of the American Jewish World Service (AJWS) and the American people through the United States Agency for International Development (USAID). The contents are the responsibility of the Women's Commission for Refugee Women and Children and do not necessarily reflect the views of AJWS, USAID, or the United States Government.

2 'Firewood' is a generic term used throughout the chapter that also encompasses shrubs, roots, and other organic materials that displaced women and girls collect to burn or sell.

3 At the time of writing, the Women's Commission is spearheading an effort to establish an Inter-agency Standing Committee (IASC) Task Force on Fuel to address all fuel-related co-ordination issues.

5 Negotiating violence and non-violence in Cambodian marriages

Rebecca Surtees

Domestic violence has been increasingly recognised as both a social problem and an issue of human rights in recent decades. In Cambodia, development discourse and programmes have increasingly acknowledged the existence and widespread impact of domestic violence in both advocacy and applied interventions. Coming to terms with, and addressing this violence is urgent. This in turn necessitates a finely tuned understanding of the interplay of social structures, culture, and domestic violence. By locating the elements that promote and perpetrate domestic violence, we are better able to understand why and how this violence occurs, as well as how it can be targeted through interventions. In considering the work of two Cambodian NGOs – Cambodian Women's Crisis Centre (CWCC) and Project Against Domestic Violence (PADV) – we can identify key elements of successful domestic violence interventions in Cambodia. The success of these approaches is in their skill at acknowledging and accommodating the cultural terrain upon which domestic violence is played out, while simultaneously challenging and re-conceptualising the degree to which domestic violence is considered acceptable and permissible.

Qualitative data indicates that between 15–25 per cent of Cambodian women are beaten by their husbands (WGWRC 1994), and 73.9 per cent of women in a national household survey were aware of at least one family which suffers domestic violence (Nelson and Zimmerman 1996). Research also indicates that domestic violence is an issue in families across the socio-economic spectrum; education, age, and income have no correlative effect on the use of violence by intimate partners (Nelson and Zimmerman 1996). As one Cambodian woman observed to me, 'It happens a lot, to my friends, to my family...Many women in Cambodia are hurt by husbands' (interview, July 1998).

Not only is the violence widespread: it is also severe. Over half of abused women in the national household study sustained injuries; more than 50 per cent of women were struck with an object, and 9.1 per cent of injured women had been tied up and hit. Equally disturbingly, 36.4 per cent of women reported having been threatened with a knife or gun, and 5.5 per cent of women reported being stabbed or shot at by their abusive spouse (Nelson and Zimmerman 1996). One woman told of being attacked by her husband with an axe. Another woman spoke of being beaten with whatever was at hand, explaining, 'he beats me with the lock and chain from his *cyclo*, he whips me with a plastic rope, he slaps my face, he pushes me down and kicks me. He punches me with all his might. He beats me with a bamboo rod... He grabs whatever is near him' (Zimmerman 1994, 81).

But uncovering a glaring social problem is one thing. Accounting for it and addressing it in appropriate ways is another. To understand and redress domestic violence, it is critical that we analyse and understand the cultural terrain upon which this violence occurs. Our starting point must necessarily be a contextual understanding of marriage in Cambodian society, and the meanings this holds for Cambodian women themselves. As critical is an understanding of social attitudes to domestic violence and how these contribute to and mitigate domestic violence. As Kleinman argues, 'everyday practices [are] the appropriate site to understand how larger orders of social force come together with micro-contexts of local power, to shape human problems in ways that are resistant to the standard approaches of policies and interventions programs' (2000, 227).

Women as wives and mothers — status within Cambodian marriages

Cambodian society is centred around the family and household, in which 'the bonds between husband and wife, siblings, and especially parents and children, are the strongest and most enduring relations found in village social organisation' (Ebihara 1974). While the conflict and turmoil of recent years has done much to disrupt social structures, this observation remains salient.

Women's role within this template is primarily as wife and mother; marriage and parenthood are important signifiers of status within Cambodian society (Ledgerwood 1990). Women are tasked with the care of the children, responsibility for the household and household economy, and ultimately with ensuring the success of their husbands. Buddhism – to which 95 per cent of the population adheres – also privileges the status of wife and mother, in that the growth and survival of the Buddhist monastic order *(sangha)* is dependent on women's donations of sons, food, and money (Keyes 1984; Ledgerwood 1990).

In Cambodia, as is the case throughout South-East Asia, women gain an important public value through domesticity. They gain prestige as mothers, and official status as elders, worthy of respect. Women are able to exploit this status in their economic ventures and for financial gain (Wazir 1995).

As Wazir argues, 'motherhood diffuses boundaries between the public and domestic spheres and gives women the legitimacy to explore other forms of personal or social activity outside the family' (1995, 19).

Compelling evidence abounds of the privilege attached to the roles of wife and mother. For example, Ledgerwood (1990) recounts instances of Cambodian women who no longer lived with their abusive husbands, but nevertheless displayed photos of their husbands in their homes, in places of respect. Further evidence is found in the increased prevalence of polygamy in Cambodian society, a practice which was not traditionally widespread. The dearth of men caused by the war (1970–1975) and the ensuing civil turbulence, which endured until 1998, forced many women to choose between being a second wife or remaining unmarried. While the status of second wife is less valued, given the primacy of family and women's role within it in the Cambodian social order, some researchers argue that many women prefer to be second and third wives, rather than to remain unmarried (Ledgerwood 1996; Baldwin *et al.* 2000).

Social acceptance of domestic violence

Social acceptance of domestic violence is also a factor in its perniciousness. In Cambodia, many men feel it is their right to beat their wives for 'legitimate' reasons, which generally centre on a wife's failure to fulfil her familial responsibilities. Beating is a legitimate punishment for preparing unappetising food, being sexually unreceptive, or ineffective child-rearing techniques. In situations of domestic violence, the question is thus always what the woman has done to deserve it (Ledgerwood 1990).

Acceptance of domestic abuse is reinforced in literary texts and proverbs. For example, the *chbap srey* (the woman's code)[1] advises women to: 'Follow the command of the husband like a slave; dread your husband's heart for fear of otherwise being insulted or beaten; cook well and never dare to eat until your husband returns home; suppress your emotions to avoid the risk of having your husband insult you; even if your husband has a terrible temper, you must never dare to reply' (quoted in Zimmerman 1994, 26; Pou 1988).

Social acceptance also leads in some cases to institutional acceptance. One research study found that 48 per cent of police surveyed did not consider domestic violence a crime, and only 17 per cent of police officers who witnessed a man whipping his wife would arrest the man (Women's Resource Centre no date). Even in the NGO community, increasingly oriented towards human rights, women and men workers betray varying degrees of acceptance of this violence. For example, one Cambodian female human-rights worker strongly disagreed with her agency's interference in an instance of domestic violence, arguing that the woman might have done something to merit the assault (interview, May 1998).

However, while domestic violence is socially accepted, it is important to emphasise that it is not encouraged. There are social mechanisms to discourage violence. For example, there is a view that, by resorting to physical violence, one lowers oneself in the eyes of the community (Ledgerwood 1990; McLellan 1996). But this needs to be read in context. If a man beats his wife for no reason, shame might play a role. However, if he beats her for socially acceptable reasons (i.e. lax household responsibilities, infidelity), shame is not likely to be an issue (Ledgerwood 1990). Family intervention may also discourage domestic violence, with research indicating that 'more than twice as many women whose parents are dead are abused as women who live with their parents' (Nelson and Zimmerman 1996, 29). However, while families may intervene to stop the violence, they may also subsequently encourage women to return to their husbands. As one mother advised her abused daughter, 'Please go back home. Don't be afraid of your husband, he won't beat you until you are dead. At most he will just hit you until you are unconscious. If he beats you to death, I will bury your bones' (Zimmerman 1994, 26).

Another factor which makes domestic violence so pernicious in Cambodia is that it is seen as a private, family issue rather than as a public and social problem. However, to read and understand domestic violence as a public issue means that it appears in its true light, as one of many manifestations of social violence, rather than as a form of violence which is outside the domain of public awareness and significance. To promote this understanding of domestic violence is neither a simple nor an insignificant undertaking. Indeed, one of the major obstacles in combating domestic violence everywhere in the world is that it is commonly conceptualised as a private issue rather than a public concern. This is dangerous for a number of reasons. First, it suggests domestic violence can be understood in isolation, outside of the social and political context in which it is perpetrated. As Marcus argues, 'all too often, it is distinguished from other forms of punishable violence in a society; this distinction confines it to the category of "discipline", or response to "provocation"; it is minimised or denied, or viewed as individual and aberrant, rather than a culturally justified and endorsed systemic practice designed to silence and to coerce a clearly identifiable population' (1994, 17). It permits a focus on the individual as a sufferer of violence, and an ignorance of the fact that such violence is systemic (Surtees 2000).

Second, seeing domestic violence as a private affair permits society to ignore the specific, gendered nature of domestic violence. Women suffer domestic violence because they are women, and they suffer it at the hands of their intimate partners. The punishment (or lack thereof) for perpetrators of domestic violence further supports this assertion. As one aid worker in Cambodia explained to me, 'When a man is killed by a woman, the woman will go to jail. When a man kills a man, the man will go to jail. When a man kills a woman, the husband pays off the family, or nothing at all happens. It is the difference between women and men' (interview, June 1998).[2] Of course, domestic violence is not simply an issue of sanctioning men's violence against women. Were a man to beat or kill his neighbour's wife, there would be repercussions. Domestic violence is violence within marriage and the family, which has everything to do with the sexual nature of the relationship between (abusing) man and (abused) woman. Sexual relations, sanctioned as taking place within marriage, and hence the private domain, introduce a different set of social dynamics and allowances in terms of violence (Surtees 2000).

Third, seeing domestic violence as 'private' implies that the state has no duty or ability to intervene. Yet the dichotomy of public/private in the contemporary state is an overstatement. There are numerous examples of the selective intrusion of the state into the private sphere, including taxation, social security, immigration laws and marriage and family law, established religion and military service (Carrillo 1992). As Marcus has put it, 'family and state are not unrelated institutions' (1994, 26) and it is disingenuous to suggest that family issues are beyond the state's control (Surtees 2000).

If domestic violence is seen as an issue of public concern, it can be understood in terms of what it seeks to achieve and promote, which moves the focus beyond the act itself or the context in which it occurs. If we accept that violence in general is 'a strategy for asserting control and domination and creating terror', we must accept that domestic violence seeks the same objectives (Marcus 1994, 26). The fact that it is perpetrated within an intimate personal relationship does not modify, or in any way change, the objective of the violence.[3] It cannot be understood as a 'lovers' quarrel' or trivialised as a 'spat'. Further, women's experiences as victims of domestic violence must be reconsidered. While victims of 'public' violence elicit social sympathy and support, abused women are often dismissed as provoking the assault, or because it is judged by outsiders to be 'none of our business'. As a result, abused women and their experiences are 'disconnected from the social, cultural, economic and political context of domination and subordination' (Marcus 1994, 33).

From understanding to intervention

The above discussion has sketched out the social terrain upon which domestic violence is played out. Understanding this is critical in the designing of policy interventions which fit the Cambodian social context. As Kleinman observes, 'the problem may be global, but the intervention needs to be oriented to a local world' (2000, 235). Focus must be placed 'on the interpersonal space of suffering, the local, ethnographic context of action. This requires not only engagement with what is at stake for participants in those local worlds, but bringing those local participants (not merely national experts) into the process of developing and assessing programs' (Kleinman and Kleinman 1996, 18). This means that concern for human rights must always be central, but development programmes must also accommodate local cultures, to ensure that these facilitate and change, rather than form an obstacle to it (Hobart 1993).

Thus, anti-violence interventions which are feasible elsewhere may be inappropriate in Cambodia. Take, for example, the 'solution' of suggesting that a woman divorces an abusive husband. Even in situations of domestic violence, Cambodian women are very reluctant to leave their marriages. Divorce deprives women of their privileged status as wife, closes many access routes to social power, and decreases women's status (Ledgerwood 1996). As CWCC director Ung Chantoul commented to me, 'abused women have an option here at the shelter to a certain extent...we can help them get a job, we can help them with counselling...but then the women are often saying "it is hard to be a widow". We must think of what it is like to live in Cambodia without a husband' (interview, June 1998). Divorced women suffer social discrimination (Ovesen *et al.* 1996; Zimmerman 1994) and 'censure from the community acted as an extremely strong deterrent to divorce, particularly for women... a woman is marked for life, as a disgrace to her family, as an unfit marriage partner, as "used goods" ' (Ledgerwood 1990, 181). As former PADV director Sar Samen has noted, 'in Cambodia, they believe that divorce is not good for women, because it hurts the future of the children, and it's hard for the woman to live without a husband. People look down on her' (interview, May 1998).

In addition to social stigma, there are real economic hardships for female-headed households, including labour shortages and the issue of land ownership (Baldwin *et al.* 2000). For example, in one study, all of the abused women were dissatisfied with their divorce settlement, as husbands were awarded property that the women had purchased themselves, or owned prior to marriage (Zimmerman 1994).

Further, leaving the relationship does not always remove the risk of violence. Abused women risk murder and 'separation assault' – that is, the spouse continues to hurt his wife after separation (Mahoney 1994; Teays 1998). Zimmerman documented 'a great deal of circumstantial evidence of spousal murder. We learned of at least ten women who died as a direct result of beatings' (1994, 78). This was vividly illustrated recently, in the case of one woman who was nearly beaten to death by her estranged husband after she refused to have sexual relations with him (*Phnom Penh Post* 2002). For these reasons, divorce is hardly a panacea in Cambodia.

With this in mind, we can identify key points of entry, and formulate interventions by looking at the work of Cambodian NGOs on domestic violence. While the terrain is a difficult one to negotiate, it is not impossible. Two Cambodian NGOs – CWCC and PADV – have proven successful in formulating appropriate interventions in domestic violence in Cambodia. What is most compelling about the approaches of CWCC and PADV is how their interventions mesh with social norms, while simultaneously challenging the permissibility of domestic violence. For example, CWCC attempts to reconcile marriages where possible, while forcing an acknowledgement of women's rights, through the use of marriage contracts. Similarly, PADV's awareness-raising efforts confront the understandings of domestic violence as a private, family issue, outside of the scope of human rights and public intervention. These NGO initiatives should be analysed, acclaimed, and expanded.

Cambodian Women's Crisis Centre (CWCC)

The Cambodian Women's Crisis Centre was established in 1997, in response to the overwhelming rate of violence perpetrated against women, and the impunity enjoyed by the perpetrators of this violence.[4] The organisation is founded on concern for domestic violence as a violation of women's human rights, and a parallel concern to ensure abused women can make their own choices. CWCC sees its role as facilitating domestic violence survivors in making choices that meet with their needs and interests. A central choice is whether or not to leave their abusive marriage.

This choice is most frequently conceptualised as that between 'victim' (those staying in the relationship) or 'agent' (those leaving the relationship). The situation, however, is significantly more complex, particularly where social prestige is associated with marital and parental status. Leaving the relationship is not the only means by which women can express choice and agency. Women who stay in their relationships exert agency, and negotiate in ways that are camouflaged if their choice is seen simply as 'staying'. For example, in seeking to change the relationship, getting advice from friends, finding temporary shelter, having someone intervene, or setting conditions for their return, women are acting out their resistance to domestic violence within the framework of 'staying' (Surtees 2000). As Mahoney argues, 'Emphasising exit defines the discussion of violence in ways that ignore the woman's life experience and the personal and societal context of power, focusing instead on whether her responsive actions conform to societal expectations. The idea that women should leave – and that a woman acting in her own interest will always leave – is shaped by this atomistic view of agency' (1994, 74).

There is little research anywhere in the world into how abuse is successfully overcome in a relationship. Little is known about women who stay and renegotiate their relationship, or about the batterer who stops battering.[5] Nevertheless, even seemingly straightforward situations of victimisation and violence potentially hold within them possible negotiation. As Mahoney observes, 'legal and social inquiry then turn to investigation of "staying" as a problem, rather than giving attention to the help and support a battered woman needs to effectuate her goals' (1994, 76).

Significantly, it is precisely this issue of agency within 'staying' that has value for interventions on domestic violence in Cambodia. Agency as manifested in the West – divorce, separation, criminal charges, restraining orders – appears neither desirable, nor particularly plausible, from a legal, economic, or social perspective. But this does not mean that Cambodian women are simply passive. For example, Cambodian women agreeing to be interviewed for research on domestic violence are expressing their voice. Likewise, women negotiate when they seek temporary refuge with family or neighbours, or file a complaint with the village chief, or confront their husbands and demand change. Once expressions of women's actions are identified, they can be further developed, and other possibilities identified to support and enhance not only women's agency, but also their options.

A valuable illustration of encouraging women's agency (and alternatives) in cases of domestic violence comes from CWCC, in its critique of the state-administered process of marriage reconciliation (psapsaah). Conventional marriage reconciliation consists of a number of stages, and, while not uniform, follows a general pattern. The woman files a divorce complaint. The couple are then required to attend a reconciliation meeting with a Commune official. They each voice their complaints. The woman complains of abuse. The husband likely explains (and excuses) his behaviour by accusing the wife of infidelity or, more commonly, of domestic violations, like burning the rice or not disciplining the children. The reconciler then suggests how the situation might be remedied, and the husband pledges to end the abuse, if the wife drops her complaint. Generally, there are three reconciliation meetings before the court will entertain the possibility of divorce (Zimmerman 1994).[6]

The practice of Cambodian marriage reconciliation is ultimately dangerous for the abused woman. First, the mandatory nature of this form of 'reconciliation' does not address the specific risks of an abusive relationship. Second, while the law stipulates that reconciliation should not be pursued when the court finds that the complaint is based upon very serious circumstances, domestic violence researchers found no occasion where this exception clause was used (Zimmerman 1994). As such, the process violates a woman's right to live free from violence. Third, officials are inadequately trained in reconciliation, and consistently misquote and misrepresent the marriage law. Even among the informed, legal decisions do not always reflect legal parameters (Zimmerman 1994). Fourth, the process seeks a pre-determined outcome of reconciliation, and as such is a violation of a woman's right to autonomy. Fifth, the reconciliation process, as a 'no-fault' system, ultimately places at least some blame with the woman, failing to address the issue of domestic violence as a criminal assault and human-rights violation.

CWCC has developed an alternative to the above process. In its alternative intervention, CWCC oversees a legal contract between the married couple, in which the husband pledges to cease abuse if the wife returns to the marriage. However, the contract goes beyond that of mainstream reconciliation pledges, which are not binding or enforced.[7] The CWCC contract is a legal document, which includes conditions of return, and provides for legal and financial settlements for the wife, should the abuse continue and the couple separate. Provisions might include the husband's relinquishment of the family home; financial support; custody of the children; or a pledge of uncontested divorce. As Acting Director of CWCC Sun Sothy explained to me, this means that in the event that the husband violates the CWCC agreement, the victim has a legally binding document which will be of assistance when filing a complaint for divorce in court (personal communication 2003). As such, the wife is able to return home, while making her own conditions for return. CWCC provides women with negotiation tools, signalling an awareness that women's decision-making power represents a critical point of intervention for domestic violence programmes. That being said, Sun Sothy stressed that 'after signing, it does not mean that the domestic violence case is finished…CWCC gives one chance for the couple to reconcile and live together without filing a complaint in court' (personal communication 2003). In 2002, 28 domestic violence victims were staying at the CWCC shelter, of whom 12 opted eventually for divorce, while 16 opted to return to their families (personal communication 2003).

The CWCC approach avoids divorce, at least initially, while still guaranteeing the rights and safety of the abused woman, and allowing her to make choices with which she is comfortable. In contexts in which divorce is not only legally possible, but socially sanctioned and economically viable, such measures are not vital. In Cambodia, however, given the problematic nature of divorce there, such measures are important: they facilitate women's agency while protecting their rights and safety, in a culturally sensitive manner.

Project Against Domestic Violence (PADV)

The Project Against Domestic Violence (PADV) was established in 1995, as a resource, information, and training agency. PADV tackles domestic violence in large part through its awareness-raising campaigns, and profiles it as a public, rather than private, issue. That is, PADV is reconceptualising the terrain upon which this issue should be addressed. This is critical, given that current ways of categorising violence – '…public versus domestic, ordinary as against extreme political violence – are inadequate to understand either the uses of violence in the social world, or the multiplicity of its effects in experiences of suffering, collective and individual' (Kleinman 2000, 227).

In its efforts to force recognition of domestic violence as a public issue, and ensure it is tackled as such, PADV produces information materials on domestic violence. These include a video enacting a survivor's story, a television drama, radio announcement, and the first Cambodian poster against domestic violence. Perhaps the most striking example of PADV's awareness-raising efforts was its 1998 national theatre tour. This was undertaken in collaboration with the Women's Media Centre (WMC)[8] and the Prom Mahn theatre troupe. The play adopted the *ayai* style – a Cambodian improvisational theatre form using song and comedy – to convey its message in a culturally appropriate way.[9] The play contrasted the lives and fortunes of two neighbouring families. One family enjoyed a happy and good life, due in large part to the loving relationship between the husband and wife, while, by contrast, their neighbouring family suffered much misfortune and pain, due to domestic violence in their home. The drama suggested non-violent ways of settling domestic discord within families. The play raised and explored domestic violence as a public issue and a criminal act, but it did so subtly and in such a way that it did not overtly attack men and husbands. It permitted men and women to take a vantage point on domestic violence, and the means to ameliorate this violence, without loss of face or dignity (Frieson 1998; Baldwin *et al.* 2000).

For the vast majority of the audience, a drama which discussed domestic violence at all, let alone as a public issue, was novel. PADV staff also took advantage of the forum offered by performances of the drama to disseminate information about domestic violence, and the means to effect change. This information included printed matter about the law, referral agencies, and other NGOs working on domestic violence. Prior to performances, PADV staff also met with government and community leaders to provide information on the existing laws, and appropriate responses. This ensured that the issue was framed in a way in which the community and community leadership had a role to play and could assume responsibility.

The travelling drama and its associated advocacy activities generated extensive attention in the media, as well as stimulating public dialogue on the issue of domestic violence (Mapleston 1998). This is a significant development. As one former PADV technical adviser observed, 'more organisations are talking about domestic violence as a category of violence... People have started to talk about domestic violence as a human rights issue' (interview, May 1998). As such, PADV's theatre tour represents a valuable means of profiling this assumed private issue, and situating it firmly and correctly in the public domain.

As Marcus argues, 'Often the recasting takes what is designated as a "personal situation" and identifies it as a social and political issue. Often, recasting provides a foundation for a re-viewing of an issue in new ways. In turn, this re-viewing may result in the emergence of new and different assessments and evaluations of a problem. Finally, this re-viewing may lead to the development of innovative strategies for the future' (1994, 25).

Through this 'recasting', PADV has pushed the parameters of what can be discussed publicly. The play gave persuasive examples of why domestic violence could not, and should not, be seen only as an issue of the domestic sphere. And it equipped public actors – officials, neighbours, community leaders – with the information they needed to tackle the issue in the public domain. Of course, this is not to say that this public recognition and recasting was a straightforward process which is now complete. Everywhere in the world, it has been a long and arduous battle to situate domestic violence in the public sphere. However, PADV's work is noteworthy as an important step in this direction.[10]

Conclusion

In Cambodia, marriage and domestic violence are so embedded in social systems that development initiatives cannot target these issues in a cultural vacuum. Without acknowledging and exploring the presence and meaning of domestic violence in marriage, it is impossible to tackle it.

This should not be taken to mean, however, that there is no space for internationally informed and formulated interventions in Cambodia. The universality of domestic violence reveals many commonalities of experience and, thus, potential for programmes which incorporate elements which have proved successful in other contexts. Nor is this an argument in the vein of cultural relativism where traditional resolutions are 'ideal' because they are 'cultural'. Too often women suffer violence precisely in the playing out of traditional features of a culture. Rather, what I argue is that space must be provided for Cambodian women (and men) to design and implement domestic violence interventions which are grounded in local cultural perspectives (Surtees 2000). As Desjarlais argues, 'perhaps it is precisely in the clash between worldviews, in the tension between symbolic systems (how reality is defined, the body held or experience articulated) that some...insights emerge' (1992, 18).

Significantly, by combining international standards and an understanding of cultural and social structures, one can formulate interventions which respect human rights, while simultaneously maintaining or evolving desirable elements of the social order. Both CWCC and PADV have done precisely this, in their efforts to combat domestic violence in Cambodia. These interventions mesh with cultural norms and the established social order, while simultaneously seeking to redress the prevalence and permissibility of domestic violence. Such interventions and perspectives must be further acclaimed and expanded.

This article was originally published in Gender & Development, *volume 11, number 2, July 2003.*

References

Ang Choulean (1986) *Les Etres Surnaturels dans la Religion Populaire Khmere*, Paris: Cedoreck.

Baldwin, H., J. Benjamin, and Krishna Kumar (2000) 'War, Genocide and Women in Post-Conflict Cambodia' (Working Draft), Washington DC: USAID.

Ball, M. and Kuch Nren (2002) 'Cambodia: Debate set for Domestic Violence Draft Law', *Cambodia Daily*, available at http://www.ahrchk.net/news/mainfile.php/ahrcnews_200211/2746/ (last accessed 30 March 2007).

CAMBOW (2003) Press Statement, 15 January 2003, posted to twcc listserve on 13 January 2003.

Carrillo, R. (1992) *Battered Dreams: Violence against Women as an Obstacle to Development*, New York: UNIFEM.

Desjarlais, R. (1992) *Body and Emotion: the Aesthetics of Illness and Healing in the Nepal Himalaya*, Philadelphia: University of Philadelphia Press.

Dworkin, A. (1997) *Unapologetic Writings on the Continuing War against Women*, New York: The Free Press.

Ebihara, M. (1974) 'Khmer village women in Cambodia', in C. Mattiassons (ed.) *Many Sisters: Women in Cross-Cultural Perspective*, New York: The Free Press, 305–47.

Frieson, K. (1998) *The Role of Women's Organisations in Post-Conflict Cambodia*, Washington: Center for Development Information and Evaluation, USAID.

Hobart, M. (1993) 'Introduction', in M. Hobart (ed.) *Anthropological Critique of Development: the Growth of Ignorance*, London: Routledge, 1–30.

Keyes, C. F. (1984) 'Mother or mistress but never a monk: Buddhist notions of female gender in rural Thailand', *American Ethnologist* 11(2): 223–41.

Kleinman, A. (2000) 'The violence of everyday life: The multiple forms and dynamics of social violence', in V. Das, A. Kleinman, M. Ramphele, and Pamela Reynolds (eds.) *Violence and Subjectivity*, Berkeley, LA and London: University of California Press, 226–41.

Kleinman, A. and J. Kleinman (1996) 'The appeal of experience; the dismay of images: cultural appropriations of suffering in our times', *Daedalus* 125(1): 1–24.

Ledgerwood, J. (1996) 'Politics and gender: negotiating conceptions of the ideal woman in present day Cambodia', *Asia Pacific Viewpoint* 37(2).

Ledgerwood, J. (1990) 'Changing Khmer Conceptions of Gender: Women, Stories and the Social Order', Ph.D thesis, Cornell University, Ithaca, New York.

Mahoney, M. R. (1994) 'Victimization or oppression? Women's lives, violence and agency', in M. A. Fineman and R. Mykitiuk (eds.) *The Public Nature of Private Violence: the Discovery of Domestic Abuse*, New York and London: Routledge, 59–92.

Mapleston, C. (1998) 'Theatre tour highlights domestic violence', *Bayon Pearnik*, Phnom Penh, March, 3(23): 7.

Marcus, I. (1994) 'Reframing "domestic violence": terrorism in the home', in M. A. Fineman and R. Mykitiuk (eds.) *The Public Nature of Private Violence: the Discovery of Domestic Abuse*, New York and London: Routledge, 11–35.

McLellan, J. (1996) 'Silent screams and hidden pain: barriers to the adaptation and integration of Cambodian women refugees in Ontario', in W. Gales, H. Moussa, and P. Van Esterik (eds.) *Development and Diaspora: Gender and the Refugee Experience*, Dundas, Ontario: Artemis Enterprises, 238–55.

Nelson, E. and C. Zimmerman (1996) *Household Survey on Domestic Violence in Cambodia*, Phnom Penh, Cambodia: PADV/MWA/IDRC.

Ovesen, J., Ing-Britt Trankell, and Joakim Ojendal (1996) *When Every Household is an Island: Social Organisation and Power Structures in Rural Cambodia*, Stockholm, Sweden: Uppsala University and SIDA.

Oxfam (1998) 'Nothing Can Stop Me Now: Report on the International Oxfam Workshop on Violence Against Women', Sarajevo, Bosnia. 30 November – 4 December 1999, available at http://www.law-lib.utoronto.ca/Diana/fulltext/VAWsucc.htm (last accessed 30 March 2007).

Phnom Penh Post (2002) 'Police Blotter', 11(23), available at http://www.phnompenhpost.com/TXT/current/stories/police.htm (last accessed 30 March 2007).

Pou, S. (1988) *Guirlande de Cpap*, Paris: Cedoreck.

Surtees, R. (2000) 'Cambodian Women and Violence: Considering NGO Interventions in Cultural Context' (MA Dissertation), Sydney, Australia: Macquarie University.

Teays, W. (1998) 'Standards of perfection and battered women's self-defense', in S. French, W. Teays, and L. Purdy (eds.) *Violence against Women: Philosophical Perspectives*, Ithaca, NY: Cornell UP, 57–76.

Wazir Jahan Karim (1995) 'Bilateralism and gender in Southeast Asia', in Wazir Jahan Karim (ed.) *'Male' and 'Female' in Developing Southeast Asia*, Oxford: Berg, 35–73.

WGWRC (1994) 'Wife abuse in the family: violating the rights of women in Cambodia', in UNICEF/SSWA *Fire in the House: Determinant of Intrafamilial Violence and Strategies for its Elimination*, Bangkok, Thailand: UNICEF, 171–80.

Women's Resource Centre (WRC) (n.d.) *Report of the Survey on Domestic Violence*, Phnom Penh, Cambodia.

Zimmerman, C. (1994) *Plates in a Basket Will Rattle: Domestic Violence in Cambodia*, Phnom Penh, Cambodia: Asia Foundation/USAID.

Notes

1 The *chbaps* are prescriptions for proper behaviour and comportment. There are *chbaps* for all human relationships – *chbap srey* (woman's code), *chbap proh* (man's code), the *chbap kun cau* (grandchildren's *chbap*), *chbap baky cas* (*chbap* of ancient advice), *chbap keru* (inheritance *chbap*) (Ang 1986).

2 In one instance, I recall a neighbour intervened in a situation of domestic violence and was injured by the abusive husband. Charges were brought against the husband for his assault on the neighbour. No charges were laid for the assault of the wife.

3   The significance of this understanding cannot be overstated. As Dworkin
    argues, 'It is easy to say that men beat women in order to express domination,
    to exercise control, these are easy sentences to say. But I need you to think
    about what they really mean…When we talk about battery, we have to remember
    that we are talking about every aspect of a human life, every single day,
    all the time. The problem of human freedom has never been considered from
    the point of view of a woman's life' (1997, 157–8).

4   A domestic violence law is currently being debated in the Cambodian National
    Assembly (Ball & Nren 2002). The law was formulated by the Ministry of
    Women's and Veteran's Affairs in 2001 with inputs from civil society. NGO
    efforts to advocate for, articulate, and pass domestic-violence legislation has
    been ongoing since 1996.

5   One study found that 27 per cent of women who reunited with their abusive
    spouse experienced violence within six weeks and 57 per cent experienced
    violence within six months. That is, more than 40 per cent of women reported
    no violence for six months after returning to the relationship. In another study,
    more than 50 per cent of abusive husbands arrested their abuse out of fear of
    divorce or the desire to rebuild their marriages (Mahoney 1994).

6   Divorce generally involves at least three stages of reconciliation; months of
    waiting in between; extensive cost; travel to the court; court delays; social
    pressure from family, neighbours, and officials; and continued abuse from the
    husband. Further, it is not uncommon that the judge simply refuses to grant a
    divorce. As one survivor explained, 'I went to the local authorities for help,
    but they would only arrange reconciliation' (Oxfam website 1999).

7   Only one of the 28 women who attended reconciliation meetings said it was
    successful. Some women reported that the reconciliation process did more harm
    than good. Several were beaten immediately afterwards (Zimmerman 1994).

8   Women's Media Centre (WMC) was established in 1993 to produce media
    material on a range of gender issues, as well as to monitor and analyse the
    representation of women in the Cambodian media.

9   The play was performed in 39 rural communities in five provinces, reaching more
    than 250,000 people in total (Baldwin *et al.* 2000).

10 Such 'recasting' efforts continue in the present. Most recently, in January 2003,
    PADV, as a member of the Cambodian Committee of Women (CAMBOW) was
    involved in implementing public hearings on domestic violence at which
    victims shared their stories and experiences of domestic abuse with govern-
    ment representatives. As PADV director Hor Phally explained, this initiative
    seeks 'to give the problem a human face and provide a comprehensive picture
    of the effect of domestic violence on society as a whole' (CAMBOW 2003).

6 Social policy from the bottom up: abandoning FGC in sub-Saharan Africa

Peter Easton, Karen Monkman, and Rebecca Miles

Introduction

Female genital cutting (FGC) or female genital mutilation (FGM) – less precisely termed 'female circumcision' – is a centuries-old cultural practice in parts of sub-Saharan Africa and in a few contiguous areas of the Muslim world, such as Egypt and Yemen. Inaccurately identified with Islam, FGC is not sanctioned by the Koran. It has also spread in recent years via migration to the Far East, Europe, and North America. It is estimated that over 130 million women and girls worldwide have undergone the procedure, and two million more are subjected to it each year (Population Reference Bureau 2001).

FGC involves partial or total removal of the female external genitalia and is usually performed on pre-pubescent girls aged four to twelve as part of their rites of passage. In Senegal and Mali it is sometimes performed on baby girls as young as one month old. FGC is practised for a variety of social and cultural reasons:

> The ritual cutting is often an integral part of ceremonies...in which girls are feted and showered with presents and their families are honored...The ritual serves as an act of socialization into cultural values and an important connection to family, community, and earlier generations. At the heart of all this is rendering a woman marriageable, which is important in societies where women get their support from male family members, especially husbands...The practice [of FGC] is perceived as an act of love for daughters...Because of strong adherence to these traditions, many women who say they disapprove of FGC still submit themselves and their daughters to the practice. (Population Reference Bureau 2001:6)

The social function of FGC rests, in some traditional societies, on a long-standing concern to control the perceived threat of overt female sexuality to the web of inter-familial affiliations that marriage cements; however, the practice can have a number of severe health consequences on the women who undergo it. Short-term repercussions may include:

...severe pain, shock, haemorrhage, urine retention, ulceration of the genital region and injury to adjacent tissue...Long-term consequences include cysts and abscesses, keloid scar formation, damage to the urethra resulting in urinary incontinence, dyspareunia (painful sexual intercourse) and sexual dysfunction and difficulties with childbirth. (WHO 2000)

These effects can significantly compromise a girl's lifetime health outlook, although the severity of consequences depends on the procedure used.

The issue was adopted as a major health concern by WHO in 1982 and recognised as a human-rights issue in the 1990s. Strategies for promoting the abandonment of the practice include legislation, medicalisation (training health professionals to perform the procedure under sanitary conditions), religious condemnation, information, 'just-say-no' campaigns, educational efforts, and attempts to institute alternative rituals. According to Mackie (2000), few have had widespread or locally sustained effects because in many cases such strategies have failed to recognise the need for locally generated initiatives to reform such social conventions.

Among the few successful strategies has been an approach developed by Tostan, a rural village empowerment programme that originated in Senegal. The Tostan programme did not at first explicitly focus on FGC, but it embraced it when a number of local women participants decided that combating the practice was their biggest concern and organised to promote its abandonment. Tostan's approach has since been replicated with modifications in Burkina Faso, Mali, Guinea, and Sudan. The story of its development and dissemination – presented and analysed below – provides insight into linkages between non-formal education and social change from the bottom up.

The Tostan experience[1]

Tostan's original mission did not include combating FGC (Easton 1998, 2000; Easton and Monkman 2001; UNICEF 1999, 2002). In Senegal, FGC is practised among about 50 per cent of the population. Only a very small proportion of the country's dominant ethnic group, the Wolof, observes the custom; but the practice is widespread among some of the other main groups in the country – including the Pulaar, the Bambara, and the Mandinka, while it has also been adopted by fragments of the Serer and Diola peoples.

The Tostan initiative got underway in the late 1980s as an attempt to devise non-formal education and literacy programming for rural Senegalese women grounded in their own perception of problems and based on their own learning styles. The word *tostan* itself is Wolof for 'breakthrough' or 'coming out of the egg'. The programme has been continuously supported by UNICEF, and at times it has enjoyed the tolerance and the active endorsement of the government of Senegal. After a trial period in the Kaolack region, the programme was officially launched in

Wolof-speaking villages surrounding Thiès in the central agricultural basin of Senegal and in Pulaar-speaking communities in the region of Kolda, south of the Gambia. It was aimed primarily at women but was also open to men, who accounted for about one-fifth of registrants.

A participatory orientation

A curriculum for the programme was devised in a highly participatory and iterative manner. Designers held a series of workshops with rural women to identify their felt needs, to develop and test curricula that reflected their concerns and used language and cultural forms familiar to the participants, and to anchor the approach in a Senegalese version of 'women's ways of knowing' (Belenky *et al.* 1986). Tostan staff were concerned to break with the then-traditional approaches to literacy programmes, where women struggled over exercises that had little practical application in their lives. The Tostan model that emerged used a problem-solving approach based on the women's perception and prioritisation of their own needs.

Six modules, requiring 18 months' study in all, constituted the initial Tostan curriculum. The programme started with an introductory session on problem solving and continued with modules on hygiene, oral rehydration, immunisation, leadership skills, feasibility studies for local projects, and project management techniques. Literacy lessons in the language of the participants were interwoven throughout. The objective was to enable women to get to grips with their most pressing problems and to acquire the skills to design and manage their own projects as means of addressing those needs. Participants were also encouraged to 'adopt' non-participating adults and – collectively – a non-participating community.

Tostan provided learning materials, training for local facilitators, the bulk of their salaries, and outside monitoring services. The village was responsible for recruiting participants, building and furnishing a learning centre, housing and feeding the facilitator, contributing to the facilitator's salary, and establishing a management committee to supervise these activities. Villages typically organised one or two classes with a maximum of 35 adults each. Facilitators originally came from the community itself, but, with the increasing diversity of curricula, Tostan staff and participants decided to bring in people with greater knowledge and teaching experience. These were generally 'graduates' of other Tostan programmes in the area or literate young people with the requisite interest and skill. Facilitators were paid about $25 a month for each class they taught, of which about $5–10 was provided by the village. The willingness of villages to accept these obligations is testimony to the importance they gave 'second-chance' and problem-solving education for women in a rural environment strongly affected by male out-migration, but also witnesses the attraction of programming that might attract new resources for local development, as Tostan in fact later did.

Follow-up provisions

The village improvement projects and income-generating activities that typically followed the education modules were a significant part of the attraction and momentum of the programme. With the aid of a variety of donors, Tostan tried whenever possible to make available small amounts of seed capital and microcredit for communities and groups that took the initiative to organise and propose projects. Initiatives typically included well-baby clinics, improvements to local water supply, small livestock projects, consumer co-operatives, collective farming efforts, and crafts marketing. The follow-up activities added to the successful aura of the programme and helped increase demand for it. They also created another incentive for men, who were often involved in (but seldom controlled) the management of the resulting initiatives.

As the Tostan programme gained in popularity, participants began requesting further training and new knowledge after completing the 18-month course. To meet the demand, Tostan set about developing a programme of 'continuing education'. The first step was once again to conduct needs assessment in each targeted region in order to ascertain what topics should be addressed. The next step involved participatory development of the related curricula, devised by teams who worked closely with local students and teachers. Four modules of particular local interest were added at this time: human rights, women's health, early childhood development, and sustainable natural resource management. Two months were allotted to the study of each. Not all supplementary modules were implemented in all communities. Uptake depended on the level of local interest and the willingness of donors to underwrite Tostan's related costs.

The first two of these topics quickly generated a great deal of interest. Attendance at sessions on human rights and women's health – which included sessions on issues of women's sexuality that had never before been so openly discussed – broke all records, and lessons were disseminated by word of mouth around a much broader community. During the participatory research phase, Tostan staff discovered the depth of oppressive experiences from which this reaction sprang – stories of girls who had died or had their health permanently impaired by FGC, or tales of women worn out by repeated childbirth who risked death because families and medical personnel refused to allow them access to family planning. In addition, the concept of human rights and the evidence of its international endorsement seem to have struck a chord with a rural population quite aware of its disadvantage compared to urban areas and the industrial world and not far removed from a history of repression. Programme designers realised that the human-rights component provided a means of addressing health issues as well, and of fostering a consciousness-raising, empowering experience that allowed women to open up for the first time about topics that had traditionally been taboo and created a platform for involving both women and men in social problem solving.

'Human rights' thus became an integral part of the message, and the focus of the modules was progressively broadened to include men's health. Drawn by this approach, either by sheer curiosity about issues of such importance to women or out of interest in the broader human-rights agenda, a greater number of male participants began to appear in the classes.

Confronting FGC

In these circumstances, something remarkable happened in one village outside Thiès – the community of Malicounda-Bambara. Women (and a few men) from the village had just completed the full Tostan training programme, including the 'continuing education' modules on human rights and health. When participants sat down to decide what 'problem' they most wanted to address in their post-training phase, a resounding choice was made: get the community to abandon FGC once and for all. The initiative caught Tostan staff almost totally by surprise, and it had multiple repercussions over the months that followed.

The women began by approaching local authorities and other villagers to win support for a declaration of intent to abandon the practice, and they succeeded. On 31 July 1997, the villagers of Malicounda-Bambara made a collective statement renouncing the practice in perpetuity in front of 20 invited Senegalese journalists. The declaration was broadcast on national television and through other media. There was some immediate opposition from conservative religious and political leaders to what the women of Malicounda-Bambara had done, as much in reaction to the 'shame' of talking publicly about a taboo topic as to the substance of the declaration. Despite the controversy, however, Nguerigne-Bambara, a neighbouring village of similar lineage that had also completed the Tostan training programme, decided to imitate Malicounda-Bambara's example. Significantly, the effort there was led by a woman who was herself a traditional 'cutter' and knew the potential effects of FGC only too well. A third village, Kër Simbara, began actively discussing the idea. Then a critical event occurred.

The turning point

Concerned by these events, Demba Diawara, the much-respected 66-year-old imam of Kër Simbara, came to talk with Tostan representatives and the women of Malicounda-Bambara. Diawara was disturbed by this challenge to traditional mores and asked to address the group. But the women of Malicounda-Bambara suggested that he first talk with his own female relatives about their experience and feelings, and then he could return to discuss the matter. Diawara did as he was told, and he got an earful. The elderly imam came back, persuaded that the women were right – and was ready to help. He also had some important advice to give, though.

Diawara pointed out that there were two major problems with the way in which things were being done. 'We are part of an inter-marrying community', he said, 'and unless all the villages involved take part, you are asking parents to forfeit the chance of their daughters getting married.' Second, he felt that there was a real problem of the choice of language and approach. These are taboo topics, Diawara insisted, and they should not be discussed lightly or inconsiderately. The people who crusaded against FGC in the past had done so in front of mixed audiences and used terms and images that shocked the villagers. They had treated the practice as a disease to be eradicated and its practitioners as social pariahs. That is no way to change a culture, or to help it change itself, the imam pointed out.

So Diawara and the women of Malicounda-Bambara outlined a careful strategy that consisted of the following:

- Go to all the villages in the inter-marrying community and start by reaffirming personal relationships.

- Do not tell the villagers what to do, but rather what Malicounda-Bambara and Nguerigne-Bambara had done, and why. Then let them tell their own stories and make their own decisions.

- Avoid using graphic terms or demonstrations for taboo activities. Refer to FGC simply as 'the custom', as everyone knows what is meant. (In Senegalese, Bambara 'customs' in the plural refer to a whole set of cultural traditions; 'the custom' in the singular refers to FGC alone.)

- Avoid condemning practitioners either implicitly or explicitly for practices they have been performing in good faith.

On the basis of these agreements, the imam set out on foot, accompanied by his nephew and the woman cutter from Kër Simbara, to ten other villages within the marriage community. It was a ground-shaking experience, analogous – in its own way – to the 'speak bitterness' campaigns of revolutionary China or the truth commissions of post-apartheid South Africa. Women opened up and told stories of daughters who had died from haemorrhage, contracted infections, or experienced long-term psychological distress from the FGC trauma. Cutters and men talked, too. No systematic inducements were offered to traditional cutters to abandon their practice and nothing was said to condemn them. The approach focused more on drying up demand than on forbidding supply.

In the end, all ten villages visited decided to join the original three in opposing FGC. Fifty representatives of the 13 communities, representing 8000 rural people, met on 14 February 1998 at Diabougou – one of the villages that had joined the grassroots coalition – and declared 'never again'. The news multiplied the impact of Malicounda-Bambara's initiative.

The movement next jumped to the Casamance region of Kolda – in southern Senegal below the Gambia – where a majority of the Fulani ethnic group traditionally practised FGC and Tostan programmes were already underway. A first group of 14 villages studied the health and human-rights modules, listened to the news of Malicounda-Bambara, resolved to take action in their own environment, and enlisted four additional communities within their socio-marital network to make a joint declaration in the village of Medina Cherif on 12 June 1998.

National debate and grassroots dissemination

Since the original breakthrough in Malicounda-Bambara, the movement has evolved along two paths: out front in the media and international forums, and on the ground. For once, the out-front publicity does not seem to have outstripped the local reality, and the activity has remained largely wedded to its village manifestations.

Media attention was quick in coming, both to Senegal and abroad. In October 1997, a feature article on the 'Oath of Malicounda-Bambara' came out in the French newspaper *Le Monde*. Tostan representatives have since been invited to numerous conferences, assemblies, and events to relate the story of the movement against FGC. In almost every instance, promoters have made sure that local people speak for themselves, sometimes through interpreters. The local champions of the movement – the elderly imam and the women cutters and organisers – have made presentations to the British parliament, the German Ministry of Development and Cooperation, the EU, an international women's rights conference, and various UN committees. More significantly, they have travelled to neighbouring countries – Burkina Faso and Mali – to talk with others facing similar problems.

But outside attention has had its downside. Endorsement of the Oath of Malicounda-Bambara by the Senegalese President Abdou Diouf – significant, even if he himself is from the majority Wolof (few of whom practise FGC) – led to a move in the country's Assemblée Nationale to pass a law abolishing the practice and dictating severe penalties for violators. The allies of Tostan were immediately concerned and went to Dakar to testify against the law, not, obviously, because they wanted to maintain FGC, but because they firmly believe official abolition and sanction are not the way to go. They believe laws should not be dictated from the top down but follow changes made at the local level. As the imam from Kër Simbara put it in reference to his own ethnic group, 'Try to tell Bambara people what they must do about their own customs and you have a fight on your hands'.

He was right. The law was passed despite these words of caution, and a general outcry ensued. In protest, one traditional cutter in the region of Tambacounda made a point of performing 120 'circumcisions' in the days following the enactment of the law. Perhaps the most harmful outcome was that an influential religious leader in the north of Senegal issued a statement saying that FGC is a religious practice and must continue. This greatly hampered the activities of the women in that area, as his followers did everything to prevent open discussion of the issue.

Developments on the ground unfolded quite differently. Additional villages in the Thiès and Kolda regions rallied to the cause. New grassroots movements took hold, not without strong opposition at times, in the Futa Toro and the Sine Saloum areas of Senegal, with women in the latter coastal area canoeing from island to island to spread the word. The more recent evolution of events, described in Easton and Monkman (2001) in greater detail, resulted in over 700 communities throughout the country making their own declarations by June 2001 and in growing demand from human rights and women's health advocates in neighbouring countries for help in initiating similar movements.

An indigenous strategy for policy change

Analysis of the Tostan experience and local response to it reveals a strategy with three distinct elements.

First, the approach was *collective*. It explicitly recognised that families cannot abandon a deep-rooted cultural practice if there is no collective will to change the incentive structures and at least some of the objective conditions that hold it in place. When 13 related villages endorsed the Malicounda-Bambara initiative, they, in effect, changed the marriage-market conditions in which people *could* comply.

Second, the strategy adopted was grounded in the *local context* and evoked some of the strongest values and practices of ambient culture – parental love, Koranic piety – to challenge other practices. It came across more as a movement for internal consistency and liberation than as an outside condemnation. No one talked of the 'eradication' of FGC, as if it were a plague to be stamped out, but rather of its conscious 'abandonment'. The presence of an imam who could remind people that Islam never dictated such a practice was also instrumental. In addition, men's support was critical to the development of the movement. One articulate cutter, Oureye Sall, was highly influential as well. She explained that she stopped the minute she learned of the harm she could potentially be causing, saying, 'I was making 5000 FCFA (about $18) for one operation, but if a girl must pay 50,000 FCFA (about $180) for medical care, I did not have the right to continue'.

Third, the tactic was *empowering* – that is, while rooted in personal testimony and the transmission of new information, it left resolution and action up to the initiative of each community and its members. It cast the problem of FGC in the larger frame of women's health and human rights – topics of importance to men too. The result was people who not only voluntarily adhered to the initiative but were also ready to spread the word.

Marketing and disseminating an innovation: the Village Empowerment Programme

As noted, the Tostan experience awakened strong interest outside Senegal as well and the organisation was increasingly solicited to disseminate its 'FGC strategy' and support or advise those interested in similar results elsewhere. The attention has created both opportunities and challenges. Tostan has always been dependent on outside funding. Though it costs only about $40 per participant per cycle to implement the programme, participating communities cannot fully cover the cost, and so the organisation tends to offer only the programmes that outside funders choose to underwrite.

Given Tostan's apparent success, more donors were willing to offer support and those already involved were ready to raise the stakes, but most asked Tostan to trim down its programme and to focus on the four modules directly relevant to FGC: human rights, problem-solving skills, community hygiene, and women's health. Literacy elements were relegated to the continuing-education phase of the programme, and emphasis was placed on immediate and highly focused change. The new strategy was called the Village Empowerment Programme (VEP).

This is the model that is currently being replicated in other African countries. Two of the worthiest early requests for assistance, in Tostan's eyes, came from human-rights and public-health organisations in Mali and Sudan. The Wallace Global Fund (WGF) in Washington DC underwrote this extension because it offered an opportunity to see whether the Tostan approach could work in societies where FGC was a nearly universal practice rather than the custom of half or less of the population, as in Senegal. WGF insisted, however, that the project provide for the external evaluation of results – and we were brought in to perform that function.

The results of the evaluation are now being analysed for Mali; and data collection is at last concluding in Sudan, where diplomatic problems initially made it difficult for outside evaluators to get visas. At this point, it appears that there have been good results at both sites. Attendance and interest have been strong. The programmes actually implemented have varied somewhat from the Tostan VEP model, both because of the need to adapt to local timing and circumstances and because of problems of implementation – but this does not seem to have seriously compromised results.

Participants in both Mali and Sudan have set up FGC committees as well as other units concerned with village hygiene and particular local projects. The women involved (and, in Mali, men as well) turn out to be enthusiastic about working with health, human rights, and FGC issues. They have encountered both resistance and support from other segments of local society, but the difference between the minority-culture status of FGC in

Senegal and the overwhelming majority allegiance to the custom in Mali and Sudan does not seem, at least at this point, to have impeded the work to any significant extent.

In Mali, where classes included both men and women, some of the men involved – evidently motivated by the factors mentioned above – were very helpful in facilitating women's participation as well as in designing and implementing the projects that evolved from the training sessions. They also appear to have supported women in leadership roles, to the surprise and gratification of some of the facilitators. The groups formed in Sudan were composed exclusively of women, though half of the facilitators were men, a fact that raised little objection. Both projects had discussed whether or not to restrict enrolment to women, with the usual pros and cons having to do with the dangers of either silencing women or marginalising the effort.

Neither in Mali nor in Sudan has there yet been a public written declaration of FGC abandonment, though the matter is still under discussion. The idea of the public declaration is to reach a much larger audience and eventually to provoke a large-scale convention. It remains to be seen whether that is the only way participants can achieve the abandonment of the practice in their communities, and whether they will adopt the same formula of alliance among contiguous villages developed in Senegal. Nevertheless, in at least three of the villages in Mali there is strong evidence that no cutting has been performed on girls since the topic was debated in the programme in July 2000.

It is not clear to what extent continued activity around FGC depends on the momentum created and sustained by other projects. Both in Mali and in Sudan there is some confusion about just what form follow-up will take outside collective FGC initiatives per se. That dimension of the Tostan approach, which acquired increasing importance in the original programme with the encouragement of village improvement projects and women-directed income-generation activities, remains somewhat vague in the stripped-down VEP model. Participants in most areas are interested in follow-up activity, but the donors' commitment does not currently include that, and it remains to be seen whether participants can undertake such initiatives on their own.

Lessons learned, questions raised

The material presently available for drawing lessons from the Tostan programme and its replication suggests a number of working hypotheses, and it highlights a variety of tensions whose resolution has been critical to the programme's success.

Abandonment versus eradication of FGC

Approaching FGC as a social custom that people can abandon through local mobilisation – under supportive conditions – appears to produce markedly better results than treating it as a scourge to be eliminated principally through outside stricture and legislation.

As a Sahelian proverb puts it, 'Send a child where he wants to go.' Tostan's approach stands out from approaches that frame FGC as 'bad', which implies that participants are also bad.

Cultural practices make sense in the context of their social function. FGC is practised because culturally it has come to represent marriageability of daughters as well as 'religious beliefs, initiative rites, or the hierarchy of women' (Izett and Toubia 1999). It is 'an essential element of social integration that ensures virginity before marriage and chastity afterwards'(UNICEF 1999). In some places where women are infibulated they are re-circumcised periodically, often after giving birth, in order to make sex more pleasurable for husbands (Khalifa 1994). This is a culturally defined obligation of marriage. These practices will continue unless beliefs and social expectations can be separated from cultural practices. People abandon cultural practices, from foot binding to the forced feeding of newborns every four hours, when they understand the negative consequences and find a different way to address the social function. Finding ways to ensure the marriageability of daughters and the fulfilment of marital obligations through means other than FGC is therefore critical.

Some deeper gender-related issues remain, however. The cultural belief in the need to protect women's virginity (but not men's), marriage as a (the) measure of success and validity for women, and the construction of sex as a woman's obligation in marriage (but a man's right) indicates the long road that remains to be travelled in achieving a more balanced version of women's – and human – rights. Abandoning FGC as a practice that negatively affects women's health is important, but it does not necessarily dismantle other gender-based practices that are harmful to women psychologically, economically, and/or socially.

Cultivating collective initiative

Because FGC is a collective cultural pattern with benefits and sanctions anchored in a broad system of social behaviour, collectively initiated action tends to be more effective in achieving its abandonment than individual 'just-say-no' tactics.

The original Malicounda-Bambara initiative emerged as a result of local women's collective reflection and problem solving. The local imam and the former cutter's insistence that families could be expected to abandon the custom only if a large part of their social network did so as well was at least equally important. Parents were bound to the practice not just by cultural tradition or social convention but by the fear that their daughters would be unmarriageable if they were not cut. The decision of the 12 intermarrying communities surrounding Malicounda-Bambara to abandon FGC in effect changed the marriage market. The group did something that individuals acting alone could not have achieved.

Mackie (2000) has pointed out the striking parallel here with abandonment of foot binding in China. FGC is obviously a strong social convention linked to cultural notions of marriageability, much as foot binding was. It is dependent on a group consensus that perpetuates the links between a painful practice and deeper cultural meaning. Manufacturing a new social consensus is not an individual affair. As with other social conventions like driving on the left (or right) side of the road, it is nearly impossible and often dangerous to make change individually – and such efforts do little for the greater social good. A critical mass must agree to reform practice and must make the change in concert (Mackie 2000).

The centrality of human rights

An environment of attention to human rights – and to women's rights and health concerns in particular – seems to constitute the most favourable setting for locally initiated abandonment of the practice.

Human rights seem to have become the governing metaphor and focal point in the Village Empowerment Programme, partly because it so nicely links individual needs with social policy, and gender equity with democratisation. Recasting women's rights as human rights places them at the centre of international attention and gives them legitimacy. Women's rights are assumed by some to benefit only women, while human rights benefit society at large. The nexus of human rights and women's health points to FGC as a primary manifestation of the combination of these issues. It provides a clear frame for analysing the cultural dynamics of FGC (as well as related problems such as early and forced marriage). How much the curricular focus guided participating communities in this particular direction is unclear, but the potency of the linkage stands out clearly.

The empowerment theme

Local empowerment is a corollary of human rights but poses a contradiction that has not been entirely resolved. An empowerment or problem-solving approach implies no outside imposition of targets for collective action. What if participants decide on a different priority issue?

This dilemma has been made potentially more acute by the stripped-down version of the Village Empowerment Programme. Donors are interested primarily in the FGC outcome, and support is somewhat less clearly available for other kinds of action and learning. What the Malian and Sudanese communities do in the future with respect to FGC may be instructive, in comparison to the Senegalese communities, where the programme was expanded. Initiating an expanded programme in Mali and Sudan would have provided an instructive comparative opportunity.

Donor influence in project agendas, goals, and strategies is common and is often criticised in the development literature (e.g. Crewe and Harrison 1998). Some development literature also criticises the way in which women's needs and interests have historically been marginalised in development projects (e.g. Kabeer 1994; Moser 1993). Yet growing numbers of projects, such as this one, focus directly on issues that affect women's lives. When is outside influence useful in getting important issues heard, and when does it sidetrack local concerns?

Similarly, we can examine the ways in which project staff may have steered the discourse toward FGC and away from other issues of interest to participants. Staff of the Sudanese project are also involved in initiatives for human-rights education, sometimes in the same communities. This dual valence seems to have strengthened the appeal of the Sudanese programme, both among the women enrolled and within the broader community. Questions remain about how the women might have responded in the shorter and longer term without that dual emphasis.

Men's roles

As the linkage between women's concerns and empowerment and community well-being is established, it is essential to involve men in the programme and in deliberations involving FGC.

The programmes in both Senegal and Mali seem to have become a crucible for new male roles in rural West African society. Navigating that route has been a fruitful experience and one that appears to have reinforced, not diminished, the centrality of women. However, the balance and the structure of participation by women and men remain delicate. It is easy to fall back into patterns of inequitable gender relations and jeopardise the agenda-setting and process dynamics of a programme such as Tostan. Family relations and social relations are both worth paying attention to so that men's participation continues to provide support but does not take over or exclude women.

The Malian project worked with mixed-sex groups, but women continued to make up the majority of participants. The Sudanese groups included only women, though three of the six facilitators were men, and the effort enjoyed active support from men in the community. The involvement of community leaders (male, usually) added further legitimacy to the undertaking. The support of husbands, husbands-to-be, and other male family representatives is also important, as their preferences or criteria in choosing a bride are critical when the abandonment of cultural practices is in question. Elder women are also key actors, since they have significant control over decisions concerning their daughters and granddaughters and, sometimes, daughters-in-law as well.

Although a significant number of men participated, women remained in the numerical majority in the Malian projects, and facilitators were trained to encourage women to take the initiative. In Sudan, the male facilitators and the project director were very sensitive to the importance of giving women a voice and systematically encouraged them to speak out.

Clarifying potential follow-up: the economic connection

The problem-solving focus that is central to the broad integrated approach works best when participants have access to seed capital for their new enterprises — whether through bank loans, microcredit, or charities — or when they have enough of their own pooled funds to meet this need, plus the juridical facilities for creating new associations and businesses.

The difficult issue here has to do with how tightly the approach is tied to external benefactors and NGO largesse. As a Hausa proverb succinctly puts it, 'It takes water in the belly to draw [more] from the well.' The rapid and largely spontaneous spread of the Village Empowerment Programme across whole regions of Senegal poses the question of follow-up. When outside assistance is available, does it enable or constrain choices? To date, the availability of credit and resources for follow-up activity seems to have been a critical element in programme success.

Implementation: perils and surprising opportunities

Though the broad integrated approach relies on a great deal of local and women-driven initiative, programmes that have been successful to date also need the implementation guidance of an effective support organisation.

This fact poses questions for replication and extension, and highlights the importance of concomitant capacity-building opportunities for implementing organisations. There must be clarity in the agreement between Tostan and the implementing NGO about expectations, roles, processes, and payments. As mentioned above, the staff in Sudan were involved not only in FGC but in human-rights education as well, but they seemed able to intertwine the two initiatives where appropriate and keep them separate at other times. Nonetheless, the staff's lack of experience with project-management concerns limited their effectiveness.

In Mali, the NGO staff were also involved in a variety of endeavours, and at a certain point this dispersion of effort seemed to deny the project there the dynamism noted in the Sudanese and Senegalese villages. Village-level support kept it going. Given the frequently precarious state of NGO finances, a broad integrated approach may mean tending to the health and capacity of the 'mother' institution as much as to the 'baby' programme, while seeking creative accommodations with its parallel commitments. A Sahelian proverb encapsulates the issue: 'Support the mother and the child will drink its milk in due time.'

Group sovereignty

From preliminary evidence, the difference between minority and majority FGC cultures does not pose insurmountable obstacles to the replication and extension of the broad integrated approach.

While only half of Senegalese women practise FGC, 94 per cent of Malian women and 89 per cent of Sudanese women do (El-Goussy 1999:29).

This implies a more pervasive social norm that may constrain the cultivation of collective initiative, as discussed above. In interviews, however, Sudanese women seemed to be aware of other practices and other options; they knew that not everyone practises FGC. And initial results from the Mali programme suggest that participants felt quite able to promote abandonment of the practice in their communities, despite the unanimity of social norms in their environment. A long-term assessment of results will be instructive, both in terms of the strategies used to address FGC (or other issues), and in terms of the ability to sustain changes or abandonment of practices.

The perils and potentials of philanthropic marketing

International NGO largesse provides critical support for such innovative grassroots initiatives, but the layered dynamics of philanthropic marketing can create demand pressures that risk skewing strategies in the field and short-circuiting empowerment. The programmes discussed seem in good measure to have circumvented these dangers by virtue of the loosely coupled nature of monitoring and supervision: in short, they did pretty much as best they could with the funds available. But availability of resources for one type of activity and lack of outside support for another inevitably creates a somewhat distorted local policy environment, only surmountable to the extent that beneficiaries can play multiple sources off against each other and/or generate some of their own local capital.

Acknowledgements

The three authors evaluated the Tostan programmes in Mali and Sudan. An earlier version of this paper was presented at the 46th annual meeting of the Comparative and International Education Society (CIES), Orlando, Florida, 6–9 March 2002. We appreciate the thoughtful comments of Sydney Grant and those of the anonymous reviewers.

This article was originally published in Development in Practice, *volume 13, number 5, November 2003.*

References

Belenky, M. G., B. M. Clinchy, N. R. Goldberger, and J. M. Tarule (1986) *Women's Ways of Knowing: The Development of Self, Voice and Mind*, New York, NY: Basic Books.

Crewe, E. and E. Harrison (1998) *Whose Development? An Ethnography of Aid*, London: Zed Books.

Easton, P. (1998) 'Senegalese women remake their culture', in *IK Notes* (Indigenous Knowledge Notes) No. 3 (December), Washington, DC: World Bank, also available at http://www.worldbank.org/afr/ik/iknotes.htm (last accessed 14 March 2003).

Easton, P. (2000) 'Senegal: grassroots democracy in action', in *IK Notes* (Indigenous Knowledge Notes) No. 16 (October), Washington, DC: World Bank, also available at http://www.worldbank.org/afr/ik/iknotes.htm (last accessed 14 March 2003).

Easton, P. and K. Monkman (2001) 'Malicounda-Bambara: the sequel. The journey of a local revolution', in *IK Notes* (Indigenous Knowledge Notes) No. 31 (April), Washington, DC: World Bank, also available at http://www.worldbank.org/afr/ik/iknotes.htm (last accessed 14 March 2003).

El-Goussy, H.S. El-Din (1999) 'FGM – will it ever stop?', *Sudan Dispatch* (July):26–32.

Izett, S. and N. Toubia (1999) *Learning About Social Change: A Research and Evaluation Guidebook Using Female Circumcision as a Case Study*, New York, NY: Rainbo.

Kabeer, N. (1994) *Reversed Realities: Gender Hierarchies in Development Thought*, London: Verso.

Khalifa, N.K. (1994) 'Reasons behind practicing re-circumcision among educated Sudanese women', *The Ahfad Journal – Women and Change* 11(2):16–32.

Mackie, G. (2000) 'Female genital cutting: the beginning of the end', in B. Shell-Duncan and Y. Hernlund (eds.) *Female 'Circumcision' in Africa: Culture, Controversy, and Change*, Boulder, CO: Lynne Rienner, also available at http://tostan.org/news-fgc.htm (last accessed 14 March 2003).

Moser, Caroline (1993) *Gender Planning and Development: Theory, Practice and Training*, New York, NY: Routledge.

Population Reference Bureau (2001) *Abandoning Female Genital Cutting: Prevalence, Attitudes and Efforts to End the Practice*, Washington, DC: Population Reference Bureau, available at http://www.prb.org/pdf/AbandoningFGC_Eng.pdf (last accessed 14 March 2003).

UNICEF (1999) 'A Centuries-old Practice: A Deadly Tradition', New York, NY: United States Fund for UNICEF, available at http://www.unicefusa.org/issues99/jan99 feature4.html (last accessed 14 March 2003).

UNICEF (2002) 'Tostan: a breakthrough movement', in *State of the World's Children 2002*, New York, NY: UNICEF, available at http://www.unicef.org/sowc02/pdf/sowc2002-eng-p7–31.pdf (last accessed 14 March 2003).

WHO (2000) 'Female Genital Mutilation', in *Fact Sheet No. 241*, Geneva: WHO, available at http://www.who.int/inf-fs/en/fact241.html (last accessed 14 March 2003).

Notes

1 Portions of the description of Tostan programmes are taken from a paper prepared by the authors for *IK Notes*, a web and hard-copy bulletin of the Indigenous Knowledge Programme of the World Bank. See Easton and Monkman (2001). See also Tostan's website at http://www.tostan.org.

7 Constructing an alternative masculine identity: the experience of the Centro Bartolomé de las Casas and Oxfam America in El Salvador

Susan Bird, Rutilio Delgado, Larry Madrigal, John Bayron Ochoa, and Walberto Tejeda

'And what is this about masculinity?' 'Is it about men making ourselves "more manly"?' 'Is it for men with sexual problems, for gays?' Sample of questions asked regularly during the masculinity workshops with Salvadoran men. (Madrigal and Tejeda 2003)

Introduction

The year 2006 marked the fifteenth anniversary of the signing of the peace accords in El Salvador, which brought an end to a brutal 12-year armed conflict that resulted in more than 75,000 military and civilian deaths, 8,000 people disappeared, 12,000 physically disabled, and 1.5 million displaced. This small Central American country of 6.7 million people continues to suffer from old wounds still unhealed from the war period, and from new wounds as current economic and social crises bring immense income disparity, high levels of out-migration and urbanisation, and unchecked gang violence.

As a result of this, society in El Salvador remains violent. Figures show the murder rate for 2005 to be higher than for 1989, the bloodiest period of the war, and although the majority of murder victims are men, the rate of assassinations of women has risen considerably over the last five years: between 1999 and 2004, approximately 1,000 women were murdered. This phenomenon is referred to as femicide by some women's organisations in El Salvador (and in Guatemala and Mexico), and represents an extreme example of more widespread gender-based violence against women. For during the same period, seven out of every ten Salvadoran women suffered some kind of gender-based violence (hereafter referred to as GBV).[1]

Despite these alarming figures, GBV against women is not considered to be a serious problem by many people in El Salvador. Indeed, a poll of attitudes and opinions on violence against women carried out in 2005 by

CS Sondea, a Salvadoran research NGO, revealed that 56.4 per cent of the population sees it as normal behaviour for a man to strike a woman. This reflects understandings of acceptable masculine behaviour in El Salvador, which emphasise control, physical force, and the treatment of women as possessions, lacking rights of their own.

Against this backdrop, seven organisations joined together in 2005 to create the Campaign for the Prevention of Gender Violence in El Salvador. Centro Bartolomé de las Casas (CBC), Asociación de Mujeres Salvadoreñas (AMS – Association of Salvadoran Women), Instituto de la Mujer Salvadoreña (IMU – Salvadoran Women's Institute), Asociación de Agricultores Salvadoreños (AGROSAL – Association of Salvadoran Agriculture Workers), Movimiento Salvadoreño de Mujeres (MSM – Salvadoran Women's Movement), Instituto de Derechos Humanos de la Universidad Centroamericana (IDHUCA – Human Rights Institute of the Central American University), and Oxfam America designed the campaign to raise awareness and mobilise public opinion, to generate knowledge to promote new ways of prevention, and to advocate for improved policies and practices to prevent and eliminate all forms of GBV.

The Campaign 'Entre vos y yo, una vida diferente' (between you and me, a different life) addresses the topic of GBV with proposals and positive messaging for building change. Where past efforts have concentrated on denouncing specific cases of GBV against women, this campaign aims to influence attitudes and behaviour surrounding gender roles and GBV, in order to change the cultural factors that give rise to gender-based discrimination and violence. This focus on prevention also changes the perception that GBV is a women's issue, or that men are the enemy. Indeed, an important aspect of the campaign consists of working with men. This approach seeks to open dialogue between men and women on building equitable relationships, and to help men explore their experience and understanding of gender roles and relations, and culturally constructed concepts of masculinity.

Why work with men on GBV?

Working with men on the prevention of GBV against women may seem like an impossible task or a naïve proposition, considering the small number of men currently willing to participate in prevention projects. But not to work with men is to stop short of effecting real and lasting change. Men are the main perpetrators of GBV against women. This reality leads us to ask: why does a man become an aggressor, and what can we do to change this? Within the campaign, programmes working with men seek to influence the cultural factors that support acceptance of GBV, with the message that prevention is the responsibility of men and women. It includes work with men of all ages, and incorporates study of the causes as well as the impact of GBV.

Men invited to participate in these programmes begin by reflecting on the construction of masculine identity in society and relationships between men and women. Two factors are commonly present in GBV: violent expressions of masculinity and unequal gender relations Violent behaviour in men produces violence against women. In other words, in the context of El Salvador, men can be a *risk factor*. This is an important concept for men to come to terms with.

Despite this reality, it would be a mistake to identify men as a risk without questioning the factors that create this risky behaviour. Men are not born violent. Growing attention given to the problem of men and violence shows the importance of environment and socialisation, culturally dominant ideas and beliefs regarding acceptable masculine behaviour, and images and stereotypes present in men's lives. Yet these same images and stereotypes can be a source of hope: the hegemonic cultural model of masculinity that generates GBV against women is deeply ideological but not unchangeable. The masculine model has changed over time and is not the same in all situations within a society. Perhaps most importantly, it is not uniform for all men within the male population of a given society, nor is it consistent for all ages (Madrigal 2006, 58).

As the socialisation process for men is not uniform, many do not agree that GBV against women is acceptable. In a culture with high levels of violence and aggression, many men have grown up witnessing GBV or being victims themselves. While some repeat this violent behaviour within their own family and relationships, others reject it and look for ways to transform behaviour patterns that lead to violence. Men as former victims can become a social force for change and violence prevention, and working with men can help change our understanding of the causes of violence and violent behaviour.

As with other examples of violent behaviour, if men do not develop the skills to find non-violent outlets for their emotions, it is very unlikely that coercive laws, regulatory measures, or stricter sentences will contribute to a significant reduction in GBV (Ferguson *et al.* 2005, 37). Although working with men to change their attitudes and behaviour patterns can be a slow process, initial results of existing work in this field provide hope that more men can support the prevention of violence, rather than legitimising or reproducing it (Welsh 2001, 62).

Many male survivors of violence, as well as survivors of socialisation mechanisms that reproduce violent behaviour, are ready to listen to other ideas. They seek out organisations with positive messages that avoid placing blame, and get involved in projects that understand their situation, and are prepared to work with them even if their engagement with the issue is at a fairly low level. In addition, many men in positions of power and influence reject GBV against women in their personal and professional lives. Their behaviour may in turn influence other men, and encourage them to join efforts to prevent GBV.

The Campaign for the Prevention of Gender Violence included a specific focus on men in two strategies: formation of critical thought and leadership development.

Formation of critical thought

As part of an effort to deepen our understanding of the issues affecting women and violence in Salvadoran society, the organisations opened spaces for dialogue, learning, and alliance building, ensuring that the responsibilities of men regarding GBV were highlighted as a cross-cutting issue throughout the dialogue. The coalition also designed and carried out a certificate course on gender-based violence for NGO representatives and public officials. The course covered four areas: human rights; gender and human rights; the prevention of gender violence from the perspective of public policy; and gender-based violence and the construction of masculine identity. Participants included representatives from 18 state institutions and 14 civil-society organisations. The 46 graduates were enthusiastic in their evaluation of the course, describing the positive changes in their personal lives, as well as ways they are now working for change within their workplaces.

University professor G. Pichinte said: 'Now the national university has interest in masculinities as a cross-cutting theme in undergraduate programmes', while Myrna Carcamo, the gender co-ordinator in a rural women's organisation added, 'We are creating a gender issues office in my organisation, including workshops with men and women, research and local advocacy'. Rosalio, a social worker for the Department of Family Services, commented 'I have incorporated the masculinities perspective to prevent GBV in my work. Now, I take some cases of men involved in crimes against women, to help them reflect on possibilities for change'.

Leadership development

Four of the six organisations in the campaign have extensive experience of working on women's leadership development. Through local projects that train women and young people on local advocacy, risk management, economic and human development, women's groups have brought the campaign's message on GBV to 18 municipalities in creative ways, such as organising youth festivals and theatre workshops. In 2005, the above-mentioned feminist organisation AMS sought the co-operation of the CBC to complement their campaign work. The CBC launched a masculinities training programme with a group of men identified as allies in the municipal government structure. The organisations also carried out specific training activities with young leaders working on the prevention of GBV in suburban areas of San Salvador.

These activities are discussed in the following section.

The Masculinities Programme

The phenomenon of GBV against women has been thoroughly researched and documented in terms of its consequences, expressions, and legal and criminal characteristics. But there is still work to be done in the area of working with men to prevent GBV. The CBC's Masculinities Programme is an attempt to prevent and modify risk factors that influence GBV, and to change cultural ideals that tolerate or legitimate violence. Men work to change their own habits and create alternative idea patterns, seeking to sustain deep and lasting change. In turn, the programme motivates men to lead by example, and encourage other men to change their own behaviour.

The programme consists of different activities, including awareness raising and leadership capacity building, producing materials and methodologies for use at the community level, and research on masculinities in the context of El Salvador. The programme looks particularly at points of connection between violence and sexual/ reproductive behaviours. The organisation's most significant activities are 'masculinities workshops', allowing male participants to explore how gender identity and gender relations are shaped by social expectations.

The CBC masculinities workshops implement three initial strategies for working with men: creating an environment of trust and confidentiality, reconnecting emotion with the physical body, and group reflection on the personal and social construction of masculinity. Each strategy incorporates learning through participatory techniques, such as co-operative games and collective art, personal reflection, such as meditation and individual exercise, and group reflection, such as discussion and analysis of videos and other materials.

Many men report that the most significant changes in their own attitudes, behaviour, and self-awareness occur when the theoretical aspects of the training are verified by practices in daily life. We have found that combining a theoretical discussion with reflection on personal experience is very helpful when dealing with a subject as intimate and subjective as personal identity. There are emotional responses from participants: confusion, anger, expectation, and some satisfaction and liberation. Almost all participants continue questioning their male socialisation long after the training has ended.

Initially, course activities can be carried out with diverse groups of men, as well as in different spaces and in different ways. During the certificate course mentioned in the previous section, 12 men participated in a combination of traditional coursework in a classroom setting and 'experiential learning', which began with encouraging participants to put their personal gender experience into context, and moved on to physical movement and emotional interaction. Participants had the opportunity to put concepts discussed in the classroom to the test, and to qualify personal experiences through a theoretical lens. The experiential learning process touched on aspects of complicity in acts of violence, remaining silent and failing to challenge GBV, aggression, and practical steps men can take to prevent GBV.

As part of the programme, male members of the Municipal Council of Concepción Batres, a rural municipality in eastern El Salvador and former war zone, took part in a five-day training workshop. During this training, participants were able to detect the violence in their own lives, identify the process of masculine socialisation that they had experienced, and learn simple tools to change their behaviour. Participants reported that they had very few opportunities in their lives to play outside of competitive sports, and still fewer opportunities to express their deepest feelings, except through laughter or rage. They felt restricted by the male gender stereotype they were expected to conform to, that of the 'true man' – physically and emotionally strong, free, fast, smart, and with many girlfriends whom he treats as his possessions. After the training, the men who had taken part continued to hold periodic follow-up and self-help meetings, as well as supporting actions to prevent GBV in the workplace and the family.

In another recent project, CBC has worked with bus drivers and employees of a public transportation co-operative which serves riders between San Salvador and the nearby municipality of Santa Tecla. The CS Sondea poll mentioned previously shows that a majority of the population perceives the public transportation sector as one of the most abusive to women, in terms of verbal aggression and age discrimination towards passengers. Since February 2006, 120 men have been participating in an 18-week workshop, carried out in weekly blocks of four hours while the bus drivers are on a break for vehicle maintenance. The main focus of the workshops has been awareness raising around physical and emotional actions, attitudes and behaviours at work, and different expressions of violence. The low drop-out rate (of 120 participants, only five stopped attending) shows the enthusiastic and committed response of the men involved.

Impact on men's lives

Results from the masculinities workshops show initial shifts in attitude that may lead to long-term change. The following testimonials are reaffirmed by interviews with people close to the participants, such as immediate male and female family members, co-workers, and facilitators.

In the majority of the cases monitored, men said that the way they viewed themselves had begun to change, as had the way they interacted in their personal relationships. They also felt an improvement in their ability to express their feelings and emotions, to see beyond their own self-interest and welfare, and a better appreciation of the role and value of their wives, children, and other family members.

Rosalio, a social worker from the Department of Family Services, said '[The module on masculinities] in the certificate course helped me to think especially about my home and the environment in general, to understand and comprehend myself better. My understanding and communication with my family has gotten better. I have adopted a new attitude about being a man, I have understood the role that we men are playing in society, and above all, I've started a process of transformation in the search for a male profile different [to that] of the macho, possessive, egotistical [man].'

Often, the process of transformation generates tension with other men. Within a group of men, such as male family members or co-workers, men frequently uphold stereotypes regarding acceptable masculine behaviour. In this context, the fact that men who have completed the masculinities workshops feel able to affirm a different type of masculinity without aggression or violence towards others, calmly and with conviction, shows evidence of the impact of the training.

Municipal Council member René, who participated in the masculinities workshops in Concepción Batres, said, 'On the street, I've had a different attitude. It's gotten surprised reactions from a lot of men. I have assumed my place as a man and have made important decisions that have been difficult to understand for the rest of the men I usually meet. But my new attitude towards men after the [masculinities workshops], has made them understand little by little my decision and will to change. I have improved my conduct and my rebellious attitude. I have felt a lot of motivation and courage to tell other men about the importance of the masculinities workshops. My relationship with women after the process is different, one of more respect and collaboration in everything I can, and sharing my vision of masculinity'.

Recognising one's own capacity for violence is further evidence of a change in attitude. This recognition is fundamental to allowing participants to begin deconstructing the machismo[2] to which many men in El Salvador feel the need to conform, and the violent masculinity that accompanies it, characterised by egoism, and an inability to see the world from the point of view of women. Participants also expressed changes in their views of others, especially of women. Discussing and coming to accept the idea that women are subjects with rights of their own generated reflection amongst participants about their own masculinity, and how it shaped their attitudes to others. Rosalio affirmed, 'If I as a man am affected, all of my relationships are going to be affected: workplace, family, and social relationships. I should say that the [masculinities workshop] has caused a positive conflict in me...it has helped me do a self-evaluation of my behaviour as a man. For example, I asked myself, what characteristics of the hegemonic male model do I have with my family, my children, my wife, with other women and other men? How and what have I done that has helped and hurt my family?'

Participants in the workshops have also shown greater recognition of women as individuals with rights, and have begun to show more respect towards others in work at the community level. In the case of the municipality of Concepción Batres, men who participated in the masculinities workshops have contributed to projects led by the local women's organisation. Observing the change in attitudes and behaviour of a male official who had participated in the training, Ana Clemencia Roldán, Project Co-ordinator for AMS, commented, 'he works with the [women's] organisation and is always talking about us, that women should be taken into account. This is after the [masculinities] workshops, it's recognising that the women are here. Before he called us the AMS women, but now he says "the women", it's like he sees more now than he saw before'. This change represents a great step in the local context: men are beginning to change their beliefs about women, and are starting to recognise them as equal partners.

In addition to changing attitudes at the personal level, the workshops in Concepción Batres also prompted participants to act in support of women's rights in their professional lives. Public officials René and Santiago supported a two per cent assignment of the local budget to women's-rights projects, and joined the local campaign to demand better policies for women. And young men who participated in the masculinities workshops are collaborating with the local women's initiative on a baseline study to assess the incidence of GBV against women in the municipality.

Given the critical situation of GBV in El Salvador, these changes, although small, provide hope of a long-term transformation. Many participants express an eagerness to train other men on masculinities. This is an important step in building alliances of men committed to acting for the prevention of GBV, and demonstrating a personal responsibility towards seeing themselves as agents of change. For example, since attending a masculinities workshop held for religious leaders, Jesus Maria Aechu, pastor of the catholic parish Saint Francis of Assisi, Mejicanos, has begun supporting the Women's Office, a local effort to help and advise survivors of domestic violence. He speaks out against GBV within his congregation and promotes the masculinities workshops to young people.

Other comments from the workshops include: 'I feel motivated, content and willing to go ahead with carrying out prevention [of violence activities] from the Department of the Family'; 'I've told other men about the importance of the Masculinities Workshops'; 'I'd like to know more about what I can do in my job with the government to help with prevention of GBV'. In interviews with female colleagues close to the participants, the same reaction has come across: 'He tells me that he can help transmit what he's learned, he wants to give others what he has received'.

This new disposition to learn and reflect can also be seen in comments made by the bus drivers who participated in the training. They frequently report to the facilitators, 'We are very interested and want to learn and change'. Luis Valencia, Co-ordinator of the Personnel Office for the 101-B public transportation co-operative, said 'In fact, since [our drivers attended] the masculinity programme, calls to the complaints hotline have decreased 75 per cent. This is a great motivation to all male employees to continue the process and a bit of appreciation of our changes by customers, especially women'.

During and after the masculinities workshops, many participants experience social pressure from men and women who, out of curiosity and fear of this 'new' masculine behaviour, reject the changes they observe in the participants. On one occasion in Concepción Batres, workshop facilitators Walberto Tejeda, John Bayron Ochoa, and Rutilio Delgado report that a woman and several men came to the room where the workshop was taking place to secretly observe what was happening. The observers saw an exercise where the participants carry out a group hug, and reacted with shame, nervousness, mocking, and fear at what they interpreted to be 'homosexual conduct'. After the session, participants were questioned by co-workers, family members, and others, about the workshop, and were the subject of jokes mocking their sexuality. In a subsequent workshop, some participants raised doubts about the process, asking the facilitators, 'What do you really want with these workshops?' One of the younger participants had to stop coming due to pressure from his older brother.

Risk analysis

We have found that the process of helping individual men to construct an alternative masculine identity is best carried out over a period of time, and in conjunction with wider activities working towards equality and the prevention of GBV. As participants begin to uncover and process the violence in their daily lives and personal histories, we begin to see higher levels of participation and self-motivation. Often, as men see this violence in a new way, they become deeply engaged in the process of change.

Moving too fast can risk participant resistance. Another risk is the pressure that participants can feel from men and women outside the process, which can become an obstacle generating self-doubt and mistrust of the motives of the organisation facilitating the process, and can lead to men dropping out of the workshops. When friends, co-workers, or family members begin to spread rumours or express doubts, participants may feel shame, anger, and frustration, and run into problems with men in their social circle, losing leadership and prestige.

Another risk is that activities with men's groups can come to dominate public activities relating to GBV prevention, reducing the importance, in the public eye, of women's organisations working to end GBV. It is important to develop frameworks for continual feedback with women's organisations, to ensure that all groups working in this field are working towards common goals. Raising self-awareness amongst men should never replace drives to increase women's empowerment, in terms of funding or leadership in public spaces.

From a Latin American perspective, masculinities work with men should avoid a purely rational, academic, or theoretical focus, even if working with men with high levels of education. Our experience suggests that an experiential, emotional, physical, and dynamic methodology is most effective, bringing in a theoretical perspective after a period of time to support participants' individual experiences.

Conclusion

While the masculinities workshops have had a significant impact on the attitudes and behaviour of individual men, which has affected their interactions with others in their communities and workplaces, it is still too early to gauge whether this programme has had any social impact at the national level. There is a need for greater collaboration with other organisations, and to develop deeper processes that allow men to continue exploring and reconstructing their masculine identity, beyond the limited scale of this programme.

When these efforts are linked to other processes of social transformation and are supported, promoted, and respected by men, we can expect wider changes in society, and can look to men as allies in the prevention of GBV against women. The most significant impact should come from the construction of a non-violent masculine identity and a cultural consensus in which GBV is de-legitimised, and violence against women is reduced. El Salvador has had many centuries of patriarchal socialisation where the concept of who and what is powerful has modelled behaviours, attitudes and ideologies, and so far, few men have been prepared to challenge this, and explore alternative masculine identities. But those who are prepared to do so should be supported, for the principle of changing men from perpetrators to preventers of GBV against women has great possibilities.

This article was originally published in Gender & Development, *volume 15, number 1, March 2007.*

References

Ferguson, H., J. Hearn, Gullvag Holter, L. Jalmert, M. Kimmel, J. Lang and R. Morrell (2004), *Ending Gender-based Violence: A Call for Global Action to Involve Men*, Stockholm: Sida.

Madrigal, L. J. (2006) 'Masculinities: hopes to change', in *Celebrating Changes: Exploring Quality and Equity of* Diakonia *in the Church*, Geneva: World Council of Churches.

Madrigal, L. J. and W. Tejeda (2003) *Compartiendo de Nuestro Pan: Una Experiencia de Trabajo con Hombres en el Área de la Masculinidad*, Guadalajara, Mexico: Ediciones Encuentro.

Welsh, P. (2001) *Men aren't from Mars: Unlearning Machismo in Nicaragua*, London: Catholic Institute for International Relations.

Notes

1 Gender-based violence (GBV) is considered to be any act of violence sustained by an individual as a result of her or his gender status. GBV can of course affect both women and men, but for the purposes of this article we are focusing on GBV against women.

2 'Machismo' is the belief in male hegemony over women and other men, played out with physical force, control, and violence. A macho man is a man who reflects these characteristics.

8 'We Can': transforming power in relationships in South Asia

Mona Mehta and Chitra Gopalakrishnan

Introduction: 'We Can' end violence against women!

Gender-based violence against women is one of the most significant mechanisms by which the state and societies retain power over women, their lives, and choices. Any attempts to engender equal worth and opportunities for women must address the issue that shackles them most – violence against them. What is worrying is that the scale and severity of abuse is on the rise in South Asia. One in every two women in South Asia faces violence in her daily life, and social customs and attitudes that support violence against women (VAW) are entrenched and institutionalised at all levels – home, family, community, society, and the state. The 'We Can' campaign is a coalition of over 600 organisations (including Oxfam GB),[1,2] collectives, and individuals working together in Bangladesh, Sri Lanka, India, Nepal, and Pakistan. From 2007, the campaign will extend to Afghanistan.

Over the next four years the campaign aims to achieve a fundamental shift in the social attitudes and beliefs which support and maintain VAW in the countries in which it works, by creating a popular movement to end VAW. This will come about through the creation of a range of local, national, and regional alliances working together to end VAW, and by different sections of the communities targeted taking a collective and visible stand against violence. Most importantly, the campaign seeks to mobilise five million ordinary men and women – Change Makers – to speak up, break the silence, and act to stop violence against women. They in turn will talk and influence ten others. In this way, the campaign hopes to symbolically link up with the 50 million 'missing women' in the region.[3]

Change Makers — challenging violence within the community

Change Makers are individuals willing to encourage others in their community to recognise various forms of violence, and create a positive environment for women by taking a stand on VAW. The support they receive includes interactive training materials, campaign communication material, and information on support services for women available locally. Change Makers work individually on a person-to-person basis, or affect thinking and strategic choices within the organisations they work in, or act as a group for better impact. Their work is supported through highly visible and co-ordinated community-mobilisation programmes, public-education events, mass media, and other traditional and non-traditional means of communication, a variety of institutions (civil-society groups, universities), celebrity endorsements, and unique 'sign ups', where an entire community will 'sign up' to end violence against women.

Sufia Begum of Jatrapur district in Bangladesh is a Change Maker for the 'We Can' campaign. She raises awareness on issues relating to violence within homes in her community, and tries to mediate when a domestic crisis is brewing. A few years ago, Sufia would hardly have dared to think or believe that the change that has occurred in her life and those of other women could be possible. Married at the age of 14, Sufia Begum was a victim of mental and physical torture, from both her husband and her mother-in-law. In addition, she was expected to do all the domestic work within the household. She had her first and only child at 16. Sufia was not allowed to leave the house, and did not have the courage to ask her husband for anything, even when her baby daughter became ill. She was sent back to her father's home with a demand for more dowry, but her father refused to part with any money, and she did not return to her marital home. Meanwhile, her daughter's condition deteriorated and she died.

Life it seemed was preparing her for even harder times. Soon her father died as well, and her brother denied her any right to her father's land or property. At that point Sufia broke her silence and fought for her rights through legal means. Seeing other women in a similar plight, she then began to work for her community. Every year for the past five years she has been elected to the Union *parishad*.[4] Sufia's own struggle began before the 'We Can' campaign, but through her involvement she has gained awareness, courage, and the potential to bring about wider change. Campaign allies help Sufia and others like her to recognise VAW as violence, sensitise them through communication material to be aware of and understand different kinds of violence, and help them to find alternatives to violence in their own lives, and in the lives of others.

Sufia says today she fully understands the devastation that domestic violence can cause to a woman, the family, and the community. She says that a few years ago, she would never have had the courage to intervene or mediate in a 'private' family matter, and believes that her own experience helps her to empathise and take action. 'As I understand the damaging and far-reaching consequences of abuse by an intimate partner, I need to speak out. I need to first gather courage to change within.' So far, Sufia has mediated disputes in 300 families and interacted with more than 1,000 individuals for the campaign. 'My message to all women is that they must break the silence, talk about abuse, and stop it. The problem appears intractable because it occurs in the private realm. But it is within the power of each one of us to stop violence in our lives and in the life of others. Only I, Sufia Begum cannot stop it, we all have to work together to achieve peace.'

Sixteen-year-old Nischal Pakhrin of Sri Nepal Madhyamik High School in Bara district, Nepal, is as determined as Sufia to help girls and women in her community to assert their rights. 'I have never understood why people look upon violence against women as normal. It is disgraceful and should not be tolerated. I often wondered how I could approach the members of my family on the issue, as I have been witness to many, many unsavoury incidents of abuse in my home. The 'We Can' campaign gave me a chance. I joined up after thinking about it a lot. I began speaking to members of my family and my community about the ills of violence against women.' Her family was aghast. Her mother and grandfather were extremely angry and said her behaviour went against their tradition and culture.

Says Nischal, 'I reasoned with them and said a culture that does not respect women is no culture at all. They found this hard to understand at first. But eventually they began to see my point of view. After gaining their support, I felt far more confident. I encouraged other girls to join me and together we approached families and requested them to allow their girls to attend school.' This may seem to be a very small step. 'But it isn't', says Nischal. 'In our community, girls are barred from going to school. Our efforts have resulted in six young girls enrolling in local schools. This fuelled our enthusiasm and we have started adult education classes with 30 women.' Nishal's success in encouraging women and girls to enter education is significant, for violence against women in South Asia encompasses not just physical abuse, but also abuse of other kinds, including the denial of women's basic rights to education, health, and job opportunities.

Ram Kison takes a different approach. He tries to bring harmony into the lives of women and men through song and theatre. A singer in a 'We Can' youth cultural troupe in Ranchi, Jharkhand, eastern India, Ram and his group travel from village to village, raising awareness about domestic violence. This region has been the site of armed conflict for many decades. Reflecting on the aim and methods of the two change processes, the gunmen wishing to change society through armed violence, and his cultural troupe wishing to change society through drama, he says, 'The gunmen like us want a change in society. The gunman has his guns, and we have our music. People are scared of guns, but they enjoy our performances. Our messages stay…in the hearts of people.'

Ideas in action

'We Can' is enabling thousands of men and women – like Ram Kison, Nischal Pakhrin, and Sufia Begum – to speak up and act against gender discrimination and violence in the home. What was considered a 'private' matter is increasingly becoming a visible 'public' concern, and gradually, people are beginning to talk about it and discuss it at public and private gatherings. The two messages that are repeatedly communicated are that women are no less valuable than men, and that violence against them is unacceptable. Reflective spaces for sharing, thinking, analysis, and creative writing are also helping break the culture of tolerance and silence.

Change is happening, slowly but surely. Over the last two years, the campaign has evolved into a large-scale people's movement that is bringing change in the beliefs and behaviour that support violence against women. Ordinary men and women are taking small and large steps to accept new ideas and enable women, men, and children to live safer, violence-free lives. They are together unlearning socialised ways of expressing power, and are beginning to develop alternatives that are more equal, respectful, and mindful of individual dignity.

To many, Change Makers may not appear to be extraordinary people performing extraordinary acts. A majority of them, in fact, are ordinary people trying to make a difference in their own circle of family, neighbours, friends, and colleagues by simply breaking the silence on the issue of violence against women and encouraging others to act to end this violence. Sending a postcard may not seem like much. But Ashok, a student from Gujarat in India, wrote to his friend saying he now recognised that their attitudes and behaviour towards girls in their college was harassment, and urged his friend to join him in stopping such harassment. In a small way, he is helping to spread the message. Tarek Zaman, a businessman from Gaibandha market in Bangladesh, has printed campaign messages on shopping bags and visiting cards that he hands out to his clients and fellow traders. 'People take back commodities as well as ideas', he says.

Change in societal attitudes is difficult to achieve. While reforms in laws, programmes, policies, and international agreements support such change, deeply entrenched attitudes can be changed only by people. The 'We Can' Change Makers, with the support of the growing coalition of campaign allies, are currently disseminating information on gender discrimination and violence against women, questioning norms that 'normalise' violence against women, challenging gender-biased attitudes and stereotypes, opening up a dialogue with their friends, neighbours and clientele, and generating public debate. More importantly, through their actions to make changes in their own relationships, they are spreading the message that each person has the potential to change within, and to bring change in the lives of others.

Elias Mridha, a radio and television mechanic in Bagerhaat, Bangladesh, is a committed Change Maker. In his own words, 'During a ['We Can'] meeting I realised that I had a problem. I thought that I was powerful and I can beat my wife. I assumed that beating my wife was natural. I realised how I had unthinkingly adopted a culture of violence. My father used to beat my mother regularly and I had inherited his attitude towards women.' He spoke about his violent behaviour and attitude in the group and resolved to change. He says, 'Now I realise my wife is a human being and that we are equal. We now make all our decisions and take care of our family together.' Elias has begun the process of change among his extended family and with at least 50 other families in his community. The subject of violence against women has become a standard topic of conversation at tea stalls or casual gatherings in the market place.

South Asia: gender realities

Gender violence is an extreme manifestation of unjust power relations. It stems from gender hierarchies and inequalities that perpetuate and lend legitimacy to violence against women. In South Asia, gender bias and violence against women are institutionalised at all levels: home, family, community, society, and the state. Social, cultural, political, economic, and legal factors in the region combine to leave women vulnerable to community-sanctioned violence (Oxfam International 2004).

In South Asia, the cycle of disadvantage and violence begins long before birth and continues throughout women's lives. Unborn girls are killed through sex-selective abortions. One in six deaths among female infants in India, Bangladesh, and Pakistan is due to neglect and discrimination. In this region, women endure daily beatings, harassment for dowry, verbal abuse, and acid attacks for refusing to comply with male demands. Every day, their behaviour, appearance, expression, and movement are controlled. Other women become targets of extreme forms of violence such as incest, rape, forced marriage, child marriage, being traded to settle disputes and debts, public humiliation, trafficking, 'honour' killing, and dowry deaths. The severity of the problem is on the rise (Oxfam International 2004).

One in every two women in South Asia faces violence in her home. In Bangladesh, 47 per cent of women and in Sri Lanka, 60 per cent of women suffer at the hands of their intimate partners. In India, one in five married women experiences domestic violence from the age of 15 and in Pakistan, 80 per cent of women are subject to physical violence at home and more than 1,000 women are victims of 'honour' killings every year. In Afghanistan, 50 per cent of women live with domestic violence.[5]

The pervasive culture of discrimination and gender-based violence has eroded women's fundamental rights to life, health, security, bodily integrity, political participation, food, work, and shelter. Women in this region remain deeply vulnerable and disadvantaged, and their status is amongst the lowest in the world (UNDP 2005; United Nations Statistics Division 2005).

Power: central to gender inequality and violence against women

According to economist Amartya Sen, the question of power is central to gender inequality. It throws into sharp focus the real 'capabilities' that women and men have – the power they have to do or be what they value. The more powerful party (men) obtains a more favourable division of the family's overall benefits and chores (Sen 2005), and is also able to exercise power and control over others in the family.

One reason for continued inequality within the household is that is that the weaker party (women) often speaks and acts in support of this inequality. Individual women may perceive that it is in their interests to maintain and support existing power relations, even though such belief and behaviour are in reality harmful to them (see Kandiyoti 1988). This is true especially if the alternative options are worse. A woman may 'perceive' that it is in her interest to remain within an abusive marriage if the alternative in her mind is break-up, divorce, stigma, and loss of children and economic support.

The 'We Can' campaign is based on an understanding of the congruent and conflicting interests that women and men have within the family. It builds on the analysis that such relations of 'co-operative conflict' and overt or covert forms of discrimination and violence are rooted in imbalances of power. The campaign strategy recognises that there is agency (within the constraints of unequal power) among individuals in the family, and aims to trigger and channel this agency towards positive change. For instance, the campaign builds on the existing power that men have in their relationships, and encourages them to reassess their own positions of dominance within their families and communities. Women are encouraged to action by recognising their experience as violence (and not 'normal'), and their right to a violence-free life.

The people-to-people approach: change beyond the individual

While the emphasis of the campaign is on change at the individual level, this cannot be sustained without a supportive social environment. A large number of people need to break their silence and reject ideas and beliefs supporting violence against women. Further, the change in power relations among a large number of individual relationships, family, and other community groups will need to extend to include various social and state institutions within the community and society as a whole.

We believe that the move from change in an individual to the family, community, and society can happen when people help others to change their perceptions and practices. Allison Aldred, Regional Director, Oxfam GB, South Asia, says, 'The role of "We Can" is to act as a catalyst and advocate, rather than a service provider. We hope to build knowledge and capacity of men and women in communities on how to transform the way power is used and to what ends. Our aim is to play a role in the trans-formation of power relations for gender equality by supporting civil-society organisations and individuals committed to this change.'

The impact of 'We Can' is already beginning to be felt. The people-to-people approach is working. Dr Farooque is a medical practitioner who has come into contact with the campaign. In Kapasia, the village where he works in Gazipur district, Bangladesh, Dr Farooque counsels his women patients on the health hazards they face due to violence and discriminatory practices at home. This does not fall within the limits of his responsibilities, but he willingly raises questions, listens, and even uses his influence to counsel the male partners of his patients.

Eighteen-year-old Kavitha of Chowdaripatti village, Nalagonda district, Andhra Pradesh, India, says, 'Before becoming part of the campaign, I was accustomed to remaining silent at home and accepting everything I was told. But now I request my father to accommodate my mother's needs and hear her out so that her opinions can also be taken into account. I have been explaining the contents of the campaign communication material to people in the village in the hope that men in other families will do the same as my father. I do not know whether I will succeed but I am trying.'

In Pakistan, 'We Can' campaign allies have released *Apna Faisla* – a video song dedicated to the thousand women who are murdered every year in the name of honour. Produced by Farkhanda Shaheen, it depicts the fear of a mother who lives in perpetual anxiety for her daughter's safety, in a highly traditional society where the slightest suspicion or allegation about the character of a woman may lead to her murder by close relatives. 'The idea behind the song is to create a space for dialogue on the issue of honour killing and come up with answers on how to end this practice that robs women of their right to life and dignity. As songs can be [broadcast] over and over again, we are aiming for a reinforcement of the message,' said Shaheen.

Geetha, from Periyakulam, Ampara, Sri Lanka, has dedicated her life to working with women affected by violence in her area. Geetha has been able to take on this difficult task because she herself survived violence from her husband and her in-laws. Geetha enlisted the help of the Affected Women's Forum to set up a poultry-rearing enterprise and become self-reliant.

Her dream is to enable other women who suffer violence to become financially independent.

In Nepal, a group of boys committed to the campaign have managed to convince their friends not to tease and harass girls. Some girls were being harassed during *Krishnajayanti* (the birthday of Lord Krishna) celebrations in Amlekhganj, Bara district. Seeing this, the boys who had enlisted in the 'We Can' campaign as Change Makers, rushed to intervene and persuaded the troublemakers not to indulge in such behaviour. As they were wearing 'We Can' t-shirts, the boys creating trouble stopped to listen to them. This encouraged other boys who were also part of the campaign to speak up. Some of the boys who had not worn their t-shirts hurried home to change into them and return to the venue. 'Wearing the "We Can" t-shirt made us conscious of our behaviour and responsibility and we felt we had to do something. The fact that the other boys began to look at us with respect and take us seriously has given us the confidence to speak up and convince others to believe in the values of the campaign.'

Next steps

Over the next four years, allies will continue to work through an awareness-to-action programme. Five million Change Makers will play an essential role in building a people-based movement to end violence against women. The allies believe their efforts must be united, in order to sustain a long-term commitment to the process and to reach all sections of society. They believe it is important to remain vigilant to emerging threats, develop ways of addressing them, and bring together diverse local, national, regional, and international efforts working towards ending violence.

Community efforts to challenge and change ideas and practices that deter gender equality will determine the campaign's success. Encouraging alternative and more equitable attitudes, gender relations, and behaviour will have to come from people themselves. As Sufia Begum succinctly puts it, 'It is within the power of each one of us to stop violence in our lives and in the life of others. Only I, Sufia Begum cannot stop it, we all have to work together to achieve peace.' People will have to come together to transform the way power is perceived and used.

This article was originally published in Gender & Development, *volume 15, number 1, March 2007.*

References

Bangladesh National Women Lawyers' Association (2005) 'Wife Abuse in Bangladesh', Dhaka: BNWLA.

Kandiyoti, D. (1988) 'Bargaining with patriarchy', *Gender & Society* 2(3).

Klasen, S. and C. Wink (2003) 'Missing women: revisiting the debate', *Feminist Economics* 9(2–3): 263–99.

Oxfam International (2004) 'Towards Ending Violence against Women in South Asia', Oxfam Briefing Paper No. 66, August 2004, Oxfam International, available at http://www.oxfam.org.uk/what_we_do/issues/gender/downloads/bp66_evaw.pdf (last accessed 30 March 2007).

Sen, A. (2003) 'Missing women revisited', *British Medical Journal* 327:1297–8.

Sen, A. (2005) 'Gender and cooperative conflicts', in B. Agarwal, J. Humphries, and I. Robeyns (eds.) *Capabilities, Freedom and Equality: Amartya Sen's Work from a Gender Perspective*, Delhi: Oxford University Press.

UNDP (2005) 'Human Development Report 2005, International Cooperation at a Crossroads: Aid, Trade and Security in an Unequal World', New York: UNDP.

United Nations Statistics Division (2005) 'The World's Women 2005 – Progress in Statistics', New York: United Nations Statistics Division.

Notes

1 The list of alliance members is provided on our website: www.wecanendvaw.org/Who%20are%20we.htm (last accessed 16 November 2006).

2 Oxfam GB staff members provide executive leadership to the campaign. Such leadership is critical for the strategic planning, co-ordination, and management of the campaign. A core group of 5–6 member organisations will soon be formed to gradually take on executive leadership responsibilities. Oxfam GB will remain part of the core group, but its role will shift from almost sole responsibility to shared responsibility. The core group will then create and manage representative alliance structures at national/sub-national levels.

3 The figure refers to women and girls who have died due to gender discrimination and violence, including unequal access to resources, and girl foetuses aborted through sex selection. See Klasen and Wink (2003), and Sen (2003).

4 The Union *parishad* is the lowest tier of local-government administration in Bangladesh.

5 Information provided by Bangladesh National Women Lawyers' Association (BNWLA 2005), the Sri Lanka Ministry of Child Development and Women's Empowerment, Oxfam GB Programme office in Pakistan, and the Afghanistan Independent Human Rights Commission. All available at www.wecanendvaw.org (last accessed 16 November 2006).

9 Gender violence in schools: taking the 'girls-as-victims' discourse forward

Fiona Leach and Sara Humphreys

Introduction

The recent two-year global United Nations (UN) Study on Violence Against Children (UN 2006) provides stark evidence both that violence in and around schools occurs worldwide, and that there is now international recognition that the issue needs to be addressed. The study drew on consultations held in nine regions of the world, questionnaires completed by governments, and submissions from specialist agencies and other stakeholders, including children. The report includes an examination of the scale and nature of violence against children in school, covering corporal punishment, bullying, gang violence, and gender violence, as well as in other locations such as the home, the workplace, and the street.

Existing research into gender violence in schools is limited and has focused on investigating sexual harassment and abuse.[1] Researching sexual matters is a sensitive issue, especially when children are involved and when Western researchers like ourselves are describing the 'developing' world (itself a problematic labelling). In so doing, we are engaging in the complex and problematic activity of constructing social 'truths' about 'others'. We are therefore conscious of the need to avoid oversimplified and implicitly judgemental accounts.

We start by examining some key concepts and definitions surrounding gender violence, before moving on to a brief overview of its scope and various manifestations in schools (reported in English), highlighting some key issues (see Dunne *et al.* 2006 for a more detailed account). We note that most research to date has focused on girls as victims of gender violence within a heterosexual context and suggest that other types which need to be researched more fully include homophobic violence, girl-on-girl violence, and student-on-teacher violence.

We then move on to look at interventions designed to address gender violence in schools. The pool of resources to draw on is not extensive, as most work in this relatively new area of research has focused not surprisingly on identifying and understanding the issues around gender violence rather then on developing interventions, although we note that 'the act of identifying an issue can in itself constitute an intervention' (Leach and Mitchell 2006, 4–5). Nevertheless, we briefly outline a number of interesting interventions from across the developing world, some working with young people (both mixed and male-only groups), others with teachers and trainee teachers, and with communities. While we highlight some general principles on strategies for change, we recognise that successful interventions are likely to be based on context-specific understandings of complex issues.

Gender violence as a field of study

Heightened awareness of the existence of gender violence in schools in developing countries stems from the convergence of a number of disparate concerns in gender and development. Firstly, anxieties about girls' access to formal education, as expressed at the 1990 World Conference on Education for All (EFA) at Jomtien, Thailand, accompanied by the emphatic message that schooling leads to social and economic betterment, initially obscured the fact that schools may in reality reinforce gender inequalities and constitute unsafe sites for students. Subsequently, several studies in the mid-1990s investigating girls' low participation in education in Sub-Saharan Africa identified widespread sexual harassment of girls by male teachers and negative attitudes displayed by teachers (both male and female) towards girls, including verbal and physical abuse in the classroom (Hallam 1994; Gordon 1995; Odaga and Heneveld 1995). During the same period, as the AIDS virus began to spread in sub-Saharan Africa, the school was identified as a suitable location to teach about the disease. Paradoxically, however, as the gendered dimension of the disease was belatedly recognised, the school was also recognised as a site where sexual violence and gender inequalities occur (Mirembe and Davies 2001), both of which increase girls' vulnerability to HIV infection. This, in turn, has given rise to increasing interest in issues related to gender, sexuality, and schooling (Dunne *et al.* 2006) and in transforming gender/sexual relations within schools (Pattman and Chege 2003). Given international concerns to address the HIV and AIDS pandemic in sub-Saharan Africa, it is not surprising that most school-based studies of gender violence in developing countries (available in English) have been located in this region – hence the African bias in our review. However, we stress that the problem is neither confined to Africa nor to developing countries, but is a global phenomenon (see Leach and Mitchell 2006).

Further impetus to investigate and address gender violence has come from the rise in prominence of a rights-based discourse in development, as exemplified in the UN Convention on the Rights of the Child in 1989 and the

UN Declaration on the Elimination of Violence Against Women in 1993. The latter defines violence against women as 'any act of gender-based violence that results in, or is likely to result in, physical, sexual or psychological harm or suffering to women' (United Nations 1993). Significantly, the declaration singles out female children as a particularly vulnerable group and identifies educational institutions as potential sites for gender violence, even though most research to date has concentrated on domestic or intimate-partner violence on adult women (Mirsky 2003).

Definitions

The conflation of 'women' with 'gender' contained in the above UN declaration is symptomatic of the common narrow understanding of gender violence as being primarily violence by males against females. This is reflected in the current agenda on educational development, in which 'gender' is primarily conceived as a categorical variable and the drive for gender equality focuses on improving the access and retention in school of girls 'as-a-whole' in relation to that of boys 'as-a-whole' (Cornwall 1997). In this discourse, girls' inability to access formal education has often been ascribed to poverty and/or culture (see for example Colclough *et al.* 2000) and the girls themselves have generally been constructed as victims. It is unsurprising, therefore, that studies of gender violence in schools in developing countries have used similar binary gender categories to position female students – and to a lesser extent teachers – as the victims of physical or sexual violence perpetrated by male teachers or students (see for example Leach and Machakanja 2000; Human Rights Watch 2001).

In wishing to take a broader view of what gender violence encompasses, we have avoided using the term 'gender-based violence' (GBV), even though it is common currency within the international development community. The term suggests that violence is not necessarily gendered and that forms of violence exist which are unrelated to processes of gender/ sexual positioning and broader social gender inequalities. Our view is that all violence is gendered. However, broadly speaking, gender violence within schools includes physical, verbal, psychological, and emotional as well as sexual violence; it also includes the fear of violence, both between females and males and among females or among males. Significantly, looking at differences within gender categories can also shed light on patterns of social behaviour between them (Connell 2002). These differences might relate to other social markers of ethnicity, age, location, sexuality, social class or caste, which always interact with gender. So far, very little work on gender violence, or even gender and educational development more generally, has explored these gender differentiations.[2] This is clearly an area for future work.

The research — the dominance of heterosexual violence

Given the dominant understandings of gender and gender violence outlined above, it is not surprising that the primary focus in the literature has been on physical and sexual violence against female students. Studies have now been carried out in at least eight countries in sub-Saharan Africa (USAID 2003; Wible 2004), depicting a consistent pattern of sexual abuse and/or harassment of female students by both male students and teachers. Many of the studies report male teachers demanding sexual favours from girls in return for good grades, preferential treatment in class or money, and other adult men and older male students also offering gifts or money in exchange for sex. Less commonly, cases have been reported of male students being raped at school (Rossetti 2001, in Botswana; Burton 2005, in Malawi). Parental fear for girls' safety both in school and on the way to and from school has also been identified in a number of studies as a key reason for girls being withdrawn from, or not being enrolled in, school, especially in South Asia (see for example Brohi and Ajaib 2006, in Pakistan).

Some recent studies in sub-Saharan Africa have turned away from an exclusively 'girl-as-victim' perspective. They have highlighted female agency in what are termed 'transactional' sexual relationships, both among students and between teachers and students (Nyanzi *et al.* 2000; Luke and Kurz 2002) and have also noted that girls may bully boys (Wood and Jewkes 2001). Acknowledgement of female agency and/or complicity in the gendered landscape is critical, even if the 'choices' are limited within broader gendered constraints, since it highlights the need for interventions to work with girls and boys, and students and teachers, to understand more complex and often contradictory interactions.

In most countries, relationships with students, whether coerced or consensual, are a violation of the teachers' code of professional conduct, yet cases are rarely reported or pursued (Leach and Machakanja 2000). Even when regulations demand that teachers should be dismissed, very little is done; at most, a teacher might be transferred to another school. This discourages students from reporting cases. Prosecutions are also made more difficult when the family of a girl made pregnant by a teacher withdraws their initial complaint in order to agree a financial settlement with the man involved. This is more common in rural areas. Although reports have concentrated on male teacher/female student relations, there have also been some reports of liaisons between female teachers and male students (Mensch and Lloyd 1997, in Kenya; Pattman and Chege 2003, in Zambia), which imply the negotiation of different gender/authority power relations.

Outside sub-Saharan Africa, the few studies that have been conducted into violence in schools have been couched in genderless terms. These have been predominantly quantitative and often involve self-report questionnaires about students' or teachers' experience of violence (including corporal punishment and bullying). While they have sometimes offered some gender-disaggregated data, they have not been analysed within a theorisation of gendered power relations. In Latin America and the Caribbean, violence in schools is usually associated with guns, gang violence and drug-trafficking (see for example Guimarães 1996, Abromavay and Rua 2005), illustrating how schools get caught up in broader social conflicts. Yet the association of these forms of violence with hypermasculinity (stereotypical traits of masculinity based on virility, aggression, and strength) and their gender-differentiated effects have generally not been explored. Standing *et al.*'s (2006) study of schools affected by conflict in Nepal is a recent exception.[3]

Forms of gender violence are also culturally specific. Examples include 'acid attacks' against young women[4] and 'eve-teasing' (sexual harassment) in South Asian contexts, and 'jack-rolling' (gang rape) in South Africa. Further, as the recent rise to prominence of cyber-bullying in North America has shown,[5] forms of gender violence are also dynamic, with new manifestations emerging and evolving.

Regardless of contextual variations, the causes of gender violence are similar, originating in structural gender inequalities in various social arenas. In school they are rooted in the formal and informal processes of schooling, which serve to establish the gendered norms of behaviour in what is commonly termed a 'gender regime' (Connell 2002). Studies in sub-Saharan Africa show that these informal processes include allocating higher status public tasks to boys and more domestic private tasks to girls (e.g. male students ringing the school bell for assembly, girls cleaning the classroom floors), allowing boys to generally dominate the physical and verbal space in class, and tolerating sexual harassment (Leach *et al.* 2003; Dunne *et al.* 2005). In practice there is likely to be more nuanced gender differentiation. Authoritarian teaching practices, competitive assessment procedures, and narrowly focused curricula often exclude particular groups of learners. For example, students from minority ethnic groups can feel marginalised when their cultures are omitted from, or undermined by, curriculum materials. These are all processes which sustain inequalities and in so doing promote the conditions for gender violence. The social practices of schooling both operate within, and serve to sustain, a gender regime which presumes the naturalness of heterosexual attraction (even as it attempts to suppress it), promoting aggressive masculinities and compliant femininities while discouraging other ways of being.

The studies in Africa have shown that double standards operate in terms of 'permissible' female and male sexuality in school (Pattman and Chege 2003). Despite considerable variations among individuals and institutional contexts, the dominant expectation is for female students to be simultaneously sexually inexperienced yet available and desirable, whereas male students are expected to demonstrate physical superiority and (hetero)sexual prowess through 'winning' girlfriends. For boys, this often involves competing for partners with other males (including teachers) and negotiating for position in a gendered hierarchy based on age and authority. Thus, 'bullying' and 'fighting' become normalised in a 'boys-will-be-boys' discourse. Students who do not conform to expected gender identities are targeted. Attempts are made to regulate their behaviour – sometimes through overtly violent means, such as physical and verbal abuse by teachers or other students, but often through less visible forms of violence which are 'normalised' as 'teasing', 'playing', or 'gossiping' (Dunne *et al.* 2006).

Less well-recognised forms of gender violence in schools

Although corporal punishment is one of the most obvious and widely reported forms of school violence, which sometimes results in serious injury, truancy, or drop-out (Hart 2005; UNICEF 2001), it has not usually been framed in gendered terms. However, it is strongly linked to performances of aggressive masculinity and its persistence and widespread abuse implicitly endorses physical violence in school relations, which play out differently among female and male students and teachers (Humphreys 2006). In the nexus of gender and age/authority relations, corporal punishment of female students has been rationalised by some girls as socialising them to become obedient mothers and wives, while the harsh beating of male students by male teachers is interpreted as the dominant male asserting authority over the younger male, and a toughening up process as rite of passage into male adulthood. In contrast, female teachers are said to prefer verbal chastisement to caning, as male students, particularly older ones, may contest female authority and refuse punishment as a means of asserting their perceived masculine superiority.

Another largely unexplored form of gender violence is violence by girls, possibly because girls are generally perceived as victims, and dominant understandings of femininity do not associate girls with violence. Cases have been documented in South Africa of female students being physically violent towards other female and male students, and sexually taunting boys (see for example Wood and Jewkes 2001). Violence by girls is often less overt and physical than that by boys, and hence less easily recognised. Yet some girls complain about the negative impact of other girls 'gossiping' (Leach *et al.* 2003); when this involves spreading false rumours or ostracising girls, it constitutes a subtle form of aggression.

While homophobic violence has been identified as a serious issue in schools in many developed countries, such as the UK, USA, and Australia (Warwick *et al.* 2004), little is known about its prevalence in educational settings in the developing world. Its existence is likely to be widespread, however, given the reported aggressive policing of heterosexual boundaries within schools, which often takes the form of verbal insults, including sexual taunts and homophobic comments. The latter are particularly directed at boys (Morrell 1998). A five-country study in Southern Africa has indicated some of the difficulties that gay and lesbian students experience in negotiating identities in schools in the face of considerable harassment and pressure to conform to heterosexual norms (Human Rights Watch and the International Gay and Lesbian Human Rights Commission 2003). This is another area which needs further research.

Interventions

As noted above, gender violence in schools is a relatively recent area of research and few initiatives have been developed to tackle it. Most of those documented are small-scale and context-specific. Most also originate in sub-Saharan Africa, where concern over high HIV and AIDS prevalence among young people has led to initiatives to promote sexual health messages in schools (including messages about the risks of multiple sexual partners and forced sex), and to provide advice on how to deal with sexual abuse or violence. Some school-based interventions address both girls and boys, others only girls or only boys. Others seek to raise awareness among teachers and trainees and to provide skills to address the problem. Less common are programmes involving parents and communities. In addressing violence against girls, recent interventions have recognised the need to work with boys as well as girls in a context that tries to unravel the complexity of gender dynamics – this is a welcome development in moving beyond the 'girls-as-victims' discourse. We will outline some innovative work in each of the following categories: mixed student groups, boys, teachers, and communities. There is little available information about the impact of many of these interventions, especially where they are small-scale: this is a shortcoming that needs to be addressed.

Despite being context-specific, most of these interventions share a common set of methodological principles. The most important of these is a commitment to behaviour change and a belief that this can only be brought about through participatory methodologies inspired by PRA (Participatory Rural Appraisal), and learning through reflecting on experience ('experiential' learning). This process is sometimes facilitated by the use of visual media such as drawings, film, drama, video, and interactive websites (Leach and Mitchell 2006). A second important principle is a commitment to seek out and value children's knowledge, opinions, and perspectives, and for adults to engage in an open and democratic partnership, minimising the traditional adult–child power imbalance. A third principle is creating a non-threatening and safe environment in which young people can openly discuss sensitive topics, question traditional views, express fears, and seek advice. This encourages and facilitates self-reflection, and provides space to learn and rehearse new behaviours.

Working with mixed groups of young people

The most common type of school-based initiative seeks to raise awareness and bring about behaviour change through the curriculum, usually in life skills or health promotion lessons. In one example from Uganda, a small action research project (Mirembe 2006) questioned how the official message of the AIDS curriculum – that negotiation and partnership in sexual relationships are fundamental to HIV prevention strategies – could be effective while the school allowed sexual harassment and aggressive male behaviour towards girls to go unchallenged. Research showed that students found the conventional AIDS lessons boring, irrelevant, and a waste of time. The project provided them with the opportunity to determine their own topics for discussion in the AIDS lessons, and to work collaboratively with the teacher on how the curriculum should be delivered. Female students identified issues of gender inequalities both in school and outside as of immediate concern to them. By linking these concerns with the spread of HIV and AIDS, the curriculum was adapted to address issues such as sexual harassment and male students' domination of the classroom, leading to the development of an agreed set of class rules and a more positive learning environment for both girls and boys. A commitment, with staff support, to promote similar changes across the whole school followed. Through this more democratic approach to teaching and learning, students were able to work out their own manageable solutions to problems.

Another curriculum intervention with mixed groups is the Auntie Stella activity pack and website, which provide opportunities for adolescents to talk about sexual and reproductive health and relationships in school lessons in a proactive and imaginative way (TARSC 1997). First developed in Zimbabwe, *Auntie Stella* is based on a series of 40 letters, each written in the style of a missive to a newspaper agony aunt, with an accompanying reply. The topics include violence and coercion in sexual relations, male teachers propositioning girls for sex, and transactional sex. The approach is for small, mixed sex groups to work on their own, reading a letter and discussing the identified problem through guided questions. They then turn to Auntie Stella's reply for advice and suggestions and to a number of supplementary activities, such as role-plays, quizzes, research projects, song-writing, and storytelling, designed to assist them in exploring how that particular issue affects their lives and what they can do about it. This process encourages critical thinking and reflection, and helps young people to assess risks and options, while also increasing their confidence and ability to communicate, negotiate, and strategise. It also emphasises the importance of building social networks, and a more supportive and youth-friendly social environment.

Working with boys

Working with adolescent boys to address aggressive masculinity and sexual violence is a relatively new field of activity. Initiatives have usually been located outside the school context, although some work in collaboration with schools. One well-known example is Program H in Latin America, now also in India (Barker 2005), which focuses on helping young men question traditional norms related to manhood and violence and to promote health and gender equity. Program H's educational programme includes a manual series and video designed to promote attitude and behaviour change. Activities are usually led by a male facilitator and consist of role plays, brainstorming exercises, discussion sessions, and individual reflections on how boys and men are socialised, including positive and negative aspects of this socialisation, and the benefits of changing certain behaviours. These activities are supplemented by a social marketing campaign which taps into male youth culture through radio spots, billboards, posters, and dances to promote gender-equitable lifestyle changes and changes in community and social norms relating to what it means to 'be a man'. This programme has been systematically evaluated through an in-depth two-year impact study covering a range of PROMUNDO activities in Brazil. It revealed that positive changes in male attitudes towards gender equity and male lifestyle behaviour were maintained up to a year after exposure to the programme.

In South Asia, where a culture of silence usually surrounds issues of sexuality, sexual relations and HIV and AIDS, a project called 'Let's Talk Men' has used film to open up discussion of such topics among children aged 10–16 in order to challenge entrenched gender stereotypes and raise awareness of the damaging effects of male violence against women (Seshadri and Chandran 2006). In facilitator-led workshops, four specially produced films were screened, featuring various real-life and fictional male characters who present different models of masculinity. These include boys portrayed as artistic, kind, caring, and sensitive. The subsequent discussions encouraged boys to talk about their experiences of gender and sexuality and to understand how masculinity and violence are social constructs, not givens. The project worked with quite young children in the belief that promoting alternative models of masculine behaviour has to start early, when children are in the process of constructing their gender identity. Film was used to promote the message, in recognition of the fact that visual media, especially cinema and television, rather than family conversations, provide children with information about gender, sex, and sexuality. Visual media, which usually project conservative images of women and men in highly unequal gender relations, offer a potentially powerful tool for subverting and challenging such images.

Working with teachers

A number of projects have worked with both experienced and trainee

---

teachers to raise their awareness of the damaging effects of gender violence in school and to provide them with strategies and skills to tackle it. This can be a challenging task in countries where the education system is particularly hierarchical and authoritarian, and where teaching methods are largely didactic and based on rote-learning, as such interventions require a fundamental change in the teacher–student relationship.

In South Africa, a training manual for teachers entitled *Opening our Eyes* has been introduced to address the very high levels of gender violence in schools (Mlamleli *et al.* 2001). It starts from the belief that teachers must first possess knowledge and understanding about gender inequality and violence themselves in order to implement a curriculum of change. The eight interactive workshops show school staff what is happening in their schools and how they can respond to gender violence. The manual aims to heighten awareness of what constitutes gender violence and why it exists, increase awareness of the links with HIV and AIDS, provide tools and strategies for addressing gender violence, and contribute to 'whole school' strategies to develop a safe learning environment.

A small project at Kenyatta University, Kenya, started from the position that, if teachers are to tackle violence in their schools effectively, they first need to confront their own gendered experiences (Chege 2006). Twenty male and female volunteer trainee teachers were asked to keep a diary over a five-month period in which they relived important incidents of violence in their lives, which they then shared in oral narratives at regular group meetings. By encouraging future teachers to reflect on their own childhood experiences of violence, it was hoped that more effective strategies for transforming schools into non-violent spaces and more pupil-friendly pedagogies might emerge. Violence by teachers emerged as the key theme in the diaries, with most recalling being beaten or insulted by their teachers. Female trainees documented numerous incidents of sexual harassment, some at primary school. The initial shock of having to confront buried memories of childhood violence through their diaries generated feelings of pain, distress, fear, resentment, and guilt. However, this process of individual reflection combined with collective analysis and shared understanding of how violence had impacted on their lives led the trainees also to experience therapeutic effects. Some expressed the intention to ensure a violent-free environment for children in their care. In this way, their memories of childhood violence were used to help construct their identities as future teachers and parents.

Working with communities

Very few interventions involving parents and communities in addressing this issue are documented in the available literature. However, two examples exist of communities which, with outside support, decided to take collective action to address the sexual abuse of girls in their schools. In Ghana, a researcher persuaded local educators to help stage a community event (a *durbar*) to create awareness in the community of the very real abusive experiences that girls encountered in and around the school (Leach *et al.* 2003). Key to the event's success was the support of the local chief and elders, who mobilised interest and created strong pressure on the community to attend. The centrepiece of the event was a play performed by students about a headmaster who demanded sex of girls in his school; after the performance, invited guests answered questions from the audience and information was provided on the procedures for parents or students for reporting and following up a complaint with the authorities. The event was supported by a phone-in on national radio, with school children answering questions from the public, and newspaper reports. As a consequence of the event, an investigation was launched into sexual misconduct by teachers in one school and more girls and parents came forward to seek advice and help. Generally, girls felt safer as sexual abuse in schools was now a topic of open discussion in the community.

In rural Namibia, where many children are sent away to board in school hostels far from the family homestead, a British-based NGO worked with one local community on a long-term participatory project aimed at halting what were perceived as deteriorating adult–child relationships and unruly and self-destructive behaviour by children (Kandirikirira 2002). One negative aspect of social relations identified by the community was the demonstration of male power through violence and abuse. A prominent manifestation of this among school children was the ritual of boys breaking into the girls' hostels at night and raping them. To the boys, this was merely an evening's entertainment affirming their masculinity but for girls it was an evening of trauma and humiliation to be endured in silence. Such violence was sanctioned through the inaction of parents, teachers, and hostel wardens, who over the years had come to see it as normal 'boys-will-be-boys' behaviour. As part of the collective response to the issue of male violence, the Forum Theatre technique was used.[6] In one series of plays, children acted out provocative scenes of girls being 'hunted' by boys and sexually exploited by teachers to mixed audiences of adults and children. In this way, drama provided children, traditionally silenced by adults, with a voice and a forum to develop the skills to articulate their perceptions, reflect critically on issues of power and participation, and establish a dialogue with adults. Through the performances, adults came to realise that children's perspectives were very different from their own, and men and boys began to see their violent behaviour as destructive. A collective commitment to address the issue by adults and a greater confidence among children to report abuse led to a decline in the incidence of 'hunting' and sexual abuse by teachers, and improved relationships generally between adults and children.

Conclusion

In the first part of this chapter, we offered a brief overview of our current knowledge about gender violence in schools in the 'developing' world and discussed some of the difficulties of definition and interpretation. Adhering to a broad definition of gender violence which encompasses many forms of violence, some of them context-specific, suggests the need to reconsider the female victim/male villain dichotomy. It also means looking beyond the more obvious sensational forms of gender violence that grab the headlines to the more invisible forms often not perceived as violence, and/or not connected with gender, and addressing the way that school processes create the conditions for further violence. More importantly, there is a need to recognise and address the complex and nuanced interactions of different forms and understandings of gender violence and their implications in specific contexts.

In the second part of the chapter we provided some examples of small-scale interventions which seek to address gender violence in schools with a range of different stakeholders. These interventions adopt an experiential approach to learning, one which engages young people as active participants in constructing knowledge and commits both adults and children to seeking solutions through behaviour change. The challenges are great: in a didactic authoritarian school culture, introducing such approaches is not easy, but if schools are to change gender behaviour (and to teach effectively about AIDS), a more open, process-oriented, and participatory mode of teaching and learning needs to be built into the school curriculum.

This article was originally published in Gender & Development, *volume 15, number 1, March 2007.*

References

Abromavay, M. and M. Rua (2005) *Violences in Schools*, Brasilia: UNESCO.

Barker, G. (2005) *Dying to be Men: Youth, Masculinity and Social Exclusion*, London: Routledge.

Brohi, N. and A. Ajaib (2006) 'Violence against girls in the education system of Pakistan', in F. Leach and C. Mitchell (eds.).

Burton, P. (2005) 'Suffering at School: Results of the Malawi Gender-based Violence in Schools Survey', National Statistical Office, Malawi.

Chege, F. (2006) '"He put his hands between girls' thighs": the role of student teachers' memories in addressing gender violence', in F. Leach and C. Mitchell (eds.).

Colclough, C., P. Rose, and M. Tembon (2000) 'Gender inequalities in primary schooling: the roles of poverty and adverse cultural practice', *International Journal of Educational Development* 20(1): 5–27.

Connell, R.W. (2002) *Gender*, Cambridge: Polity Press.

Cornwall, A. (1997) 'Men, masculinity and 'gender in development'', *Gender and Development* 5(2): 8–13.

Dunne, M., S. Humphreys, and F. Leach (2006) 'Gender violence in schools in the developing world', *Gender and Education* 18(1): 75–98.

Dunne, M. and F. Leach with B. Chilisa, T. Maundeni, R. Tabulawa, N. Kutor, L. D. Forde, and A. Asamoah (2005) 'Gendered Experiences of Schooling: the Impact on Retention and Achievement', Education Research Report No. 56, London: DfID.

Gordon, R. (1995) 'Causes of Girls' Academic Underachievement: the Influence of Teachers' Attitudes and Expectations on the Academic Performance of Secondary School Girls', Harare: HRCC, University of Zimbabwe.

Guimarães, E. (1996) 'Effects of violence in slum areas controlled by drug traffickers and gangs on schools', *Prospects* 26(2): 279–92.

Hallam, S. (1994) 'Crimes without Punishment: Sexual Harassment and Violence against Female Students in Schools and Universities in Africa', Discussion Paper No. 4, London: Africa Rights.

Hart, S. N. (ed.) (2005) 'Eliminating Corporal Punishment: the Way Forward to Constructive Child Discipline', Paris: UNESCO.

Human Rights Watch (2001) 'Scared at School: Sexual Violence against Girls in South African Schools', New York: Human Rights Watch.

Human Rights Watch and the International Gay and Lesbian Human Rights Commission (2003) 'More than a Name: State-sponsored Homophobia and its Consequences in Southern Africa', New York: Human Rights Watch.

Humphreys, S. (2006) 'Corporal punishment as gendered practice – not simply a human rights issue', in F. Leach and C. Mitchell (eds.).

Kandirikirira, N. (2002) 'Deconstructing domination: gender disempowerment and the legacy of colonialism and Apartheid in Omaheke, Namibia', in F. Cleaver (ed.) *Masculinities Matter! Men, Gender and Development*, London and New York: Zed Books/Cape Town: David Philip.

Leach, F., V. Fiscian, E. Kadzamira, E. Lemani, and P. Machakanja (2003) 'An Investigative Study of the Abuse of Girls in African Schools', Education Research Report No. 56, London: DfID.

Leach, F. and P. Machakanja (2000) 'Preliminary Investigation into the Abuse of Girls in Zimbabwean Junior Secondary Schools', Education Research Report No. 39, London: DfiD.

Leach, F. and C. Mitchell (eds.) (2006) *Combating Gender Violence in and around Schools*, Stoke-on-Trent: Trentham.

Luke, N. and K. M. Kurz (2002) 'Cross-generational and Transactional Sexual Relations in Sub-Saharan Africa: Prevalence of Behavior and Implications for Negotiating safer Sexual Practices', Washington DC: International Center for Research on Women.

Mensch, B. S. and C. B. Lloyd (1997) 'Gender Differences in the Schooling Experiences of Adolescents in Low-income Countries: the case of Kenya', Policy Research Division Working Paper No. 95, New York: Population Council.

Mirembe, R. (2006) 'Gender, AIDS and schooling in Uganda', in F. Leach and C. Mitchell (eds.).

Mirembe, R. and L. Davies (2001) 'Is schooling a risk? Gender, power relations and school culture in Uganda', *Gender and Education* 13(4): 401–16.

Mirsky, J. (2003) *Beyond Victims and Villains: Addressing Sexual Violence in the Education Sector*, London: PANOS.

Mlamleli, O., V. Napo, P. Mabelane, V. Free, M. Goodman, J. Larkin, C. Mitchell, H. Mkhize, K. Robinson, and A. Smith (2001) 'Opening Our Eyes: Addressing Gender-based Violence in South African Schools', Pretoria: Canada–South Africa Management Programme.

Morrell, R. (1998) 'Of boys and men: masculinity and gender in Southern African studies', *Journal of Southern African Studies* 24(4): 605–30.

Nyanzi, S., R. Pool, and J. Kinsman (2000) 'The negotiation of sexual relationships among school pupils in South-western Uganda', *AIDS Care* 13(1): 83–98.

Odaga, A. and W. Heneveld (1995) 'Girls and Schools in Sub-Saharan Africa: from Analysis to Action', World Bank Technical Paper No. 298, Washington DC: World Bank.

Pattman, R. and F. Chege (2003) 'Finding our Voices: Gendered and Sexual Identities and HIV/AIDS in Education', Nairobi: UNICEF.

Rossetti, S. (2001) 'Children in School: a Safe Place?' Gaborone, Botswana: UNESCO.

Seshadri, S. and V. Chandran (2006) 'Reframing masculinities: using films with male adolescents to address gender-based issues', in F. Leach and C. Mitchell (eds.).

Standing, K., S. Parker, and L. Dhital (2006) 'Schools in Nepal: zones of peace or sites of gendered conflict?' in F. Leach and C. Mitchell (eds.).

Subrahmanian, R., Y. Sayed, S. Balagopalan, and C. Soudien (eds.) (2003) 'Education inclusion and exclusion: Indian and South African perspectives', *IDS Bulletin* 34 (1).

TARSC (1997) Auntie Stella: Teenagers talk about Sex, Life and Relationships, an adolescent reproductive health pack, Harare: Training and Research Support Centre (TARSC). http://www.tarsc.org/auntstella/index.html (last accessed 30 March 2007).

UNICEF (2001) 'Corporal Punishment in Schools in South Asia', Kathmandu: UNICEF.

United Nations (1993) 'UN Declaration on the Elimination of Violence Against Women', available online at http://www.un.org/documents/ga/res/48/a48r104.htm (last accessed 30 March 2007).

United Nations (2006) 'The United Nations Secretary General's Study of Violence Against Children', available online at http://www.violencestudy.org (last accessed 30 March 2007).

USAID (2003) 'Unsafe Schools: a Literature Review of School-Related Gender-Based Violence in Developing Countries', Washington DC: Wellesley Centers for Research on Women & DTS/USAID.

Warwick, I., E. Chase, and P. Aggleton (2004) 'Homophobia, Sexual Orientation and Schools: a Review and Implications for Action', Research Report No. 594, London: Department for Education and Skills.

Wible, B. (2004) 'Making Schools Safe for Girls: Combating Gender-based Violence in Benin', Washington DC: US Academy for Educational Development.

Wood, K. and R. Jewkes (2001) '"Dangerous" Love: reflections on violence among Xhosa township youth', in R. Morrell (ed.) *Changing Men in Southern Africa*, Scottville/University of Natal: Zed Books.

Notes

1 The legal definitions of 'abuse' and 'harassment' vary across countries, as do understandings on the ground. Sexual abuse usually refers to sexual exploitation of a child by an adult (and sometimes by another child or adolescent) by virtue of his/her superior power, and for his/her own benefit or gratification. Sexual harassment is more usually associated with adult victims, such as students in higher education and employees in the workplace, and commonly involves unwelcome sexual advances of a verbal, physical, or psychological nature.

2 One exception to this is Subrahmanian *et al.* (2003), a study of social inclusion in South Africa and India, which explores how gender, race, social class, and caste interact in complex patterns of discrimination in schools.

3 This British Council-funded study explored the gendered impact on schools and school children in 11 public secondary schools in the Kathmandu valley within the context of the ongoing 'people's war'. While there was overlap in the experiences and fears of boys and girls, there were also important differences.

4 See Acid Survivors' Trust International – www.asti.org.uk (last accessed 10 October 2006).

5 See www.cyberbullying.org (last accessed 22 November 2006).

6 Forum Theatre is a form of interactive theatre developed by Brazilian theatre practitioner Agosto Boal. It is used to help communities tackle issues that they face in their lives, be they social, political, economic, or environmental. The scripted presentation of a Forum performance presents a worst-case-scenario or 'anti-model' for dealing with a social issue. After the audience has seen the play once, they are invited to stop the action on stage when they feel that a character has been disrespected, manipulated, or oppressed in some way. After identifying the problem, an audience member replaces that character and tries to change the situation for the better. For more information, see www.mixedcompanytheatre.com/forum/forum.html (last accessed 10 October 2006).

10 Gender-based violence in and around schools in conflict and humanitarian contexts

Jackie Kirk

During armed conflict, girls are subject to widespread and, at times, systematic forms of human rights violations that have mental, emotional, spiritual, physical and material repercussions. These violations include illegal detention with or without family members, abduction and forced removal from families and homes, disappearances, torture and other inhuman treatment, amputation and mutilation, forced recruitment into fighting forces and groups, slavery, sexual exploitation, increased exposure to HIV/AIDS, and a wide range of physical and sexual violations, including rape, enforced pregnancy, forced prostitution, forced marriage and forced child-bearing. (Mazurana and Carlson 2006,1)

Introduction

Sexual violence and exploitation of girls at school is a worldwide phenomenon and certainly not limited to conflict and humanitarian situations. However, for schoolgirls in conflict-affected contexts the gendered power dynamics of schools *and* of humanitarian aid converge to create particular vulnerabilities. The extent of exploitation of girls and young women by humanitarian workers in refugee camps in West Africa was highlighted in a report in 2002 (UNHCR/ Save the Children UK 2002), which pointed to the fact that teachers in NGO-supported schools in the refugee camps were also perpetrators, taking advantage of their positions, and offering good grades and other school privileges in return for sex. This reality that schools – supposed to be havens of child-oriented activity, safety, and security for children affected by crisis – may in fact create risks for girls, has been reported in a number of subsequent documents and reports. Efforts are being made to address this in a number of ways, including the implementation of minimum standards, teacher training and awareness raising, codes of conduct for teachers, and 'safe school' guidelines.

This chapter focuses on the risks of GBV and sexual exploitation in and around schools in humanitarian contexts, and on efforts that can and are being made to address this issue in and through education. It begins with a brief overview of the issues, and presents evidence of the increasing awareness of the risks for refugee, internally displaced, and other girls attending school in conflict areas and other emergency-affected contexts. The chapter then describes the comprehensive framework for addressing such issues which grew out of recently developed international standards and guideline initiatives. The third section of the chapter provides a mini-case study of the Classroom Assistants programme, an intervention being implemented by the International Rescue Committee's education programme in Sierra Leone, Guinea, and Liberia. This programme aims to address the vulnerabilities of girls in school. The chapter ends with a series of recommendations for similar programmes and for the effective implementation of these guidelines to ensure that girls and young women affected by crisis are able to access safe and protective education opportunities.

Gender-based violence and education in emergencies

In many conflict contexts, schoolgirls experience 'double' gender disadvantage; being in the minority in schools dominated by boys and men, and being a female in a context in which food and other supplies and privileges rest in the hands of men who may be prepared to compromise professional ethics and exchange these for sex. It is the sad reality that girls' determination to go to school and their understanding of education as a passport to brighter futures may put them at risk, as they try to find ways of raising fees and other costs themselves.

Advocates of education in emergencies assert that schooling for children affected by crisis can provide physical, cognitive, and psychosocial protection for students (Nicolai and Triplehorn 2003). Girls who are in school may be protected from physical harms such as gunfire, landmines, and abductions. They may also learn information and skills that will help them cope with the challenges of their situation through literacy and numeracy, problem solving, and critical thinking, and may enjoy the benefit of being in school with friends (Kirk and Winthrop forthcoming) and trusted adults, and of being engaged in different activities.

However, the reality is that for many girls, school is not a safe place, and being on the school compound may put them at risk of sexual harassment, violence, and exploitation by male students and teachers. Because of high drop-out rates, girls in the upper primary years are often in the minority and are often taught exclusively by men, whose own professional training is unlikely to have included gender awareness and gender equality. Teachers are usually members of the local community, with attitudes and actions also shaped by prevailing attitudes and practices; this means that teachers may often reinforce the gender inequalities, stereotypes, domination, and even exploitation of women practised in the community. This is especially likely when, as is the case in many emergency situations, teachers enter the profession either untrained or under-trained. Teachers may commit acts such as making derogatory comments about girls, sexual harassment, and even manipulating girls into transactional sex with the promise of good grades and other favours in school. At the same time, teachers who fail to condone and punish male students who harass girls or women teachers in the school, and who fail to act if they are aware of colleagues doing the same, are also culpable.

Safety and freedom from all forms of sexual violence is important for girls whilst they are in school. However, the journey to and from school may also put them at considerable risk. Routes to school may be long and expose students to potential violence, especially if they have to travel through bush areas, or past encampments or checkpoints of armed forces. Parents, aware of the risks of attack, abduction, and harassment, may be reluctant to allow their daughters to leave home to attend school. And girls who are physically able to access school may find that fees and other costs create another barrier for them. To cover these they may take on risky activities such as selling cooked foods from door to door, or engaging in transactional sex with older men in exchange for money or necessary items such as soap and sanitary materials.

A comprehensive framework to address GBV in education in emergencies

Gender equality is a cross-cutting theme integrated across the Minimum Standards for Education in Emergencies.[1] These Minimum Standards have been developed by the international community of education-in-emergency practitioners, policy-makers, and researchers, facilitated by the Inter-Agency Network for Education in Emergencies (INEE). They act as a tool to guide policy and programming, and to ensure that the commitments made in human-rights instruments such as the Convention on the Rights of the Child, and other agreements such as Education for All (EFA) and Millennium Development Goals (MDGs), are implemented in these challenging circumstances. This is considered essential to ensure not only that girls have equal access to the physical, cognitive, and psychosocial protection that education can provide, but also that the content and processes of education in such circumstances meet the needs and priorities of girls as well as boys. The Convention on the Elimination of All Forms of Discrimination against Women (CEDAW) and the Beijing Platform for Action, for example, are not explicitly mentioned, but the Minimum Standards can be seen to reflect their priorities in terms of girls' access to relevant and gender-responsive education.

The Minimum Standards reflect the belief that children in emergency, chronic crisis, and early reconstruction contexts have particular protection needs, some of which may, to a certain extent, be met through schooling. Protection in this context encompasses both physical and psychosocial protection. Education providers should ensure that: 'learning environments are secure, promote the protection and mental and emotional well-being of learners' (Standard 2, Category: Access and Learning Environment). Gender-specific references to protection in education in emergencies imply the need for ensuring equal access to protective education for girls. They also recognise the particular vulnerabilities of girls to sexual violence, which may be heightened precisely because they come to school. For example:

> Students, especially minorities and girls, often become targets for abuse, violence, recruitment or abduction when going to and from school. In these cases students' security can be improved by a combination of community information campaigns and by having adults from the community escort them...In addition, education programmes should include monitoring of the level of harassment experienced by girls and women.[2]

The 'Assessment' Standard of the Minimum Standards category 'Teaching and Learning' has a particularly significant Guidance Note on an 'Assessment Code of Ethics'. It states:

> Assessment and evaluation should be developed and implemented according to a code of ethics. Assessments and evaluations should be considered fair and reliable and should be conducted in a way that does not increase fear and trauma. Care should be taken that there is no harassment of learners in return for good marks or promotions within a school or programme.[3]

The significance of this Guidance Note is only fully understood in the context of the realities described above, that of widespread exploitation of girls by teachers and even head teachers, in an environment where there may be very few checks and balances in place, such as supervisory visits from education authorities, UN agencies, and NGOs.

Protection for students from sexual exploitation and abuse by teachers is also addressed more explicitly by the Minimum Standards through the recommendation of a code of conduct for all teachers and other education personnel, which includes the teachers' responsibility to promote the well-being of learners within a positive learning environment. This code of conduct should include the following clauses relating to education personnel:

> exhibit professional behaviour by maintaining a high standard of conduct, self-control and moral/ethical behaviour;

> participate in creating an environment in which all students are accepted;

> maintain a safe and healthy environment, free from harassment (including sexual harassment), intimidation, abuse and violence, and discrimination [4]

As mentioned above, gender is integrated through the Minimum Standards, without a specific chapter or section. Initial feedback from users is that complementary tools are needed, in order to help to ensure that the gender-related aspects of education in emergencies, chronic crises, and early reconstruction contexts are fully recognised. This particularly relates to the imperative to address gender-based violence. INEE 'Good Practice Guides' have been developed, and the guide on 'Girls and Women's Education' has been revised to reflect the Minimum Standards framework (INEE Gender Task Team 2006). The INEE Gender Task Team is also developing a set of 'Gender Strategies in Emergencies, Chronic Crises and Early Reconstruction Contexts' which further elaborate on Minimum Standards recommendations. So far, tools on women teachers, gender-responsive school sanitation, and gender-based violence have been developed.[5]

In addition to such education-sector-specific tools, cross-cutting international guidelines on gender-based violence and gender mainstreaming in humanitarian contexts are highly relevant for educators and education policy makers. The application of tools such as the Guidelines for Gender-based Violence Interventions in Humanitarian Settings developed by the Inter-Agency Standing Committee (IASC) Task Force on Gender and Humanitarian Assistance[6] is especially important for informing integrated, multi-sector interventions which cut across different programming areas (for example, health, water and sanitation, and education). They are also important for ensuring coherence of approach and exchange of information. These guidelines include a specific section on education (Section 9), although there are other recommendations which are equally relevant to education settings. For example, Section 10.1 relates to informing the community about sexual violence and the availability of services.

It is to be hoped that future revisions of the Guidelines will explicitly cross-reference and link to the Minimum Standards, thus making the different tools more mutually compatible and user-friendly for the non-expert education programme manager in the field. The IASC Task Force on Gender and Humanitarian Assistance Gender Handbook for Humanitarian Action[7] also has a chapter on education. In this, efforts have been made to ensure that the Handbook complements the Minimum Standards: categories articulated in the Minimum Standards are used to frame checklists for information to be collected, and to generate action points to address gender disparities and gender-based violence.

Classroom assistants in IRC-supported schools in West Africa

The International Rescue Committee (IRC) supports education for Liberian refugees in Sierra Leone and Guinea. As refugees, girls are economically vulnerable and highly dependent on external assistance; because education is so important to them, and such a critical means to improving their situation, they are desperate to succeed. Prior to 2002 there were few strategies in place to protect these girls. IRC strove to address the issue, establishing preventative mechanisms, including recruiting and training female Classroom Assistants (CAs). The Classroom Assistant programme is now being closely followed through the IRC Healing Classrooms Initiative, which is a more recent project, focused on improving teacher support and development to better meet the needs of children and young people affected by conflict. Gender is one of the key focus areas. Sierra Leone and Guinea were specifically included in the Healing Classrooms Initiative pilot country assessments in 2004 in order to learn more about how this innovative programme was affecting teaching and learning processes and experiences. Data presented in this chapter was collected during those pilot country assessments. Interviews with teachers and CAs were conducted in English by the author; and interviews and discussions with male and female students were conducted by trained local research assistants in Liberian English and local languages, and freely translated by them. Liberia, where IRC is supporting the reconstruction of the education sector in a number of different ways, including teacher and education personnel training, and Parent–Teacher Association (PTA) development, is now also included in the Healing Classrooms Initiative.

The Classroom Assistant programme was initiated by IRC Guinea in 2002, primarily as an immediate response to the UNHCR/Save the Children report mentioned above. Soon afterwards, it was adopted by IRC Sierra Leone. Although there was no documentation of abuse and exploitation within the IRC programmes, the manipulation of girls into sexual relationships with teachers in exchange for good grades or other in-school privileges was widely acknowledged. It was critical to address the male domination of the schools in order to create more protective conducive learning environments for girls. Although a long-term gender-equality intervention is to recruit more women teachers to the schools (see Minimum Standards, Teachers and Other Education Personnel Standard 1: Recruitment and selection, Guidance Note: 2 [8]) this was impossible in the short term because of the few refugee or local women with the level of schooling and the time, family support, and resources required to become a teacher. Well-educated women are usually recruited for more lucrative positions in the UN, NGOs, or other agencies in the camps. Others are unable to leave family duties or other better paid income-generation activities. This is especially true for the many refugee women who are heading households. Flexible entry requirements (for instance, applicants only need to have Grade 9 education) to become a CA open up possibilities to a larger number of refugee women.

The Classroom Assistants have an explicit mandate to mitigate abuse and exploitation of students. More broadly however, the programme was also designed to create more conducive, girl-friendly learning environments, and support quality learning for all students. One critical task the assistants perform is the collection and safe-keeping of the class grades from the teacher. This means that the students do not deal directly with the teacher when they receive their grades, and therefore helps to avoid situations in which teachers can manipulate and exploit girls for sex in exchange for altering their grades. Additionally, assistants monitor attendance, and follow up on absences with home visits. They also help the girls with their studies, in addition to supporting health-education activities, and some social-club activities, such as needlework, games, and sports.

Assessments of the CA programme in Sierra Leone and Guinea indicated that there was significant impact in improving the learning environment for girls and boys. One CA in Guinea summed it up as follows: 'Before they had many problems in the school like fighting, loving with teachers, getting pregnant, but now it is improving. Before the girls were going down, but now they are improving' (Interview with Classroom Assistant in Guinea, 2004). Students in Guinea and Sierra Leone articulated the benefits of the assistants' presence in their classrooms: there is a clear message from the girls that the classrooms are more comfortable and friendly spaces in which to learn, and that they feel encouraged not only by the physical presence of a woman in their classroom, but also by the fact that she will follow up with them on home visits. Boys too appreciate the fact that the assistants help to create calmer, more orderly classrooms, and that learning is more effective.

The initial impetus for the programme was to eliminate sexual abuse and exploitation of girls in schools. According to all those interviewed, Classroom Assistants, teachers and students, there has been a change in teachers' behaviour in schools. There is however no pre-Classroom Assistant programme data to use as comparison, and it is also impossible to say that there is no longer any exploitation of girls by teachers in school, or that the risk of exploitation does not exist. But it would nonetheless appear that there has been a significant and positive change, to which the Classroom Assistant programme has contributed, along with other inter-ventions, such as training on the IRC mandatory reporting policy, and a general heightened awareness of GBV issues within the camps. In Guinea, for example, the students talk about 'more respectful' relationships between students and teachers. As one girl says, 'Teachers are no more collecting money from students in school for grades. Students and teachers are now respecting one another' (Interview with female student in Guinea, 2004). The CAs assert that 'since we came in we put a stop to those things' that 'the teachers can't do anything bad with the students, no, nothing bad like that is happening – I haven't seen anything like that' (Interview with Classroom Assistants in Sierra Leone, 2004). They stress the importance of them being there to observe and see what is happening in the schools. 'Things have changed, the teachers don't do it [sexual exploitation of girls] – this is why the girls are so serious now. We are there to observe, so the teachers can't say, like, "This girl is beautiful."' (Interview with Classroom Assistants in Guinea, 2004).

However, despite these reported impacts, challenges remain, including the teachers' attitudes towards women in schools, and the potentially negative strategies that the CAs themselves employ. It is clear that addressing sexual exploitation in schools is a complex task, and that a relatively high level of technical support may be required by education managers and officers implementing the programme.

Many of the teachers interviewed in the assessments were positive about the impact of the Classroom Assistants. However, when the women were first introduced to the classrooms, there was a certain amount of discomfort on the part of the teachers. Teachers considered the assistants as 'sex police' and as classroom spies who would be reporting on their every move. Although the teachers are now more accepting of the CAs and have responded to their presence with more respectful behaviour, improved lesson planning and delivery, and more interaction with students, the teachers are very aware of the fact that the CAs are less educated and less trained that they are, and their expectations of them are limited to relatively menial tasks and ones which do not challenge their authority as teachers. None of the teachers talked about any real power sharing in the classroom and made it clear that when the assistant was in the classroom alone with the students, she was merely a replacement for him.

Although the Classroom Assistants may be (or at least may become) strong advocates for girls' education, the strategies they employ tend to put the onus for improving the situation solely onto the girls, implying that the girls are not serious enough about their education, that they need to study extra hard and, especially, that they need to avoid the attention of men (including teachers) and male students. 'They shouldn't wear false hair or makeup as it attracts men, and short skirt', says one CA in Sierra Leone (Interview with Classroom Assistant in Sierra Leone, 2004). Other CAs also tend to talk about the girls as if the problem lies with them, and about their own role in helping to compensate for the girls' deficiencies in comparison with the boys. One CA explains, 'Of course, sometimes the boys get angry because we are only helping the girls, but we tell them that the girls are backward and they boys are cleverer and so they [the girls] need more help.' (Interview with Classroom Assistant in Sierra Leone, 2004) The Classroom Assistants also see an important role for themselves in instructing the girls to keep away from the boys: 'We talk to them about not going around with boys,' and 'We always encourage them [the girls] and tell them of the importance of education – that they shouldn't follow men and not to jump with them. We tell them "you shouldn't wrestle with boys because in doing that it is dangerous."' (Interviews with Classroom Assistants in Sierra Leone, 2004)

Classroom assistants: conclusions and recommendations

The Classroom Assistant programme is clearly successful in creating more comfortable learning environments for girls, and has had beneficial impacts for boys too. However, we can see that the emphasis of the Classroom Assistant programme has fallen on 'fixing' the girls to better fit the school environment, with the help of women who themselves are in a relatively powerless position within the school. The complete elimination of sexual exploitation and abuse is dependent on a sustained shift of the underlying hegemonic male culture of the school, and on empowering women and girls to feel they are fully part of the school with the same rights, expectations, and opportunities as the men and boys.

The opinions of the Classroom Assistants on girls, gender equality, and empowerment are grounded in their everyday realities of camp or town refugee life, and are indicative of the prevailing social context. This means that their understandings of the barriers to successful education for girls, and the strategies that they develop for addressing these, tend to reflect rather than challenge the prevailing gender attitudes and discourses. While they clearly have agency and have bravely broken new ground to promote the girls' education, it is perhaps not surprising that they ultimately do not challenge the power and authority of the teachers. For women whose financial and social security – and that of their children – may depend on working within the status quo of the community, this could be very risky. The potential risk of sexual exploitation and abuse for the Classroom Assistants themselves – both in the school setting and in the wider community – also has to be acknowledged and mitigated against.

Lessons related to the effectiveness of the CA programme and factors for success in addressing GBV and sexual exploitation are particularly relevant today in 2007, as IRC and the Ministry of Education of Liberia are developing new education policies and strategies, and a Classroom Assistant-type programme has been initiated, linked to other efforts to increase the numbers of women teachers in schools. There is also interest in this type of programme beyond the West African context. Recommendations for developing the programme include holistic gender training for teachers and CAs on different dimensions of gender equality in education, including male–female power dynamics in the classroom, and 'team teaching'.[9] Connections should also be developed between Classroom Assistants and women's groups and services in the community to extend their support base beyond the school, and to create links with programmes from which the girls may benefit. CAs should also be given opportunities to continue their education and, if so desired, to enter teaching, for example through accelerated secondary-school courses, distance learning, and complementary vocational and skills training courses. Appropriate access strategies will be needed, such as child-care provision and study groups.

Conclusion

The Minimum Standards for Education in Emergencies, Chronic Crises and Early Reconstruction provide a holistic framework for addressing gender-based violence in education in humanitarian and early recovery contexts. These standards are complemented by other guidelines which encourage educators to work with health providers, with camp managers, water and sanitation officers, and other sector specialists to ensure that women and girls affected by crises of different kinds have a protective environment and are able to fully and safely access opportunities such as education, vocational training, and income-generating activities. It is clear, however, that guidelines need to be translated into concrete actions at the field level, and that concerted training, awareness-raising, monitoring, and follow-up activities need to be provided. The IRC experience with the implementation of the Classroom Assistant programme speaks to the need to ensure adequate and in-depth support for programme staff to implement such a complex programme sensitively. Organisations providing support for communities affected by crises need to work on ensuring that all locations and activities are safe for women and girls, and that all appropriate programming channels are used to share relevant information, skills, and awareness on gender-based violence and exploitation. The education sector has a particularly important role to play in such efforts.

Acknowledgements

Elements of this text – particularly relating to the Classroom Assistant programme – have been adapted from: Kirk, J. and Winthrop, R. (2006) 'Eliminating the Sexual Abuse and Exploitation of Girls in Refugee Schools in West Africa: Introducing Female Classroom Assistants', in F. Leach and C. Mitchell (eds.) *Combating Gender Violence in and Around Schools*, Stoke on Trent: Trentham Books, pp 207–15.

References

INEE Gender Task Team (2006) *Good Practice Guide: Towards Gender Equality/Girls and Women's Education*, available at http://www.ineesite.org/page.asp?pid=1149 (last accessed 30 March 2007).

INEE (2004) *Minimum Standards for Education in Emergencies, Chronic Crises and Early Reconstruction*, available at http://www.ineesite.org/standards/MSEE_report.pdf (last accessed 30 March 2007).

Inter-Agency Standing Committee (IASC) Task Force on Gender and Humanitarian Assistance (2005) *Focusing on Prevention of and Response to Sexual Violence in Emergencies*, available at http://www.humanitarianinfo.org/iasc/content/products/docs/tfgender_GBVGuidelines2005.pdf (last accessed 30 March 2007).

Inter-Agency Standing Committee (IASC) Task Force on Gender and Humanitarian Assistance (2006) *Women, Girls, Boys & Men, Different Needs – Equal Opportunities Gender Handbook for Humanitarian Action*, available at http://www.humanitarianinfo.org/iasc/content/documents/subsidi/tf_gender/IASC%20Gender%20Handbook%20%28Feb%202007%29.pdf, (last accessed 30 March 2007).

Inter-Agency Network for Education in Emergencies (INEE) http://www.ineesite.org.

International Institute for Educational Planning (2006) *The Guidebook for Planning Education in Emergencies and Reconstruction* (Chapter 6: Gender), available at http://www.unesco.org/iiep/eng/focus/emergency/guidebook.htm (last accessed 30 March 2007).

Kirk, J. and Winthrop, R. (forthcoming) *Creating Healing Classrooms: Education in Crisis and Post-Crisis Transitions* (working title), New York: International Rescue Committee.

Mazurana, D. and K. Carlson, (2006) 'The Girl Child and Armed Conflict: Recognizing and Addressing Grave Violations of Girls' Human Rights', paper from Expert Group Meeting: Elimination of all Forms of Discrimination and Violence Against the Girl Child, Florence, Italy, 25–28 September 2006, United Nations Division for the Advancement of Women (DAW) in collaboration with UNICEF.

Nicolai, S. and C. Triplehorn (2003) 'The Role of Education in Protecting Children in Conflict', Humanitarian Practice Network paper, London: Overseas Development Institute.

UNHCR & Save the Children UK (2002) 'Note for Implementing and Operational Partners on Sexual Violence and Exploitation: The Experience of Refugee Children in Guinea, Liberia and Sierra Leone', http://www.unhcr.ch.

Notes

1 For further details see the website of the Inter-Agency Network for Education in Emergencies (INEE) at http://www.ineesite.org.

2 Minimum Standards Guidance Note 4, 'Protection'; Standard 2, Category: Access and Learning Environment, MSEE Handbook, p 46.

3 Minimum Standards Guidance Note 3, 'Assessment': Standard 4: Teaching and Learning, MSEE Handbook, p 62.

4 Minimum Standards Guidance Note 3, Standard 2, 'Conditions of Work', MSEE Handbook, p 68.

5 See http://www.ineesite.org to access these tools.

6 See http://www.humanitarianinfo.org/iasc/content/products/docs/tfgender_GBVGuidelines2005.pdf.

7 See http://www.humanitarianinfo.org/iasc/content/documents/
   default.asp?docID=1750&publish=0.

8 'In some situations, it is necessary to proactively recruit female teachers and
   to adjust the recruitment criteria or process to promote gender parity, where
   possible and appropriate'.

9 'Team teaching' is a way of organising the classroom, and of teaching and
   supporting learning activities, in which responsibilities are shared between
   two teachers and/or assistants, thus providing a positive model of
   collaboration.

11 Reducing poverty and upholding human rights: a pragmatic approach

Meena Poudel and Ines Smyth

The key argument of the chapter is that Oxfam recognises that debates[1] around the interpretations of what trafficking is are important as they influence the kind of policies implemented to eradicate the problem and support victims. However, Oxfam adopts a principled but pragmatic approach to the issue. Pragmatic in that it looks at the problem within its socio-economic context. Principled in that it bases work in this field on Oxfam's understanding of poverty as a denial of the basic rights to which every human being is entitled, and on its perception that poverty is of different kinds, all of which need to be understood and eradicated.

Oxfam GB: poverty, rights, and the trafficking of women

Oxfam GB's mandate is to overcome poverty and suffering. In carrying out this mandate, the organisation relies on a basic understanding of poverty which stresses that:

> *All people are entitled to the rights enshrined in international laws and conventions: social and economic rights, civil and political rights, and the right to life itself, free from fear and persecution. But many people are denied these rights as a consequence of neglect or oppression. Denying people their rights forces them into poverty and keeps them there.* (Oxfam GB 2002)

In order to maximise its resources and achieve 'maximum impact', Oxfam focuses its policy and programme work on five key aims:

- the right to a sustainable livelihood
- the right to health and education
- the right to life and security
- the right to be heard
- the right to equity: gender and diversity.

A concern about the denial of human rights inherent in trafficking fits well within Oxfam's overall understanding of poverty and rights. In addition, Oxfam has prioritised certain areas of work and initiated specific interventions within a global programme to end violence against women, including that against trafficked women and girls within its fifth aim (the right to equity). There is also a commitment to work towards 'getting institutions right for women and overcoming discrimination', through which Oxfam tries to reach the institutional roots of biases in policies and practices that discriminate against women and against women, men, and children on the basis of their racial, ethnic, or other identity.

The case of Niru,[2] a Nepali woman, helps demonstrate the violence, human-rights violations, and gender discrimination that characterise trafficking in women, as well as the role of social institutions such as the family, community, labour market, sex industry, and the state in perpetuating this.

> *A recruitment agent came to my village offering jobs and my parent agreed to send my brother and me. Both of us agreed because we needed money to pay back our loan. I came to Kathmandu when I was 12 years to work in a garment factory. I worked there for a year then a recruiting manager offered me another job in India where I could get more money. They took five girls including me to India by public bus. They asked us to stay in a room with a woman and promised to bring us food. They never came back.*

> *I found myself in brothel. I had been sold for 50,000 Nepalese rupees [$700]. I had to satisfy 5 to 8 clients per night but I did not get any money – only two meals a day. I spent 7 years there and tried to escape three times but didn't succeed. During that time I could not contact my family.*

> *We were 20 girls staying in the same room. There were few rooms set aside for each girl to serve clients for sex. During my menstruation period the owner used to inject drugs into my thigh before go with client. Initially I had tuberculosis but later I was diagnosed as HIV positive.*

> *One day the police raided that brothel and I managed to escape. I stayed in the Indian Government Observation Home for six months. I was taking medicine for tuberculosis but I could not continue my medication because I had no money and the observation did not provide me with any. In the end I managed to get back home with all problems but no money.*

> *When I went back home I found out that my mother had died a year ago. My father loved me but my village refused to accept me because I was considered a bad woman. Village leaders threatened my father that he had to leave the village if he accepted me. I returned to Kathmandu and joined a group of survivors of trafficking. Now I am involved in an anti-trafficking project that raises awareness of the trafficking and the consequences to my Nepali sisters. I know I cannot change my life but I have hope that I can make a contribution*

*to society through Shakti Shamuha[3] to providing information about the
dangers to my sisters who are vulnerable to this crime. My biggest
frustration is that I cannot get a citizenship certificate because of the social
rejection, patriarchal society, and my father being prevented from
recommending me for citizenship. My father's permission is an essential
requirement. Because of my position I cannot take up invitations from abroad
to visit and establish links with other campaigns against trafficking. To me
there is no country, no system that can protect my rights, and there is no
society where I belong. Where are my rights?*

The example is a useful illustration of how human rights can be violated in
all three stages of trafficking: recruitment, work, and rescue.

Recruitment

In a typical situation, a woman or girl is recruited by an agent with promises
of a good or better job in another province or country, with false documents
supplied, if required. In extreme cases, girls and women are abducted. Once
recruited or abducted, many women and girls are forced into sex work or
controlled through debt bondage. Thereafter, threats and use of violence,
coercion, and torture are not uncommon. Basic needs such as food,
medicine, rest, and safe shelter can also be denied to the victim.

Abuse of authority by officials within state institutions is another form of
violence that trafficked women face, as is the violation of their rights to
freedom, movement, and information during transit. There is ample
evidence that corrupt officials within the police and immigration services
often exacerbate the experience of those who are trafficked (Asia Watch
1993). Countries can also benefit from tourism (including sex tourism) and,
in the case of other forms of forced labour, from the avoidance of paying
welfare benefits. They are therefore less likely to take a strong anti-
trafficking position.

Work

Niru's case illustrates some of the human-rights violations within a work
environment. These include violation of contracts, unpaid labour, unsafe
working conditions, lack of safe drinking water, lack of safe and sufficient
food, unlimited time of work, underpayment, and no right to formal
unionised labour. Debt bondage is key to the conditions of dependency and
slavery in which trafficked women and youth live. Other violations include
denial of access to health services, forced use of drugs, and exposure to
sexually transmitted illnesses and HIV and AIDS.

Rescue

Human rights may also be violated at the rescue stage of the trafficking
process. Oxfam GB's experience of working with trafficked survivors and
campaigners in Nepal shows that often the rescue of Nepali women in
Nepal and in India gives cause for concern. Survivors may be illegally

arrested by police and detained, raped, and abused in custody. They are also subjected to forced medical check-ups and treatments, particularly HIV testing. The legal process is equally arbitrary and abusive. Women are forced to testify in public in long and demanding legal proceedings, with no access to independent lawyers. They are often humiliated in court or deported without due process. This violates human-rights principles such as freedom from torture and arbitrary arrest and detention, and the right to protection, liberty, security, privacy, and a fair and speedy trial.

Niru's case also illustrates the discriminatory role of social institutions. Denial of citizenship and rejection by the community not only prevent women such as Niru from taking advantage of limited opportunities for solidarity and for improvements in their lives, but also raise fundamental questions about the limited rights that women may access as citizens, both in countries of origin and destination.

Working against the trafficking of women

The realities of trafficked women and girls differ according to country-specific contexts, reflecting the multi-faceted causes and consequences of trafficking. Oxfam's engagement with the problem also varies in different countries and regions, reflecting the priorities of partner organisations. The size of the programme and types of activities undertaken depend on a variety of factors: country and regional priorities identified by partners and staff; access to necessary resources; and the historical evolution of individual programmes.

With the exception of small-scale project work in the former Yugoslavia and in Latin America, most of Oxfam's work on trafficking takes place in Asia. In the UK, Oxfam also provides support to the Refugee Council (of which Oxfam is a founding member), particularly for information and advocacy work on international refugee and asylum issues. One example of this support is a project Oxfam funded in 1998 for research into trafficking and smuggling of refugees, called 'The Cost of Survival'. In addition, a joint Oxfam GB and NOVIB (Oxfam in The Netherlands) project supports research into best practice on the integration and re-integration of women who are victims of trafficking, through a UK-based organisation and a Dutch NGO.

Most anti-trafficking activities are carried out through partner organisations and networks, rather than by Oxfam directly. For example, in Cambodia Oxfam supports, among other national agencies, KWVC and ADHOC. KWVC is an organisation that works towards promoting women's participation and decision-making in politics, society, and economics. It aims to eliminate discrimination against women and promote laws to protect women's rights. ADHOC is a local human-rights and development organisation that plays a significant role in rights education, monitoring, advocacy, and lobbying. Both have programmes that raise awareness of women and children's rights on issues like sex trafficking and domestic violence.

Bangladesh is one of the many countries in the world where violence against women and trafficking are both widespread. Instances of violence against women such as physical abuse, rape, killing, forced prostitution, trafficking for sex and sex tourism, battering, kidnapping, sexual harassment, and acid-throwing are common. Oxfam GB works to fight the causes and consequences of trafficking in Bangladesh.

Oxfam's emergency interventions in Bangladesh often include some provision for the prevention of trafficking. For example, after the heavy rains during September 2000, when water coming from West Bengal resulted in unexpected floods in south-west and north-west Bangladesh that destroyed local people's livelihoods, Oxfam offered some support. People in these regions were severely affected. As livelihoods were destroyed there was little capacity to cope with the serious impacts of the flooding. Interruption of education, erosion of incomes, and the migration of income earners all raised the risk of trafficking of adolescents. In response, Oxfam implemented a programme that, in addition to funding rehabilitation initiatives, focused on agriculture, cash for work, winter clothes distribution, rebuilding housing and sanitation, and advocacy initiatives to raise awareness and minimise the risk of trafficking.

Oxfam GB recognises that the consequences of trafficking of women and girls are exacerbated by gender biases in institutions. Oxfam GB attempted to address this problem through support for Naripokkho, a women's organisation founded in 1983 that works for the advancement of women's rights. Naripokkho is a membership organisation that undertakes advocacy, research, and training on various issues related to women's rights and development. Violence against women has been a priority concern from its very inception. The programme supported by Oxfam monitors state mechanisms and tries to institutionalise a process of state accountability for the prevention and reduction of violence against women, including trafficking.

Examples from Nepal are also useful because they demonstrate a more systematic approach to supporting local organisations to combat trafficking.

Oxfam's anti-trafficking work in Nepal

While there has been no systematic research to determine the true extent of trafficking in women in Nepal, observers believe that most Nepali women are trafficked to India, the Middle East, and other Asian countries primarily for sex work. It is estimated that there are more than 200,000 Nepalese women in Indian brothels, with additional tens of thousands of Nepalese women in other countries who have been forced into sex work or into work in oppressive situations and inhumane conditions each year (Child Worker in Nepal Concerns Centre [CWIN] 1992).

Nepal is beset with many socio-economic problems, and the extreme poverty in some regions facilitates the trafficking of women and girls. More than 70 per cent of Nepalis live below the poverty line. The average per capita annual income is $180. There is widespread illiteracy, especially among women, 72 per cent of whom are illiterate (Central Bureau of Statistics 2000).

The flourishing trade in women is influenced by the socio-economic context. Some rural families experience great difficulties in trying to sustain themselves. While the deteriorating socio-economic conditions affect all members of society, women in particular are more vulnerable to trafficking due to the discrimination they face in household decision-making matters, and the constraints they face with regard to viable opportunities for earning a living. Families' vulnerability to the trafficking of their female members is a symptom of the desperation that exists. Socio-cultural pressures marginalise women from birth onwards, and once a woman has been forced into sex slavery, there is no going back.

Traffickers often use family members and close friends of targeted women and girls to lure them and avoid detection by authorities or communities as demonstrated by the case of Bimala (in the Sindhupalchock district, 40 km north-east of Kathmandu). Bimala and Nanu Maya were good friends, studying together in grade eight at a local school. Traffickers managed to convince Nanu to lure her friend to go to Kathmandu, with the promise of better education and a job, without informing her family. The organisation Gramin Mahila Srijansheel Pariwar (an Oxfam partner) managed to rescue Bimala from Kathmandu and return her to her family. While Nanu and her mother were prosecuted, the real traffickers escaped justice.

The aim of the Oxfam programme in Nepal is to reduce trafficking in women and to work towards making a positive impact on the lives of women. In practice, the programme has increasingly focused on two aspects of anti-trafficking work: educating communities on the mechanisms and consequences of trafficking, and supporting the enforcement of existing laws and the formulation of appropriate policies, laws, and conventions to combat trafficking. Programme activities range from the grassroots to national, regional (in South Asia), and global levels. This integrated multi-level approach aims to address the problem of violation of women's rights during the recruitment, work, and rescue stages of trafficking, as well as the institutional aspects.

At grassroots level, the work focuses on collaboration with various institutions to educate communities, and to support survivors through legal processes against traffickers. Sindhupalchock is one of the most remote of Nepal's 75 districts, with a large ethnic minority population. It is located in the central hilly region of Nepal, and shares its northern border with Tibet. Since this is one of the poorest districts in the country and among the most vulnerable to trafficking, Oxfam GB has been working here with two local organisations managed and controlled by women, and with the District Development Committee, since 1998.

At the national level the work is directed towards alliance building among relevant NGOs and advocacy groups to promote law enforcement and reform based on international human-rights conventions. At the regional level, Oxfam has worked with several of its partners, and more specifically with the Alliance Against Trafficking in Women (AATWIN) and the Asian Women Human Rights Council (AWHRC) as well as other regional feminist groups, to lobby the South Asian Association for Regional Co-operation (SAARC) to set up regional mechanisms (e.g. regional courts) to address the issue bilaterally.

At the international level, the priority has been to work with international feminist groups and advocacy networks (e.g. Global Alliance against Trafficking [GAATW] and the Asian Women Human Rights Council [AWHRC]) to tackle trafficking issues within the United Nations, including the optional protocol.

This contextual and multi-layered approach has been successful in some areas. The 'Annual Impact Report', prepared by Oxfam GB (Oxfam GB 2001) summarises some of the changes that have taken place since the programme started. There are overall improvements in the participation of women in formal politics. The five major political parties in Nepal have accepted that women should have 33 per cent of seats in parliamentary structures, as against 20 per cent (in village development committees), and 5 per cent (House of Representatives). Women's groups are lobbying to have women's names lodged as head of household, along with men's, during the national census planned for June. Women are also starting to come forward as candidates for the next district elections.[4]

The incidence of trafficking has decreased by about 15 per cent in Sindhupalchock district, as a result of legal action and campaigning against the traffickers. One hundred and fifty cases of violence against women and 75 trafficking cases have been registered. Several cases have been heard by village and district development committees, and perpetrators of violence and trafficking have been punished.

Conclusions

Trafficking in women is a complex phenomenon and an extremely sensitive one, inextricably linked to poverty, migration, work, sex, money, and violence. Oxfam's work in Nepal and in other countries provides examples of a pragmatic but principled approach to the problem.

This article was originally published in Gender & Development, *volume 10, number 1, March 2002.*

References

Asia Watch (1993) *A Modern Form of Slavery: Trafficking of Women and Girls into Brothels in Thailand*, New York: Asia Watch.

Central Bureau of Statistics (2000) *Statistical Pocket Book*, Kathmandu: Central Bureau of Statistics, National Planning Commission.

Child Worker in Nepal Concerns Centre (CWIN) (1992) *Bal Sarokar*, Kathmandu: CWIN.

Oxfam GB (2001) 'South Asia Annual Impact Report', June 2001, Oxford: Oxfam GB.

Oxfam GB (2002) 'Achieving Maximum Impact: Oxfam Strategy for Overcoming Impact', Oxford: Oxfam GB.

Notes

1   Over the years, there has been much debate about the definition of 'trafficking'. Even with the introduction of the Trafficking Protocol in 2001, disagreement remains about the interpretation of the trafficking as laid out in the Protocol.

2   Not her real name.

3   Shakti Shamuha is a campaign organisation formed by survivors, and an Oxfam partner.

4   During the national census in Nepal in 2001, women's names were recorded along with men's names at the household level. However, women are yet to be legally recongised as heads of household. Recent political development in Nepal created an environment for women to push their agenda regarding the role of women in national political processes. As a result of this push, all political parties agreed to allocate 33 per cent of seats at decision-making levels to women (this promise is also reflected in the current interim constitution). However, none of the parties met their targets. Most of the parties have allocated 10–20 per cent of seats to women, but not all of these have been filled.

12 A tale of two cities: shifting the paradigm of anti-trafficking programmes

Smarajit Jana, Nandinee Bandyopadhyay,
Mrinal Kanti Dutta, and Amitrajit Saha

Over the last decade, the issue of trafficking has dominated international development debates. The ways in which the dominant discourses on trafficking are framed are based on certain assumptions and beliefs which have now come to be taken as the 'truth', without being challenged. These discourses usually define trafficking as a process where a person loses control over their own life; they equate sex work to trafficking, and stress the restriction of movement of weaker and vulnerable sections of society. Police rescue and so called 'rehabilitation' initiatives become the cornerstone of most of the programmes arising out of this thinking. At international conferences on trafficking, as well as in the popular media, those who are involved in anti-trafficking efforts contend tenaciously that the trafficking of people across international borders has escalated dramatically in the last decade. Equally, it is asserted that the funding of activities to curb trafficking has also grown exponentially. If we stop to ponder for a minute it is clear that for both postulations to be true at the same time, something must be wrong: either with the definitions or perceptions of trafficking and the estimates of its volume, and/or because the types of anti-trafficking initiatives intended to address it have been ineffective. In this chapter we present our own understanding of this issue, based on our experiences of working with sex workers' organisations running anti-trafficking programmes.

Redefining trafficking and anti-trafficking strategies

In order to have an impact on trafficking we need to focus on two courses of action, namely, exploring the root causes of trafficking, and recognising the positive role of human agency. Durbar Mahila Samanwaya Committee (DMSC) in Kolkata, one of the largest organised groups for sex workers, defines trafficking as an *outcome* of a process where:

- people are recruited and moved within or across national borders without informed consent, and coerced into a 'job' or occupation against their will;
- the trafficked individual loses control over his/her occupation and life.

People have always left home in search of new lives, better livelihoods, or simply to seek adventure. Traditionally, women often had to hold back on exploring alternatives because of rigid gender norms and lack of opportunities. Globalisation has resulted in the realignment of social and cultural relations, and radical changes in the labour market, which means that more and more women who were traditionally confined to the home are now seeking alternative, preferred, and more viable livelihood options elsewhere.

DMSC sees this as a positive and potentially revolutionary development, creating a window of opportunity for challenging existing gender and class inequalities. However, existing political systems, with increasingly stringent anti-immigration national laws in most countries, make such migration hazardous, particularly for poor or marginalised aspiring migrants who are vulnerable to being smuggled illegally into the countries they seek to enter. As long as the current economic globalisation process privileges movement of finance capital while restricting the movement of labour or human capital across national borders, trafficking of people will continue.

Women, men, and children are trafficked for various purposes, such as marriage, agricultural labour, working in various informal sector industries, domestic labour, participating in dangerous sports such as camel racing, recruitment in armed conflict, and for sex work.

The most critical element of trafficking is not necessarily the process through which a person is trafficked, nor the nature of the job or practices for which the person is trafficked: rather, it is the *outcome* of that process that is instrumental in leaving the trafficked person with little or no option to leave the place or position in which they find themselves. Trafficked persons are recruited into various jobs, for which they can be made to work without the wages or the minimum benefits that have to be provided to regular members of the labour force. If the entire employment market, in both formal and unorganised sectors, could be regulated in adherence to national and international labour laws protecting the rights of workers, and if all workers were conscious of their labour rights, were organised, and had a role in regulating the workplace, the demand for trafficked labour would cease to exist.

Patriarchal legislation and controls

Recently, in countries across the world, more and more stringent laws have been introduced to curb trafficking in order to protect women. In effect, these laws restrict the free movement of women. Bangladesh, which is one of the major labour-exporting countries of South Asia, has enacted a law preventing single women from travelling across its borders. Not only do such laws violate the fundamental human right to mobility, and discriminate against women, they also exacerbate the vulnerability of women to being trafficked: where no legal options are available to them, they must depend on the illicit options offered by traffickers. Special booths have been set up by the state in collaboration with NGOs at the borders – although there are no visa requirements for travelling between Nepal and India – where women crossing the border are interrogated in order to verify their identity and to judge whether they may be allowed to cross the border (CARE 2001a).

It is often argued, in several forums, that restricting movement across borders, through new legislation or more stringent implementation of existing laws, prevents trafficking. In fact, these kinds of restrictions can work to strengthen the influence of organised crime. The prime motivating factor that impels people to move from villages to cities and from one country to another is their aspiration to improve their life conditions, a basic social instinct that has always shaped human civilisation. If people cannot migrate legally, they resort to illegal mechanisms. Only large, organised criminal networks have the resources and wherewithal to bypass strict state control at international borders. This in turn leads to the development of bigger and bigger crime syndicates, as has happened in Eastern Europe.

Stricter border control also increases the risks for those who are trafficked, as traffickers choose more and more hazardous routes and methods to escape detection. Moreover, such controls expose women to greater exploitation because of existing gender inequalities and social vulnerabilities.

Only global structural political and economic changes can create a new scenario where trafficking becomes redundant. For example, unrestricted movement of labour across international borders would mean that a poor woman from a developing country could travel legitimately to a rich-country market to seek employment, just as her richer and more qualified counterpart is able to. Access to legitimate avenues of migration would reduce the risk of being entrapped by a trafficker. Universal education and equal access to information would also reduce the risk of potential migrants being deceived by traffickers.

When it comes to dealing with those who have already been trafficked, no attempt has been made to implement a set of standard rules, code of conduct, or self-imposed norms by the NGOs or state agencies who implement rescue and rehabilitation programmes. Nor has any effort been made to enable the participation of those trafficked in designing a programme of rehabilitation.

It is critical that we look into the issue of participation in this regard. That the direct participation of those who are trafficked in preventing and ameliorating the effects of trafficking is both ethical and effective has been demonstrated by the experiences of the Durbar Mahila Samanwaya Committee (DMSC) in this regard (Durbar Mahila Samanwaya Committee 1998, 1999, 2001). Moreover, DMSC's expertise, based on its achievements in the last couple of years, has already been transferred to other sex-worker organisations in Bangladesh.

Tales from two cities: the realities of trafficking and anti-trafficking work

The following stories demonstrate the different realities of women trafficked into sex work. The reasons why many women and girls are trafficked into prostitution include a combination of individualised choices to improve their situation through seeking better lives and employment opportunities in cities and other countries. These choices are not afforded to them within their own setting due to poverty, discrimination, inequality, and in some cases gender-based violence.

Farzana's story: seeking a better life

Farzana left her village in 1997, determined to find new opportunities and a better life. She stayed with a friend in a city slum, who, after a couple of weeks, found her a job in a garment factory. Within a couple of months her supervisor started paying her unwelcome attention and finally proposed to her. She did not like him, so she refused. The supervisor sacked her. The sense of liberty and freedom that she had now experienced, especially after what she had known before coming to Dhaka and working, stopped Farzana from going back to her village. She was determined to find something better.

She got an offer to work in the neighbouring town of Narayanganj and took it up. However, she found herself trafficked into a brothel in Tanbazar.[1] She tried to run away but was unsuccessful, and continued to work as a bonded labourer. After a year she paid off her debt to the brothel owner and was free to leave. At this juncture she pondered over what to do next. Eventually she decided to continue in the sex trade, as many others do.

In the middle of one night in 1999, policemen broke open the door of Farzana's room in the brothel and kicked her out. Along with many other sex workers, she was pushed into a police van and taken to a remand home. At the remand home she was persistently abused, physically and sexually. Her only hope for getting out of the remand home was to accept the rehabilitation programme offered by the government. This rehabilitation package included 5000 *taka* in cash and a sewing machine. Farzana was told that if she did not accept the deal she would have to remain in the home forever. She agreed, but then the authorities stipulated that unless her parents came to take custody of her, Farzana would not be allowed to leave the home.

There was no way Farzana could get in touch with her parents and persuade them to come and 'rescue' her. By this time, however, Farzana had learnt that there were people who would pose as her parents in exchange for 4500 of the 5000 *taka*, and the sewing machine. Farzana came out of the home with many others. Having lost all her savings at the time of the eviction, all she had with her was 500 *taka*. With 500 *taka* in her pocket and no place to live, she had no other option but to take to the streets or try and find another job in the garments industry.

The role of human agency: Farzana's aspirations, choices, and risks

Farzana's story raises a number of issues. When Farzana left for Dhaka, it was not mere poverty that drove her. She risked venturing out into the unknown because she could no longer accept the circumstances under which she was forced to live at home. As soon as she had reached puberty she was withdrawn from school. She was not even allowed to study at home since her father had decided it would be a bad investment, as she would eventually marry into another family. She was not allowed to play with her friends in the fields any longer. All she did was work at home from dawn to dusk performing repetitive, mind-numbing, and unending household chores. This work would never teach her skills that could earn her a living. It was her aspiration to break free of the boundaries imposed on her as an adolescent Muslim girl in a Bangladeshi village, and her determination to get more out of life, that brought Farzana to the city. The fact that someone who was not allowed to leave home could make such a life-changing move represents a triumph of human agency. The question we have to confront now is: how far are we ready to acknowledge and respect Farzana's human agency, and accept her right to find her own destiny?

In the city, Farzana found a job. For the first time in her life she was independent. She acquired new skills and earned money over which she had control. With her co-workers she could walk in the city streets whenever she wanted. However, when she decided to extend her new-found autonomy to thwart the designs of her supervisor, she lost her job.

Farzana could have returned home at this point. But knowing what awaited her there, she did not want to forego her hard-earned freedom. So she desperately looked for another job. It was at this juncture that she was trafficked. An agent who had promised to find her another job sold her a brothel owner, making a tidy profit. The brothel owner too made money out of Farzana's vulnerability by making her work for her without wages until she had made substantial profits over and above the money she had invested in procuring Farzana.

Until the brothel owner was satisfied with her profit, Farzana was bonded and could not opt out of the condition she found herself in, however much she wanted to. It is to be noted that after overcoming the constraints imposed on her by social conditions against all odds on two earlier instances, Farzana, not having any resource other than her own free will and determination, could no longer surmount the material boundaries of her situation.

However, the period of bondage came to an end after one year. Once again Farzana was at a crossroads. She had to decide whether to continue working in the sex trade or to take her chances in other job markets. Considering all her options, Farzana decided to continue to work as a sex worker. At this point, Farzana had some control over her working conditions and was free to leave the trade whenever she wanted.

What needs to be understood is that even in such adversity, Farzana managed to escape from her trafficked conditions. At this point she can no longer be considered to be 'in a trafficked situation'. It is to be noted that all trafficking situations are time-bound and usually do not extend throughout someone's entire life, or inter-generationally. This has significant implications for future anti-trafficking approaches and strategies.

Farzana's experience of forced rehabilitation

Government policy to evict all sex workers and place them in a remand home put paid to Farzana's prospects. In violation of her fundamental rights, she was forcibly evicted from her home and workplace. She was insulted and physically abused. She was then imprisoned in a remand home, once again finding herself in a situation over which she had no control. In addition, she was sexually exploited and abused at the remand home while under the supposed protection of the state. Farzana now found herself in a situation no different from the one under which she lived when she was trafficked. This raises the question whether forced 'rehabilitation' ought to be seen as trafficking too.

The government then unilaterally decided on a rehabilitation deal for imprisoned sex workers. None of the sex workers were consulted about what they wanted, completely disregarding their agency. Secondly, they were offered no choice in the matter: if they did not accept the government package they would have to resign themselves to life-long imprisonment. The government then imposed the additional condition that the rehabilitation package would be handed over to the sex workers only with their parents' authorisation. This infantilised the sex workers, and created the conditions for further exploitation. The entire exercise clearly demonstrates how any scheme that is designed with no consultation with the intended users can be counterproductive.

Who is to blame?

Farzana found herself on the streets again, exposed to greater vulnerability than before. We have to ask ourselves, is it not the lack of appropriate work environment and conditions in formal and informal sectors, such as the garments industry and the sex trade, that facilitate perpetual exploitation of the most vulnerable groups? Had there been proper protection of labour rights in the garments industry, Farzana would not have been sacked at the whim of her supervisor in the first place. Had there been adequate trade regulations within the sex industry, Farzana or any other sex worker would not have been made to work without wages, nor would any brothel owner be allowed to employ trafficked labour. In such a case, the need for trafficking would not have arisen, as there would have been no extra gains to be made in recruiting trafficked persons. The issue here is, what role did the state play in safeguarding workers' rights and in securing workplace safety to prevent extreme forms of exploitation of workers such as Farzana? Is providing workers some control over their occupation a more appropriate or effective strategy for governments?

Sofia's story: dealing with HIV

Sofia, a friend of Farzana's who had also been evicted from Tanbazar and later remanded at the same home, decided to opt out of the sex trade. She took the help of an NGO to seek an alternative livelihood. The NGO put her in a shelter home. Immediately on her arrival, the NGO personnel took a sample of her blood, and tested it for HIV without her knowledge or consent. She was found to be HIV positive. The NGO personnel informed her of this, and very quickly, all the staff members of the shelter home came to know her status. The rules of the shelter home were that no rescued women were allowed to meet and communicate with outsiders without prior permission from the official in charge of the shelter home, and that communication could only take place at fixed hours in a month. This lack of communication meant that nobody outside of the home knew what happened to Sofia. After a couple weeks, Farzana heard that Sofia had committed suicide. Her body was not even sent for a post mortem examination, a common practice internationally following any unnatural death (Mondol 2001).

Monica's story: choosing to go back

Monica had come to Dhaka from Satkhira with her father and younger brother. Her father and brother worked on a construction site, and Monica found a job in a small shop close to the site. They found out that across the border in Barasat the wage rates in construction work were higher, and the working hours were shorter. The next season, they paid an agent to help them cross the border to Barasat in India without legitimate papers in order to find work on a construction site. Monica heard from other female workers that wages in Kolkata were even higher so she started looking for ways to find work there. One morning, Monica's father found that she had gone.

After nine months Monica came back to Satkhira bringing gifts and 5000 *taka*. She had been trafficked and sold into the sex industry, where she had worked for four months bonded to the brothel ownder who had bought her. Once the bondage term was over, she stayed on in the trade working for another brothel owner and sharing her earnings with her. Initially her family and neighbours seemed appalled by the fact that she had 'fallen' into prostitution. The local religious leader arbitrated that Monica would have to pay a fine of 150 *taka* to seek re-entry into the community. Once she paid this amount, the rest of the members of the community accepted Monica back.

Gradually Monica came to know that many women from her locality had gone through the same process, through which they managed to accumulate considerable wealth and improve their living conditions. From her savings, Monica bought a piece of land and met the costs of her mother's treatment for a long-term illness. Now Monica is preparing to go back to Kolkata to work in the sex industry for a few years so that she can support her parents and also save for her future. She is looking out for an agent who will take her across the border for a fee.

A survey conducted by CARE showed that, like Monica, 22 per cent of women who have experienced trafficking actually choose to return to the occupation into which they were trafficked (CARE 2001c). Why is Monica not afraid of being trafficked again? Quite rightly, Monica has identified the real reason for her vulnerability to being trafficked. It was her lack of knowledge that made her susceptible to being deceived and trafficked. Now that she knows how the sex industry works and has control over the capital she has, she is confident that she can determine the terms under which she works. If women at risk of being trafficked were provided with information of how the market works, and were guaranteed control over the work conditions, the possibility of being trafficked into slavery-like conditions would be hugely reduced.

There are hundreds of Farzanas, Sofias, and Monicas, all of whom could tell a similar story, if we would only stop to ask them. In the course of our work in Dhaka and Kolkata, the numerous Farzanas, Sofias, and Monicas have recounted these experiences to us. To us these narratives raise a number of important questions. Should we address the process or the outcome of trafficking? Should we be shocked and horrified by these stories or concerned with the interests, opinions, and life-strategies of those trafficked? If the basic objective of our anti-trafficking efforts is to enhance the well-being of the individual and help improve her livelihood options, then the role of that individual and that of other third parties involved in the individual's rescue and rehabilitation should come under thorough scrutiny. The processes of deceit, coercion, and exploitation, which define trafficking, are not perpetrated by traffickers alone; in the name of rescue and rehabilitation, agents of the state and private actors may also employ such tactics. There is no code of conduct followed by all these agencies to ensure the protection of the rights and dignity of the victims while carrying out their work. NGOs participating in a consultative meeting recently held in Dhaka strongly recommended the development and inclusion of codes of conduct while dealing with anti-trafficking programmes (CARE 2001b).

DMSC's programme approach

Following our principal objective to dissociate sex work from all criminal associations, DMSC entered into the arena of anti-trafficking activities in 1998 and quickly developed a strategy to stop the trafficking of women and children into sex work in Kolkata. DMSC sees sex work as a contractual service, negotiated between consenting adults. In such a service contract there ought to be no coercion or deception. As a sex workers' rights organisation, DMSC is against any force exercised against sex workers, be it by the client, brothel keepers, room owners, pimps, police, or traffickers.

DMSC's programme approach is very simple. Members of DMSC keep a strong vigil in the red light districts through a group of volunteers who intercept any new entrants into the area, make enquiries about where they have come from, their relationship with the people accompanying them, if any, and thoroughly examine the role of brother owners and landlords in the process of their recruitment. They can effectively stop the entry of any under-age woman, or women who are being coerced into the trade. They do this in two ways. Firstly, being in the trade themselves they are able to identify cases of trafficking much more easily than an outsider could. Secondly, as members of a very organised labour force in the city, they can exert their power to remove or 'rescue' such women from the clutches of any unscrupulous brothel owners and pimps who have procured them. In most cases, trafficked women are counselled and sent back to their homes or to boarding schools (when the person is a minor) with the help of the Ministry of Social Welfare, but without involving the law-enforcing authorities in general.

The process is not as simple as it appears to be. Contrary to popular belief, the people who usually challenge or resist DMSC's anti-trafficking interventions are not the traffickers, or others with a stake in the sex industry. It is the state and its law-enforcing authorities which create the greatest barrier.

Madhabi's story: 'sacrifice a life' or obey the law of the land?

As a teenager, Madhabi had fallen in love with a distant relative, Mukul. Her parents did not endorse Madhabi's love affair. When her parents insisted that she end her relationship with Mukul and marry a man they had chosen for her, Madhabi ran away from home with Mukul. They rented a room in the suburbs of Kolkata and started living together. Mukul had neither income nor the skills to find any job in the city. They managed to survive during the first couple of months by selling Madhabi's jewellery.

One morning, Mukul left home in search of a job and did not return. Two days later Mukul's friends turned up saying they had come to take Madhabi to a hospital where Mukul has been admitted following a serious accident. Travelling for more than an hour by bus and tram they arrived at a place that Madhabi did not recognise. Confused, she found herself in an unfamiliar street. 'How could it be a hospital?', she mumbled. She had never seen so many women standing in the street, talking so loudly.

As she hesitated, Mukul's friends dragged her to the staircase of the nearby building. At that very moment they heard a harsh voice from behind asking them to stop. Unknown to Mukul's friends DMSC volunteers had followed them since their arrival into the red light area, finding their movements to be suspicious.

Madhabi was brought to the DMSC office for counselling and other support. The other volunteers found Mukul lurking in the brothel Madhabi was being taken to and took him and his friends to the local police station. After a brief dialogue, the officer in charge asked DMSC members to hand Mukul and Madhabi over in order to register a case of trafficking against Mukul. The officer argued that without taking custody of Madhabi, who was purportedly being trafficked, no case could be booked against Mukul. The volunteers returned to the DMSC office. A debate soon ensued, with other members of DMSC joining in, which continued for couple of hours without reaching any conclusion.

What was being debated was Madhabi's fate. Should she be handed over to the police in order so that Mukul would be punished or should she be allowed to follow a course of action of her own choice? DMSC members knew that putting Madhabi in police custody could mean indirectly 'forcing' her into the sex trade, which she did not want to engage in. Usually when a trafficked woman is rescued from the sex trade and put into police custody, the police accommodate her in the government remand home, which is notorious for corruption and for unofficial linkages with the trafficking racket.

In DMSC's experience, the brothel owners who recruit trafficked women have a system worked out by which they can pay a bribe to the remand home authorities in order to have the woman returned to them. They then extract the amount they had invested – often inflating it considerably – from the trafficked woman by making her work without wages. Moreover, the process through which Madhabi would have to pass once put in the hands of the law-enforcement system, from police custody, to judicial custody, to remand homes, is both lengthy and hazardous. The police and the caretakers of the remand home are likely to treat her with no dignity, and may sexually abuse her.[2] At the end of such a process, her already restricted options would be reduced to none whatsoever.

So, none of the representatives of the DMSC were inclined to hand Madhabi over to the police. On the other hand not doing so would result in the traffickers going unpunished. This posed the biggest dilemma to the members of the organisation. Their accumulated experience over the period had shown them that they would have to follow one or the other of the two possible courses of action. One is to obey the norms and rules of the state. The other is to respect Madhabi's wishes and take a stand outside the law so as to reverse the outcome of trafficking for her, and enhance her options to improve her life chances. Most DMSC members opted for the second path.

Sex workers' organisation and action

During the last two years, DMSC has recovered 47 trafficked women, of whom 35 were minors, and taken them to safe custody. We have repatriated four minors from Bangladesh and two from Nepal, and have helped 12 Indian minors to return home.

DMSC runs a primary prevention programme providing alternative livelihood training to those who do not want to continue in sex work as part of its broader aim to respect the choices of individuals. Training has been provided to 112 adolescents and 32 adults in skills such as silk-screen printing, toy making, and clay modelling. In addition to reducing young adults' vulnerability to sex work, DMSC has in the last year recruited 25 daughters of sex workers as teachers on their on-going education programme for sex workers and their children. They are provided with on-the-job training, which they may later use to seek alternative employment.

DMSC has reduced the economic vulnerability of sex workers and their children by running a savings and credit programme through the sex workers' co-operative institution, Usha Multipurpose Co-operative Society Limited. It has a membership of about 3500, representing different brothels in Kolkata.

DMSC also trains sex workers from neighbouring countries in order to make cross-border anti-trafficking efforts more effective. It acts in close collaboration with sex workers' organisations and supporting NGOs in Bangladesh and Nepal, particularly in the repatriation of trafficked persons.

Challenges

DMSC has faced some major challenges,[3] including strong opposition from law-enforcing authorities who criticise DMSC for taking the law into its own hands and violating the constitutional boundaries between the state and civil society. Although DMSC succeeded in creating a support base within local police institutions, without which they could not have carried out their anti-trafficking activities at the field level, contradictions with the legal and judicial system remain. This poses a constant threat to DMSC's intervention in this arena, as its extra-constitutional role can be used against it.

The broader political context, which extends beyond the red light districts but profits from the exploitation and trafficking of sex workers within the sex industry, has started making moves, in various guises, to oppose DMSC's efforts to stop trafficking into the sex trade.

The prevalent positions and practices of NGOs, both local and international, also pose a challenge to sex workers' interventions in trafficking. This conflict is on the one hand an ideological one. Sex workers and trafficked persons who take the initiative to deal with their own problems as actors in development, rather than passive recipients, are challenging the conventional role of NGOs and the enlightened middle classes working on *behalf of* the poor. On the other hand, there is an immediate conflict of interest. If more and more sex workers' organisations gain the capacity and the confidence to implement intervention activities themselves, NGOs will become apprehensive that their role as mediator will gradually become redundant.

In fact, sex workers' and trafficked persons' demands for the right to self-determination and autonomy represent an ideological challenge not just to the prevalent development practices by NGOs, but to all discourses that reduce marginalised people, particularly women, to being submissive victims of their circumstance, devoid of human agency, and unable to steer their own destiny unless 'rescued' through the benevolence of others.

Self-regulatory boards: a way forward

To overcome all these challenges, DMSC has been institutionalising the process of their anti-trafficking interventions through establishing self-regulatory boards. DMSC has so far established three local self-regulatory boards in Kolkata, and is in the process of setting up similar boards in all red light areas. Sixty per cent of the members of these boards are sex workers, and the rest are comprised of the local elected representatives of the people, representatives of the state, legal professionals, and medical doctors.

The primary objectives of these boards is to prevent exploitation and violation of human rights within the sex trade; to initiate comprehensive development programmes for the sex workers' community; and to ensure the community's right to self-determination. The boards are involved in various programmes such as mitigating violence against sex workers; establishing channels of information within the red light area through which the board members can monitor whether any children are being trafficked into sex work or whether anyone is being made to work against her will; identifying those who have been trafficked, and encouraging them to seek the help of the self-regulatory board; trauma counselling of those recovered, and providing them with health services if required; repatriation of those who are recovered, with representatives of the boards accompanying them; establishing ways of keeping in touch with those who are repatriated, with the help of collaborative sex workers' organisations and NGOs in their native countries, to ensure that they are not stigmatised or re-trafficked.

It seems to us that this unique approach can open up new ways of designing and implementing anti-trafficking programmes, and can help us to think through and re-frame the development discourse and practice on anti-trafficking programmes globally.

This article was originally published in Gender & Development, *volume 10, number 1, March 2002.*

References

CARE (2001a) Proceedings of a workshop on 'Cross-border Trafficking Prevention', organised by CARE Bangladesh in Dhaka, October 17–18 2001, Dhaka: CARE Bangladesh.

CARE (2001b) Minutes of a consultative meeting organised by CARE Bangladesh, Dhaka, 10 September 2001, Dhaka: CARE Bangladesh.

CARE (2001c) 'Report of Ethnographic Study', unpublished report of the Anti-trafficking Project of CARE-Bangladesh, Dhaka: CARE Bangladesh.

Durbar Mahila Samanwaya Committee (DMSC) (1998) 'Seven Years Stint at Sonagachi: DMSC, Human Development, and Social Action', Kolkata: DMSC.

Durbar Mahila Samanwaya Committee (DMSC) (1999) 'Second State Conference of the Sex Workers Report: 30th April to 1st May 1999', Kolkata: DMSC.

Durbar Mahila Samanwaya Committee (DMSC) (2001) 'Millennium Milan Mela', Kolkata: DMSC.

Mondol, P. (2001) 'HIV, Death and Justice: The Dhaka Experience', poster presented at the 6th ICAAP conference held in Melbourne, October 2001.

Notes

1 Tanbazar was the largest functioning brothel in Bangladesh, till July 1999. In the middle of the night, the Law Enforcing Department organised a brutal 'raid' and evicted all inhabitants of the brothel, some 4500 sex workers. The incident was widely covered in local newspapers.

2 Focus group discussion with DMSC members, held in their Kolkata office, 26 November 2001.

3 Interview with Angura Begum, Secretary, DMSC, Kolkata, 27 November 2001.

Conclusion

Geraldine Terry

There are no easy answers to the question 'how can gender-based violence best be eradicated?' Women's organisations, international development NGOs, and human-rights campaigning bodies have succeeded in bringing GBV out into the open as a human-rights violation and a development concern, but the barriers are still formidable. The sad fact is that in many countries, they have hardly been dented, let alone destroyed. As several contributors to this volume argue, GBV can only be eliminated when severe gender inequalities are levelled out and women can claim their whole range of rights. This involves transforming deeply embedded injustices such as women's low representation in governments and parliaments, which affects policy priorities and resource allocations, and women's lack of assets relative to men. Until these and other issues are addressed, women will continue to be vulnerable to GBV. This brief conclusion outlines, in very broad terms, some critical current trends likely to affect the context of efforts to eliminate GBV. It then draws out some lessons suggested by the articles in this volume, including promising strategies at different levels.

Critical current trends

The rise of identity politics and cultural relativism

Since 9/11, the so-called 'war on terror', led by the US government with the UK government a keen ally, has provoked a backlash in regions such as the Middle East, hardening cultural relativist challenges to the universality of women's human rights, and fuelling GBV in many forms. The UN Special Rapporteur has noted that, in some countries, identity politics, including religious fundamentalisms, underlie state inaction on GBV, or worse, government attacks on women's human rights.[1] Elsewhere, religious fundamentalist groups are opposing governments' efforts to tackle GBV; for instance, Oxfam has documented the resistance of Islamist groups in Pakistan, India, and Sri Lanka to government moves to strengthen women's rights in rape cases.[2] However, there are other religious fundamentalisms involved in this general negative trend, notably the US Christian right (which exerts great influence over the Bush administration's reproductive health policies in the global South), and the Vatican. Whether it is the murder of women by Hamas vigilantes in Gaza, the Vatican's entrenched opposition to the use of condoms in Africa or the US 'global gag' rule that has denied funding to reproductive health organisations working in the global South, women's rights, and their vulnerability to GBV, are involved. Cassandra Balchin of Women Living Under Muslim Laws argues that, in the near future, Islamist fundamentalist tendencies will strengthen in the Middle East, North Africa, and other parts of the Islamic world, as global inequalities are perpetuated.[3]

New technologies

In South and East Asia, North Africa, and the Middle East, a general preference for sons rather than daughters is expressed through sex-selective abortions, as well as female infanticide and the systematic neglect of girl-children. A study in India, for instance, estimated that prenatal sex selection and infanticide have accounted for half a million missing girls per year for the past two decades,[4] while according to Oxfam International, there are 50 million fewer women in South Asia than there should be.[5] Ann Elisabeth Samson of the Association for Women's Rights in Development researches the potential impact of new technologies, including reproductive technology and information and communications technologies (ICTs), on women's ability to exercise their rights. She points out that they can have both negative and positive impacts. For instance, ultrasound can make women safer during pregnancy, but it is being misused to discover the sex of foetuses and enable sex-selective abortions. ICTs also have an ambivalent role, because they can be used by GBV perpetrators as well as by women's organisations in their advocacy, campaigning, and organising. Some of the ways ICTs enable, encourage, or disseminate GBV are; Internet pornography, including child pornography, chat rooms that allow sexual predators to exploit children, and video games that glorify violence, including GBV. As ICTs spread to parts of the world where access is currently limited, these manifestations of GBV will spread too.

Climate change

Climate change, the challenge of sustainable development, and poor women's human rights in the global South, including their right to be free from violence, are closely bound together. Climate change disproportionately harms developing countries, both through extreme weather events like cyclones and floods, and through longer-term changes such as droughts and increased soil salinity. Sub-Saharan Africa, in particular, is thought to be vulnerable, although other parts of the global South, such as Bangladesh, are also very exposed. Women with a low income in developing countries are often identified as the group most vulnerable to climate change, although as yet there is a dearth of research in this area. The Stern Review, published by the UK's Treasury Department in 2006, predicts a 'vicious cycle' whereby the impacts of climate change harm gender and development goals, which in turn exacerbates poor women's vulnerability to the impacts of climate change.[6] Women's distinctive vulnerability is partly due to the gendered division of labour and associated likely increases in the burden or work for women and girls. For instance, as Ulrike Röhr of German organisation Genanet has pointed out, when clean drinking water becomes scarce, women and girls have to spend longer each day collecting it. Water shortages also often lead to increases in water-borne diseases, and because it is usually women who look after sick family-members, this again increases their workload. If poor women in the global South have to spend even more time on such reproductive work than they do already, that means less time and energy for earning an independent income, learning to read, or getting involved in local politics. All of this will put basic human rights further out of their reach, and increase their vulnerability to GBV.[7]

Any initiatives designed to promote poor people's adaptation to climate change, or climate-change mitigation, should also promote gender equality. There is certainly potential for synergy; Chapter 4 in this volume shows how initiatives to provide solar cookers to women in displaced people's camps both helps to protect them from GBV during firewood collection and mitigates carbon emissions.

Aid modalities and the failure of mainstreaming

Focusing on official development aid, the changes in the way Northern donors channel funds to the global South and transitional economies may be counteracting efforts to reduce GBV. The current policies, which have been developing since the mid-1990s, were formally encoded in the Paris Declaration of Aid Effectiveness in 2005. Through them, governments and multilateral agencies are trying to improve the quality and effectiveness of aid, using national Poverty Reduction Strategy Papers (PRSPs), direct budget support to governments in the global South, and a focus on internationally agreed priorities such as the Millennium Development Goals (MDGs). In theory there is potential to improve aid effectiveness in relation to gender goals through these processes, but there is a major problem, in that few, if any, governments in the global South prioritise gender concerns. Researcher Tina Wallace has outlined some challenges for UK NGOs concerned with gender and development issues. They include working with partner organisations in the South to find ways of integrating gender concerns into the PRSPs and the MDGs, and more generally, finding new policy spaces where gender issues can be raised and addressed. In a presentation given in 2006, she said that official aid donors now require women's NGOs and civil-society organisations in the global South to access most of their funding from their own governments, while at the same time holding those same governments accountable on women's human-rights issues.[8] It is a naïve, possibly a dangerous, expectation. Many activists and women's organisations fear that the 'new aid architecture', as these policy shifts are called, is deflecting resources away from women's organisations already grossly under-funded.[9]

However, there is a ray of light piercing this bleak prospect. Although the picture for women's rights overall is gloomy, women's-rights organisations in several regions report that it is easier to obtain funding for GBV-related activities than it was in the past. It is a paradox that, although some donors may be interested in initiatives which specifically set out to reduce GBV, those same institutions are not interested in committing funds to programmes that would reduce women's vulnerability to GBV by supporting their empowerment.

At the same time as aid modalities in general have been changing, there is a recognition among women's-rights activists that the strategy of gender mainstreaming adopted by the international community in the Beijing Platform for Action is moribund, having failed to deliver results.[10] In fact, all too often it has been counter-productive, with women's human-rights issues rendered invisible by mainstreaming rhetoric, and at worst, mainstreaming being used as a thin excuse not to address these issues. Some women's organisations in the global South have found that official lip-service to mainstreaming, as well as the new aid modalities outlined above, have been responsible for a drying up of funds from bilateral and multilateral agencies.[11] There is a need to revitalise mainstreaming and recognise that its effectiveness depends on a twin-track approach that includes initiatives specifically targeting women as well as the comprehensive integration of gender-equality objectives into policies and programmes. Otherwise, donor-funded development activities will fail to assist poor women's empowerment, in effect colluding with the GBV status quo.

Lessons, strategies, and promising developments

A new, stronger, UN women's agency?

The UN is in the process of reform, and women's-rights advocates have been lobbying for the creation of a powerful, well-resourced women's agency, which they argue is needed to make the UN system responsible for women's needs. At the time of writing, it seems that the panel making recommendations on the shape of the new UN structure has listened to the suggestions of women's organisations and networks. According to the UK's Gender and Development Network, 'The Panel proposes to establish a new agency for gender equality with more resources and operational responsibilities than the current fragmented entities. The agency would be led by an Under-Secretary General, which is a strong financial and political rank that includes a seat at all decision-making tables'.[12] However, it is not clear that UN member states will accept the recommendations without weakening them.

National-level strategies; legislation, criminal justice systems, and public education

At national level, the first stop is for governments to bring their own legislation on GBV into line with their international commitments. According to a recent UN report, 102 out of 192 UN member states still have no specific legal provisions on domestic violence, marital rape is not a prosecutable offence in 53 countries, and only 93 states have some legislative provision prohibiting human trafficking. Moreover, the report notes that existing legislation is often inadequate and/or implemented in a patchy fashion.[13] In Chapter 3 of this volume, Prieto-Carrón *et al.* point out that no government in the Mexico and Central America region has brought its national laws into line with its international commitments on GBV. However, improvements in legislation need to go hand in hand with complementary measures in the criminal justice system, health, and education sectors. This includes training judges and police and health-care workers and running awareness-raising programmes through the education system.

Public education campaigns complement strategies of strengthening legislation and improving the responses of the criminal justice system, because they are a way of creating popular pressure on governments to act. Many of the chapters in this book (such as Chapters 2 and 7) highlight the priority of large-scale initiatives to change men's and women's attitudes to GBV. In particular, several suggest that more needs to be done to change men's attitudes; see Chapter 4 and Chapter 7 for instance. Although Chapter 7 on the Centro Bartolomé de las Casas shows that small projects working with individual men have been effective, the authors point out that the challenge is to scale up such impact to the national level. Referring specifically to South Asia, Oxfam International lists the main goals of anti-GBV public education campaigns as: removing the stigma from women who face violence; changing perceptions that GBV is a private issue; uncovering its prevalence; making it unacceptable; and in general encouraging more equitable attitudes, gender relations, and behaviour.[14] The We Can campaign documented in Chapter 8 is an exciting development. It will be interesting to see what impact it has, and what lessons can be transferred to and adapted by other regions with high levels of GBV.

Increasing resource flows

Several authors in this volume (e.g. Kirk, Mehta and Gopalakrishnan, and Poudel and Smyth), argue that GBV will only be eradicated when women and girls are empowered to claim their whole spectrum of rights. In Chapter 3, Prieto-Carrón *et al.* call for aid donors to increase funding for programmes that promote gender equality, as a starting point for addressing GBV. But from the development aid perspective, the funding landscape for women's empowerment is bleak. This is due to a combination of reasons, including donors' perceptions that gender inequalities are being handled through 'mainstreaming', the sense that gender issues are 'out of fashion', and the new aid modalities already outlined. According to the Association for Women's Rights in Development (AWID), women's organisations in all regions are 'in a state of survival and resistance', with groups in Latin America and Central and Eastern Europe facing the biggest challenges.[15] The irony is that, even in narrow terms of aid efficiency, it makes little sense for donors to fund specific GBV initiatives while neglecting to address the root causes of women's vulnerability. Although AWID sees signs of hope in the growth of funding-streams from women's funds (such as the Netherlands' Mama Cash), private trusts, and individual donors, these are unlikely to expand enough to replace official development aid funding. AWID warns that women's organisations must find 'new forms of movement building around money', rather than competing with one another for scarce resources. AWID itself has started a new project, Fundher – Moneywatch, dedicated to tracking and analysing funding trends for women's organisations and movements.[16]

The gender-budgeting movement, which involves the gender analysis of government budgets and spending programmes, offers another approach concerned with increasing resource flows to work on GBV and women's rights more generally.[17] Over 50 countries have had gender-budget initiatives of one sort or another, many led by civil society. In the words of Debbie Budlender, Co-ordinator and Editor of the South African Women's Budget Initiative, and a foremost expert in this type of policy work, 'The "added value" of focusing on the budget is that the budget is the most important tool of policy of any government. Stated simply, no other policy tool of government will work unless money is allocated to implement it.'[18] In the view of Yakin Ertürk, the UN Special Rapporteur on Violence against Women, gender-budgeting initiatives could be a useful tool in holding governments to account on anti-GBV initiatives, by uncovering how much is allocated to anti-GBV initiatives, and monitoring its disbursement.

One of the most effective ways Northern women's-rights organisations can support their Southern partners is by lobbying their own governments for increased development aid allocations to women's organisations, both for anti-GBV work specifically and for women's-rights initiatives in general. US-based Women's Edge's Coalition, Amnesty International (USA), and The Family Violence Prevention Fund are jointly planning to introduce the 'International Violence against Women Act' into the US Congress in 2007.

The idea is to integrate anti-VAW activities into all USAID's programmes. A different strategy, but one also concerning resources, is to try to lever change in the global South through aid conditionality; Chapter 3 in this volume includes mention of a call to the EU Parliament to make aid to the Central American region conditional on governments ending impunity for femicide.

Expanding knowledge, improving information, and assessing impact

Several chapters in this book mention the lack of data on the prevalence of GBV in its many manifestations. An important strategy for addressing GBV is to call for governments to cover gender-based violent crimes in all relevant reports and surveys, disaggregating statistics according to gender as well as other factors. Such data can be used to generate public awareness as well as improving understanding and informing public policy. Given that accurate and reliable data is frequently lacking, some women's organisations have themselves undertaken such research. For example, in Chapter 3, Prieto-Carrón *et al.* mention that in Central America, where it is not even known how many women have fallen victim to femicide, the women's network Red Feminista has set up a research group to monitor the murders of women across the region. However, conducting research is a resource-intensive strategy that may be beyond the reach of many women's organisations.

As Leach and Humphreys point out in Chapter 9, there is a need for more research on GBV *among* men and *among* women, as well as between men and women. Human Rights Watch and Amnesty International campaign against human-rights violations based on sexual orientation, including governments' violence against lesbians, gay men, bisexuals, and transgender individuals in countries as diverse as Iran, Jamaica, and Latvia, and this is helping to push out the boundaries of GBV thinking.

Another area where more work is needed is impact assessment; both Hayes and Kirk allude to this in Chapters 1 and 10. To some extent, problems around assessing the impact of anti-GBV programmes, such as the frequent lack of baseline data, resources, and expertise, are shared by other types of development activity. Others are specific to GBV; for instance it is often not discussed because it is seen as a 'private' issue, and there is sometimes physical risk involved for both researchers and women who take part in surveys. One of the reasons why impact assessment is important is linked to funding. Today, many donors, influenced by private-sector values, want to see black and white evidence of effectiveness within a short timeframe. However, as Hayes argues in Chapter 1, tackling GBV involves a change in attitudes and behaviour that is hard to measure and often take years to bring about. WOMANKIND's efforts to evaluate the effectiveness of its support for the annual '16 Days of Activism' campaign (in which many women's organisations all over the world are involved), like the evaluation of the We Can campaign, may yield useful generic lessons.

GBV in conflicts

The protection of women and girls should be at the heart of agency programming in conflict and post-conflict situations. In Chapter 10, Kirk draws attention to the Guidelines for Gender-based Violence Interventions in Humanitarian Settings, developed by the Inter-Agency Task Force on Gender and Humanitarian Assistance, and the Minimum Standards for Education in Emergencies, both of which she sees as very useful. However, the challenge now is to translate these and other similar sets of guidelines into practice, which in her view means training, awareness-raising, and monitoring implementation. In Chapter 4, Chynoweth and Patrick highlight the need for agencies to develop and implement co-ordinated, multi-dimensional strategies that bridge relief and development.

Looking beyond the activities of humanitarian relief agencies, recent developments indicate two important live issues for the UN and the international community. Since the late 1990s, war-crimes courts have taken up rape cases and successfully prosecuted perpetrators of sexual violence as war criminals, for instance in the Balkans. However, there are complaints that many crimes of sexual violence, in Africa and elsewhere, are still not being punished, because of inadequate investigations and prosecutions. At the time of writing, the International Criminal Court's (ICC) Chief Prosecutor is investigating war crimes in Darfur, including rape, and campaigners are watching to see how the Court handles these cases.[19] According to Brigid Inder, executive director of the NGO Women's Initiative for Gender Justice, one of the best ways of preventing GBV in conflict situations is 'for the ICC to be seen to prosecute and convict those responsible and signal that rape and gender based crimes are considered amongst the gravest crimes'.[20]

Continuing evidence that some members of UN peacekeeping forces are themselves perpetrating GBV has cast a shadow over international jurisprudence achievements. In late 2006, prior to a UN Conference on Eliminating Sexual Exploitation and Abuse by UN and NGO Personnel, the BBC publicised evidence of just such abuse, including rape and child prostitution, within two of the UN's largest peacekeeping missions, in Haiti and Liberia. The Assistant Secretary General for UN Peacekeeping Operations admitted that sexual abuse is widespread, while a representative of NGO Refugees International deplored a 'culture of silence' in some UN peacekeeping forces.[21] This shows as clearly as anything can the limitations of paper commitments on GBV, in either humanitarian or development settings. They can only be a first step, and their effectiveness depends on comprehensive and vigorous implementation and enforcement. Participants at the UN conference committed themselves to ten strategic goals to end GBV by members of peacekeeping operations, including improving training for personnel, banning the re-hiring of soldiers who have committed abuse, and preventing retaliation after allegations of sexual abuse are made.[22] It is crucial that the UN fulfils the promise of former UN Secretary General Kofi Annan to end impunity for members of UN peacekeeping operations who sexually abuse and exploit women and girls.

Following on from that promise, for International Women's Day 2007 the UN chose as its theme 'Ending Impunity for Violence Against Women and Girls'. The fact that GBV is now an avowed priority on the international agenda is a big achievement for the individual women and men, women's organisations, development NGOs, and human-rights groups who have campaigned against GBV over many years. It is easy to forget how much ground has been gained in the struggle to eliminate GBV, with such slender resources. For instance, since 2003, the number of states with legislation against domestic violence on their books has increased from 45 to 89.[23] On the other hand, GBV is still systemic and prevalence rates are high in many countries. As well as getting adequate legislation into place, the most significant hurdle of the next few decades will be to change public attitudes so that GBV becomes socially unacceptable. Women's organisations cannot do this alone; governments must take the lead and show they have the political will to eliminate the violence that blights so many of their citizens' lives.

Notes

1   United Nations (2006) 'The Due Diligence Standard as a Tool for the Elimination of Violence against Women', Report of the Special Rapporteur on violence against women, its causes and consequences, Yakin Ertürk, Commission on Human Rights, paragraph 66.

2   Oxfam International (2004) 'Towards Ending Violence against Women in South Asia', Oxfam Briefing Paper No. 66, p 11.

3   Personal communication.

4   J. Prabhat et al. (2006) 'Low male to female sex ratio of children born in India: national survey of 1.1 million households', The Lancet 367: 211–18. Cited in United Nations (2006) 'In-depth study on all forms of violence against women', Report of Secretary-General.

5   Oxfam International (2004), op.cit.

6   HM Treasury (2006) Stern Review on the Economics of Climate Change, p 114.

7   From an interview with Ulrike Röhr in G. Terry (forthcoming, 2007) Women's Rights, Oxford and London: Oxfam and Pluto Press.

8   From a presentation by Tina Wallace, 'The new aid architecture and its implications for UK NGOs working on gender issues', given at a meeting of the UK Gender and Development Network, February 2006, available at: http://www.gadnetwork.org.uk/gadn-meetings.html, last accessed March 2007.

9   For instance, see C. Clark *et al.* (2006) 'Where is the money for women's rights?', Association for Women's Rights in Development.

10 For instance, see P. Donovan (2006) 'Gender Equality Now or Never: A New UN Agency for Women', Office of the UN Special Envoy for AIDS in Africa; and C. Clark *et al.* (2006) *op.cit.*

11 C. Clark *et al.* (2006) *op.cit.*

12 Gender and Development Network (2007) 'Information Round-up: February', p 3.

13 United Nations (2006) 'In-depth study on all forms of violence against women', Report of Secretary-General, p 89.

14 Oxfam International (2004) *op.cit.*, p 14.

15 C. Clark *et al.* (2006) *op.cit.*

16 Clark *et al.* (2006) *op.cit.*

17 See Diane Elson (2006) 'Budgeting for Women's Rights: Monitoring Government Budgets for Compliance with CEDAW', New York: UNIFEM.

18 D. Budlender (2002) 'Gender budgets: what's in it for NGOs?', *Gender & Development* 10(3), available at: http://www.oxfam.org.uk/what_we_do/issues/gender/gad/gender_budgets.htm?searchterm=budlender, last accessed March 2007.

19 Institute for War and Peace Reporting, 'International Justice Failing Rape Victims', 5 January 2007, available at: http://iwpr.net/?p=tri&s=f&o=328311&apc_state=henh, last accessed March 2007.

20 Institute for War and Peace Reporting, *ibid.*

21 BBC World Service (30 November 2006) 'Evidence of sexual abuse by UN peacekeepers uncovered', available at: http://www.bbc.co.uk/pressoffice/pressreleases/stories/2006/11_november/30/un.shtml, last accessed March 2007.

22 BBC News (5 December 2006) '"Zero tolerance" for UN sex abuse', available at: http://news.bbc.co.uk/1/hi/world/americas/6208774.stm, last accessed March 2007.

23 UNIFEM (2007) 'The Issue: Violence against Women and the International Response', available at: http://www.unifem.org/campaigns/trust_fund_10th_annivesary/the_issue.php, last accessed March 2007.

Resources

Compiled by Julieanne Porter

This section presents useful resources for further study under the following headings:

- Conflict and humanitarian settings
- Education
- Health
- 'Honour' crimes
- Men and boys
- Property rights
- Research methodology
- Sexual minorities
- Trafficking
- General gender-based violence resources
- Organisations

Conflict and humanitarian settings

Forced Migration Review (2007),
http://www.fmreview.org/FMRpdfs/FMR27/full.pdf

This issue of *Forced Migration Review*, available free online, explores the challenges and opportunities for combating sexual violence in conflict, post-conflict, and development recovery contexts. Articles cover a range of issues, from sexual violence against men and boys to violence and HIV and AIDS transmission, and stem from conflict areas as diverse as Sudan, the Thai–Burma border, Palestine, and Colombia.

Forgotten Casualties of War: Girls in Armed Conflict (2005), Save the Children,
http://www.savethechildren.org.uk/scuk_cache/scuk/cache/cmsattach
/2800_Forgottencasualties33395.pdf

This report identifies a 'hidden army' of girls, some as young as eight, who are abducted against their will to live life in the army, and who are often overlooked in efforts to release children from armed groups. The authors argue that proper funding from the international community, and working with local communities with reintegration, is essential in ensuring these girls can regain some sense of normal life.

Fuel Provision and Gender-Based Violence: Fuel-efficiency as a Prevention Strategy (2005), Stephanie Ziebell, UNIFEM
http://www.womenwarpeace.org/issues/violence/fuelandgbv.pdf

This document explores links between women's roles in the provision of fuel for the household, and their vulnerability to gender-based violence, in displaced settings. After identifying gaps in knowledge, such as the environmental impact of fuel collecting and the causes of GBV in the context of displacement, the author then recommends strategies for improvement, for instance developing firewood-conservation protocols and using confidence building and rule-of-law training in GBV as a response strategy.

Gender-based Violence Tools Manual: for Assessment and Program Design, Monitoring and Evaluation in Conflict-affected Settings (2004), Reproductive Health Response in Conflict Consortium, 122 East 42nd Street, New York, NY 10168, USA, tel: +1 212 551 3000, email: info@rhrc.org, website: http://www.rhrc.org

This manual was developed for use by international and local professionals with experience of addressing gender-based violence in the communities in which they work. Organised into three categories – assessment, programme design, and programme monitoring and evaluation – the tools aim to improve data collection of gender-based violence in humanitarian settings. In particular, as well as being informed by international standards, the manual is adaptable to working within specific local situations, and urges community engagement. It is a useful manual for humanitarian professionals, and it is also available online in Arabic.

Guidelines for Gender-based Violence Interventions in Humanitarian Settings: Focusing on Prevention of and Response to Sexual Violence in Emergencies (2005), Inter-agency Standing Committee, 8–14 avenue de la Paix, 1211 Geneva 10, Switzerland, tel: +41 22 917 1438, website: http://www.humanitarianinfo.org/iasc/content/subsidi/tf_gender/gbv.asp

The primary purpose of this guide is to enable humanitarian actors to plan, establish, and co-ordinate minimum multi-sector interventions to prevent and respond to sexual violence during the early phase of an emergency. Topics covered in the guidelines include: planning and preparedness, co-ordination, assessment and monitoring, protection, human resources, water and sanitation, food security and nutrition, shelter and site planning, non-food items, health and community services, education and schooling, and community education. At the end of each of these topics is a useful bibliography of key reference materials. An excellent straightforward guide, with a CD-ROM and quick reference chart, available in Arabic, English, French, and Spanish.

Innocent Women and Children: Gender, Norms and the Protection of Civilians (2006), R. Charli Carpenter, Ashgate, Gower House, Croft Road, Aldershot, Hampshire GU11 3HR UK, Tel: +44 (0) 1252 331551, email: info@ashgatepublishing.com, website: http://www.ashgate.com

This book challenges current understandings of gender constructs in international attempts to protect war-affected civilians. It pays attention to the invisibility of the *civilian* male in the construction, dissemination, and enactment of the laws of war. The author argues that gender influences the activities of three sets of actors: states and 'belligerent' forces, transnational advocacy networks, and humanitarian practitioners. Using case studies, particularly focusing on the Balkans, the book seeks to inform humanitarian policy-making and to reverse the trend to normalise wartime violence against civilian males. Although the study is grounded in gender theory, development practitioners, scholars, and activists will find it an accessible and enlightening read.

'Psychosocial Challenges and Interventions for Women Affected by Conflict' (2006), *Critical Half* 4(1), September, http://www.womenforwomen.org/documents/CH5.pdf

Articles in this journal issue highlight the psychological and social difficulties encountered by conflict-affected women. The authors discuss ways to design effective programmes that facilitate healing and encourage women's active participation in the reconstruction of their communities. Case studies from Afghanistan, Indonesia, and the UK specifically focus on the effects of gender-based violence.

Sexual and Gender-Based Violence against Refugees, Returnees and Internally Displaced Persons: Guidelines for Prevention and Response (SGBV Guidelines) (2005), UNHCR, http://www.unhcr.org/cgi-bin/texis/vtx/protect/opendoc.pdf?tbl=PROTECTION&id=3f696bcc4

These guidelines offer practical advice on how to design strategies and carry out activities aimed at preventing and responding to sexual and gender-based violence (SGBV) among refugees, returnees, and internally displaced persons. As well as an overview of SGBV and a chapter on guiding principles, remaining chapters discuss prevention, response, the special needs of refugee children, an action framework, monitoring and evaluation, and gender-related persecution when determining refugee status. A useful resource for all actors involved in humanitarian and refugee response.

Sexual Violence Against Women and Girls in War and Its Aftermath: Realities, Responses, and Required Resources (2006), Jeanne Ward and Mendy Marsh, UNFPA,
http://www.unfpa.org/emergencies/symposium06/docs/finalbrussels briefingpaper.pdf

Sexual violence and the torture of civilian women and girls both during and after conflict has been a growing phenomenon in recent years, due to the changing nature of warfare. Military engagements between national armies have been supplanted by civil wars, and this paper considers the increasing violence against women and children in armed conflict and its aftermath. The first section outlines the scope of the problem; the second discusses how NGOs have responded to date. The final section assesses this response, and argues for inter-agency multi-sector strategies in future interventions.

Violence against Girls in Africa during Armed Conflicts and Crises (2006), Florence Tercier Holst-Roness, ICRC
http://www.icrc.org/Web/Eng/siteeng0.nsf/htmlall/violence-girls-conference-110506/$File/International-Policy-Conference.pdf

This paper explores the many ways in which girls experience violence during armed conflict or crises in Africa. It makes it clear that, although legal provisions are clear, they are not necessarily easy to apply in practice. The author has six categories of recommendations: continuous promotion of the rule of law (military codes and training materials to include a prohibition on rape and all other forms of sexual violence); protection measures in the event of displacement; restoring family links (where appropriate); protection measures for girls in disarmament; demobilisation and reintegration processes; and understanding the situation of girls using disaggregated data.

Your Justice is too Slow: Will the ICTR fail Rwanda's Rape Victims? (2005),
Binaifer Nowrojee, UNRISD,
http://www.siyanda.org/static/nowrajee_justicetooslow.htm

Widespread sexual violence was directed predominantly against Tutsi
women throughout the Rwandan genocide. Yet ten years after the genocide,
the International Criminal Tribunal for Rwanda (ICTR) has handed down
only 21 sentences. This paper exposes the squandered opportunities that
have characterised sexual-violence prosecutions over the past decade at the
ICTR. The author calls for lessons to be learnt so that future international
tribunals seriously consider the notion of international justice from the
perspective of rape victims.

Education

Combating Gender Violence in and around Schools (2006), Fiona Leach and
Claudia Mitchell (eds.), Trentham Books Limited, Westview House,
734 London Road, Stoke on Trent, ST4 5NP, UK, tel: +44 (0) 1782 745567,
email: tb@trentham-books.co.uk, website: http://www.trentham-books.co.uk

Violence in and around schools is a global phenomenon, but the gender
dimension has been largely ignored. This is the first comprehensive account
of the nature and scale of gender violence in schools across the world. It will
increase awareness and understanding of gender violence in school
settings, and usefully presents innovative strategies to address it. Many
chapters focus on participatory methodologies for working with young
people on reducing violent and abusive behaviour in school, including
through curriculum development and teacher education. Other chapters
deal with gender, youth, and sexuality in the context of HIV and AIDS.

'Gender violence in schools in the developing world' (2006), M. Dunne,
S. Humphreys, and F. Leach, *Gender and Education* 18(1), Routledge, 4 Park
Square, Milton Park, Abingdon, OX14 4RN, UK, tel: +44 (0) 20 7017 6000,
email: tf.adhocprocessing@tfinforma.com,
website: http://journalsonline.tandf.co.uk

Reviewing recent research written in English, this article traces
conceptual connections between gender/sexual relations and gender
violence in schools. The authors consider *implicit* gender violence, which
relates to everyday institutional structures and practices, and *explicit* gender
violence that relates to more overtly sexualised encounters. Within these
contexts, gender violence perpetuated by student on student, teacher on
student, and student on teacher, is addressed.

Scared at School: Sexual Violence against Girls in South African Schools (2001), Human Rights Watch, 350 Fifth Avenue, 34th floor, New York, NY 10118-3299 USA, tel: +1 212 290 4700, email: hrwnyc@hrw.org, website: http://www.hrw.org

For many South African girls, regardless of their social status, violence and abuse are an inevitable part of the school environment. This report documents school-based sexual violence, reviews school and state responses to sexual violence, explains the discriminatory impact on girls' education rights when the government does not respond adequately and effectively to gender-based violence, and sets forth recommendations to rectify these problems. The issues addressed in this book will be of relevance to schools in countries the world over.

Health

Gender-based Violence and HIV/AIDS in Cambodia: Links, Opportunities and Potential Responses (2005), Nata Duvvury, Johanna Knoess, GTZ, http://www2.gtz.de/dokumente/bib/05-0492.pdf

Cambodia is often cited as having the highest rate of HIV in Asia, and it is now understood that gender-based violence is linked to this develop-ment. This report argues that the interrelation between these two issues is important in light of four new trends in Cambodia in the transmission of HIV: from husband to wife, through 'sweetheart' relationships, from mother to child, and a growing acceptance of gang rape. It recommends further research into understanding the 'link' between gender-based violence and HIV, the socialisation process of boys, the root causes of violence, and participatory action research in rural communities to transform gender norms.

Strengthening Resistance: Confronting Violence Against Women and HIV/AIDS (2006), Cynthia Rothschild, Mary Anne Reilly, and Sara A. Nordstrom, CWGL, http://www.cwgl.rutgers.edu/globalcenter/publications/strengthening.pdf

Strengthening Resistance focuses on the points of intersection in the social, political, and public-health crises of violence against women, and HIV and AIDS. The report highlights nine advocacy initiatives from different countries including Nicaragua, India, and Uganda, and offers recommendations addressed to activists and policy makers alike. It also contains a useful resource section for further study into these linked issues.

Violence against Girls and Women: Implications for HIV and AIDS in Africa
(2006), African Child Policy Forum,
http://www.africanchildforum.org/Documents/VaG_and_Women_
Implications_for_HIV_AIDS_in_%20Africa.pdf

The link between gender-based violence and higher rates of HIV infection among African girls (compared to boys) is explored in this paper. It identifies strategies to reduce HIV prevalence among girls, through tackling the violence they experience in their homes, at school, and in the community.

WHO Multi-country Study on Women's Health and Domestic Violence against Women (2005), WHO,
http://www.who.int/gender/violence/who_multicountry_study/en

This report, based on interviews with 24,000 women worldwide, documents the prevalence of intimate-partner violence and its association with women's physical, mental, sexual, and reproductive health. Aside from data on non-partner violence, sexual abuse during childhood and forced first sexual experience, the report includes women's responses such as: who do women turn to and who do they tell about the violence in their lives? Which services do they use and what response do they get? The report concludes with 15 recommendations to strengthen national commitment and action on violence against women. This report covers 15 sites in 10 countries: Bangladesh, Brazil, Ethiopia, Japan, Peru, Namibia, Samoa, Serbia and Montenegro, Thailand, and Tanzania.

'Honour' crimes

A Question of Security: Violence against Palestinian Women and Girls (2006), Human Rights Watch, http://hrw.org/reports/2006/opt1106/

Violence against women and girls in the West Bank and Gaza ranges from spousal and child abuse, to rape, incest, and murders committed under the guise of family 'honour'. Although there is increasing recognition of the problem, the Palestinian Authority (PA) has yet to take action to prevent this abuse. This report urges the PA to commit to preventing violence against Palestinian women and girls and makes recommendations to implement immediate and effective change.

Documenting Women's Rights Violations by Non-state Actors (2006), Jan Bauer and Anissa Héile, Rights and Democracy, and Women Living Under Muslim Laws (WLUML),
http://www.dd-rd.ca/site/_PDF/publications/ women/Non-State.pdf

Violence committed by non-state actors, such as members of the family, or the community, or during armed conflict, happens the world over, but takes different forms depending on the context. Covering honour and sexual crimes, family violence and sexual slavery, this manual, with a particular focus on Muslim communities, is specifically written for groups and individuals not well-versed in legal matters. It provides tools to investigate violence perpetrated against women by non-state actors, and offers explanation of the legal definitions and human-rights protection mechanisms that may help compel states to fulfil their obligation to protect women against violence perpetrated by non-state actors.

'Honour': Crimes, Paradigms, and Violence Against Women (2005), Lynn Welchman and Sara Hossain (eds.), Zed Books, 7 Cynthia Street, London N1 9JF, UK, tel: +44 (0)20 7837 4014, email: sales@zedbooks.net, website: http://zedbooks.co.uk/

The purpose of this book is to support human-rights activists, policy makers, and lawyers by explaining what honour crimes are, how they vary from country to country, and what strategies are needed to combat them. The authors seek to move the discussion around honour crimes from a culturally specific to a human-rights-based framework, and urge the reform of many national legal systems which enable men to rely on the pretext of 'honour crimes' in order to get a reduced sentence. This book crosses disciplinary boundaries, making the collection a useful read to those in fields from gender studies to history and psychology.

Patriarchal Violence – an Attack on Human Security (2006), Government Offices of Sweden,
http://www.sweden.gov.se/content/1/c6/05/68/94/42d6d51b.pdf

This international survey considers measures to combat patriarchal violence and oppression, particularly acts committed in the name of honour directed at women, homosexuals, bisexuals, and transgender persons. It focuses on how to influence and change structures to end violence and oppression in a human-rights context.

Men and boys

Dying to be Men: Youth, Masculinity and Social Exclusion (2005), Gary T. Barker, Routledge, 2 Park Square, Milton Park, Abingdon OX14 4RN, UK, tel: 44 (0) 20 7017 6000, email: tps.tandfecommerce@thomson.com, website: http://www.routledge.com

Low-income, urban-based young men (aged 15–24) face considerable challenges in societies where violence is the norm and violence against women acceptable. This study reflects on the efforts of these (predominantly heterosexual) young men to stay in school and find meaningful employment, on their interactions with young women, and on their sexual behaviour, particularly in relation to HIV and AIDS prevention. In considering the nature of gender-based violence, there is a specific focus on young men who reject violent models of masculinity and find equality in their relationships, even in societies with rigid attitudes to manhood. As one of the first books with this emphasis, it is very useful for practitioners working with young people, as well as researchers in the gender-studies arena.

Case Study Guy to Guy (2002), G. Barker and M. Nascimento, Instituto Promundo, http://www.promundo.org.br/materia/resources/files/download/CaseStudyGuytoGuy.pdf

The Guy-to-Guy Project operates in low-income communities in Brazil, and aims to engage young men and get them to question the use of violence against women. This accessible gender-sensitive study outlines previous research, and the history of the project, then discusses the project in action. In addition to survey data, qualitative research from young men in one specific community was undertaken, which focused on identifying, understanding, and eventually recruiting to the project those young men who already questioned the use of violence against women. Available in both English and Portuguese.

Masculinities, 2nd edn (2005), R.W. Connell, Polity, Marston Book Services, PO Box 269, Abingdon, OX14 4YN, UK, Tel: +44 (0) 1235 465500, email: direct.orders@marston.co.uk, website: http://www.polity.co.uk

Understanding the nature and the construction of the masculine is an important element when considering issues of gender-based violence. This new edition of a classic text discusses global gender relations, new theories, practical uses of masculinity research, and the implications of masculinity research for understanding current world issues, in a substantial new introduction and conclusion. Based on a Western idea of masculinity, it is nevertheless a useful point from which to consider not only how masculinity is constructed, but also the diversity of many 'masculinities', and attempts to pursue social justice in a gendered world.

Working with Men and Boys to Promote Gender Equality and to End Violence against Boys and Girls (2005), Save the Children Sweden, http://www.siyanda.org/docs/SCS_Regional_Workshop_Report_March _2004_Long2.pdf

This resource focuses on how to strengthen partnerships with men and boys to promote gender equality and end violence against girls and boys, in south and central Asia. The report questions constructs of masculinity, describes work currently being carried out on these issues, and makes recommendations on how to move forward. These include highlighting the need to increase knowledge on gender issues among professionals and in the school curriculum, and promoting programmes for men on parenting and responsible sexual behaviour. Including both theory and actual experiences, this is a useful resource for the activist and practitioner.

Young Men and the Construction of Masculinity in sub-Saharan Africa: Implications for HIV/AIDS, Conflict, and Violence (2005), G. Barker and C. Ricardo, World Bank Publications, http://www-wds.worldbank.org/ servlet/WDSContentServer/WDSP/IB/2005/06/23/000012009_20050623 134235/Rendered/PDF/327120rev0PAPER0AFR0young0men0WP26.pdf

This report explores the role of young men in the perpetuation of violence and the spread of HIV and AIDS in sub-Saharan Africa, and outlines the kind of interventions that can support alternative forms of masculinity. It argues that applying a more sophisticated gender analysis as it relates to conflict and HIV and AIDS is essential in order to understand how both women and men are made vulnerable by rigid ideas of masculinity and gender hierarchies.

Property rights

Dispossessing the Widow: Gender-Based Violence in Malawi (2002), Seodi Venekai-Rudo White *et al.*, Women in Law in Southern Africa-Malawi, Private Bag 534, Limbe, Malawi, tel: +265 882 9033, email: wlsa@wlsamalawi.org, website: http://www.wlsamalawi.org/

One of the most prevalent forms of violence women experience in Malawi is the dispossession of widows. Dispossession begins at marriage, derived from the construction of gender roles, and culminates in property dispossession (also known as 'property grabbing'). This book outlines the process of dispossession, perceptions of dispossessed widows, existing laws, causes (cultural, economic, gender, etc.), and community and institutional responses. The concluding recommendations will be of interest to advocates, policy makers, and researchers both inside and outside of Malawi.

Does Dowry improve Life for Brides? a Test of the Bequest Theory of Dowry in Rural Bangladesh (2004), Population Council,
http://www.popcouncil.org/pdfs/wp/195.pdf

This paper explores the association between dowry and the prevalence of domestic abuse. The theory that a dowry gives a bride more control is challenged, and the authors conclude that married females who pay a dowry are more likely to report domestic violence than those who do not.

Property Ownership and Inheritance Rights of Women for Social Protection – the South Asia Experience: Synthesis Report of Three Studies (2006), ICRW,
http://www.icrw.org/docs/2006_propertyrights-southasia.pdf

This study explores the links between women's ownership of property and inheritance rights, and their experiences of domestic violence in India and Sri Lanka. It concludes that property ownership can be a significant protective factor against violence, and that it can offer an exit strategy to women affected by violence.

Violence: The Impact of Forced Evictions on Women in Palestine, India and Nigeria (2002), Centre on housing rights and evictions,
http://www.cohre.org/store/attachments/COHRE%20Women%20Forced%20Evictions%202002.pdf

Based on three research studies from Palestine, India, and Nigeria, this report examines the types of violence women experience during the forced eviction process. As well as giving an overview of international human-rights laws to put the practice of forced eviction and the research design and methodology into context, a synthesised analysis of the three research studies is also presented. The report concludes with suggestions for future action that can be undertaken by governments and the NGO community.

Research methodology

Methodologies to Measure the Gender Dimensions of Crime and Violence (2001), Elizabeth Shrader,
http://papers.ssrn.com/sol3/papers.cfm?abstract_id=632716

Studies show that urban communities in Latin American and the Caribbean have the highest rates of homicide and crime victimisation in the world. This paper argues that violent behaviour is modifiable and therefore preventable, and offers two conceptual frameworks, one that categorises violence as being motivated by political, economic and/or social reasons, the other that divides the various causes of violence into structural, institutional, interpersonal, and/or individual causes. The author calls for standardised methodologies to measure and map violence across communities in order to develop programmes to prevent it.

Researching violence against women: a practical guide for researchers and activists (2005), M. Ellsberg and L. Heise, WHO/PATH, http://www.path.org/files/GBV_rvaw_complete.pdf

As international attention has begun to address gender-based violence, there is a need for methodologically rigorous research to guide the formulation and implementation of effective interventions, policies, and prevention strategies. This manual has been developed in response to this need. It outlines some of the methodological and ethical challenges of conducting research on violence against women and describes a range of techniques that have been used to address these challenges. Drawing on experiences from 10 countries, this accessible manual will be of interest and use to both researchers and community workers.

Violence in the Central American Region: Towards in Integrated Framework for Violence Reduction (2002), Caroline Moser and Ailsa Winton, ODI, http://www.odi.org.uk/pppg/publications/working_papers/171.html

Focusing on four countries in Central America (El Salvador, Guatemala, Honduras, and Nicaragua), this comparative study provides a conceptual framework for understanding violence in the region. The study does not simply consider gender-based violence on its own, but also the interactions between political and institutional violence and economic and social violence. The results of the study will provide NGOs and organisations with an over-arching framework for designing programmes addressing violence in the future.

Sexual minorities

More than a Name: State-sponsored Homophobia and its Consequences in Southern Africa (2003), Human Rights Watch and the International Gay and Lesbian Human Rights Commission, 350 Fifth Avenue, 34th floor, New York, NY 10118-3299, USA, tel: +1 212 290 4700, email: hrwnyc@hrw.org, website: http://www.hrw.org

This volume documents the spread of state-sponsored homophobia in Zimbabwe, Namibia, Zambia, and Botswana, and examines neighbouring South Africa and the effects of its constitutional ban on discrimination based on sexual orientation. It covers the issues of the spread of homophobic rhetoric in Southern Africa, abuse and discrimination by state actors, and violence and harassment by non-state actors. It explores the differences between the South African constitution and what happens on the ground, and then makes recommendations to enable governments to realise the rights of *all* their people.

Negotiating Culture: Intersections of Culture and Violence Against Women in Asia Pacific (2006), Yakin Ertürk, APWLD,
http://www.apwld.org/pdf/NegotiatingCulture.pdf

The consultation from which this report is derived, aimed to explain how oppressive elements of power come to dominate cultural norms in the Asia-Pacific region. The report provides in-depth presentations on different aspects of 'culture' and its effect, sometimes violent, on women. The report particularly addresses the concerns of indigenous, lesbian, gay, bisexual, and transgender women, and issues of sex-selective abortion. It also sets out effective strategies for addressing culture at the community, national, and international level.

Trafficking

Poverty, Gender and Human Trafficking in Sub-Saharan Africa: Rethinking Best Practices in Migration Management (2006), Thanh-Dam Truong, UNESCO,
http://unesdoc.unesco.org/images/0014/001432/143227E.pdf

This UNESCO report begins with the supposition that poverty is one of the main factors leading women and children to fall prey to traffickers. It attempts to unpack the interconnectedness between human trafficking and poverty in sub-Saharan Africa, critically analysing migration processes in relation to human-rights abuse. The authors' aim for the report is that it can be used as a tool for those involved in anti-trafficking work, to rethink existing interventions and advocate for sustainable change by tackling trafficking at its roots.

Sex Traffic: Prostitution, Crime and Exploitation (2005), Paola Monzini,
Zed Books, 7 Cynthia Street, London N1 9JF, UK, tel: +44 (0)20 7837 4014,
email: sales@zedbooks.net, website: http://zedbooks.co.uk/

The trafficking of women and girls for prostitution is big business the world over. In this engaging and accessible book, the focus is on the experiences of migrant women and girls who have very little choice or control over their lives. The techniques of recruitment, methods of transportation, and forms of exploitation abroad are all examined, with the final chapter considering solutions that have been proposed in countries of origin and arrival.

Special Rapporteur on trafficking in persons , especially in women and children,
United Nations Commission on Human Rights,
http://www.ohchr.org/english/issues/trafficking/index.htm

The website for the *Special Rapporteur on trafficking in persons* includes an introduction to the Rapporteur's mandate, annual reports, country visits, links to international standards, and a complaints form used to document cases of trafficking. Also available is access to all documents relating to the work of the Rapporteur, many in Arabic, Chinese, English, French, Spanish, and Russian languages.

Violence against and Trafficking in Women as Symptoms of Discrimination: The Potential of CEDAW as an Antidote (2005), Gender and Development Discussion Paper Series no.17, UNESCAP, http://www.unescap.org/esid/GAD/Publication/DiscussionPapers/17/CEDAW%20discussion%20paper%20no.%2017%20-%20revised%2023%20March%202006.pdf

This paper reviews some of the key issues concerning trafficking of women and violence against women in the Asia-Pacific region. It discusses discrimination as a common thread, and explores the potential for the use of CEDAW as a tool to reduce trafficking in and violence against women.

General gender-based violence resources

Born to High Risk: Violence Against Girls in Africa (2006), African Child Policy Forum, http://www.africanchildforum.org/Documents/Main%20Document%20(coloured).pdf

Prepared to inform discussions at the Second International Policy Conference on the African Child in May 2006, this report draws information from three areas: existing literature, thematic studies, and retrospective surveys. The experience of African girls in conflict (being forced to fight, work as servants, or become sexual slaves), refugee camps (abuse such as being forced to exchange sex for food), in schools (sexual abuse by teachers), the home, and in trafficking and child labour, are all covered. The report concludes by setting out policy and legal provisions, education and awareness strategies, making legislation and implementing laws, and ensuring that sufficient resources are allocated to programmes and initiatives aimed at addressing violence against girls.

Children and Gender-based Violence: an Overview of Existing Conceptual Frameworks (2003), Claudia Hasanbegovic, Save the Children, http://www.rb.se/NR/rdonlyres/DE6DBE61-D24F-4F88-BA1E-692872D53F51/0/Genderbasedviolencenew.pdf

This useful discussion paper outlines the different types of gender-specific abuse experienced by male and female children. It sets out the conceptual approaches of human rights, development, and gender, within which to understand the nature of gender-based violence, and the role of those who are duty-bound (parents/guardians, the state, institutions) to guarantee children an enjoyment of their rights. It concludes with good-practice recommendations to challenge gender-based violence against children, and case studies from South Asia, Bolivia, India, Nepal, and Kenya.

*Combating Gender-based Violence: a Key to Achieving the Millennium
Development Goals* (2005), UNFPA, UNIFEM, OSAGI,
http://www.eldis.org/cf/search/disp/DocDisplay.cfm?Doc=DOC20535
&Resource=f1gender

This toolkit, divided into four parts, considers the issues of gender-based violence and poverty, reproductive health, HIV and AIDS, and conflict situations. It is aimed at helping policy makers to address issues of concern, advocate for the protection of women from all forms of violence, reinforce legal mechanisms that will protect women at the national level, and end the impunity with which crimes are committed against women. The plan of action focuses on advocacy through public campaigns against gender- based violence to change policy and practice at local, national, and regional level.

Eldis Gender-based Violence,
http://www.eldis.org/gender/gender_based_violence.htm

The Eldis website is frequently updated with a wide range of reports, publications, and news, and is an essential resource for obtaining information on gender-based violence. Content is broken down into the following categories: GBV in conflicts and emergencies, domestic violence, female genital mutilation/cutting, sexual violence, programme approaches to eliminating GBV, and manuals and toolkits.

*Human Rights and Gender Violence: Translating International Law into Local
Justice* (2006), Sally Engle Merry, University of Chicago Press, Chicago
Distribution Center, 11030 South Langley, Chicago, IL 60628 USA,
tel: +1 773 702 7000, email: custserv@press.uchicago.edu,
website: http://www.press.uchicago.edu

Local communities often conceive of social justice in quite different terms from international human-rights lawyers. This volume explains how global law is translated into local contexts, and highlights the important role of activists who serve as an intermediary between different sets of cultural understandings of gender, violence, and justice. The author asks important questions about customs, how communities might use them as a site of resistance, and how economic and political conditions may affect the way customs function. The first part of the book examines the way the texts of human-rights law are framed, and the second looks at the extent to which this is appropriated into various national and local contexts.

Leading to Change: Eliminating Violence against Women in Muslim Societies (2005), Women's Learning Partnership (WLP), http://www.learningpartnership.org/docs/vawsympreport.pdf

The symposium on which this report is based provided a forum for women from Muslim-majority societies to discuss their experiences of meeting challenges and creating effective strategies to eliminate violence against women and end impunity for perpetrators of violence. Participants engaged in active exchanges on the root causes of violence, the economic, social, and developmental costs of violence, the extremist's use of tradition and religion to perpetuate violence in the private and public sphere, and the potential impact of strategies utilising positive religious and cultural interpretations.

Preventing and responding to gender-based violence in middle and low-income countries: a global review and analysis (2005), Sarah Bott, Andrew Morrison, Mary Ellsberg, World Bank Policy Research Working Paper 3618, The World Bank, 1818 H Street, NW, Washington, DC 20433 USA, Tel: +1 202 458 5454, email: pic@worldbank.org, website: http://www.worldbank.org/reference/

The knowledge base about effective initiatives to prevent and respond to gender-based violence is relatively limited, and few approaches have been rigorously evaluated. In this working paper, the authors review what is known to be more or less effective, or at least promising, to prevent and respond to gender-based violence. Definitions, recent statistics, health consequences, costs, and risk factors are analysed in the sectors of justice, health, and education. Within these sectors, laws and policies, institutional reforms, community mobilisation, and individual behaviour-change strategies are examined. The report concludes with a summary of some of the most promising approaches the authors profiled, as well as typical challenges, listed by sector.

Responding to 'Violence Against Women': How Development Interventions Address the Issue of Gender-based Violence (2006), Belén Sobrino, INSTRAW, http://www.un-instraw.org/en/images/stories/NewVoices/nv-sobrino.pdf

Based on examples from the Latin American region, this paper highlights the shortcomings of current development policies to tackle violence against women (VAW), and proposes a new framework from a body politics approach to address VAW.

Sex without Consent: Young People in Developing Countries (2006), Shireen J. Jejeebhoy, Iqbal Shah and Shyam Thapa (eds.), Zed Books, 7 Cynthia Street, London N1 9JF, UK, tel: +44 (0)20 7837 4014, email: sales@zedbooks.net, website: http://zedbooks.co.uk/

Although increasing research has been undertaken on risky consensual sex among young people, less attention has been paid to non-consensual sex. This valuable volume reveals that the interpretation of the term 'non-consensual' varies depending on gender and culture, and documents the non-consensual experiences of young people, from unwanted touch or sex through deception to gang rape. Chapters present evidence and perspectives on the non-consensual experiences of young people in developing countries, profile the magnitude of such experiences, describe some promising avenues for prevention and programming, and draw lessons for the formulation of strategies and policies to effect change. The volume shows that the subject should be of concern in multiple sectors, including for those working in the areas of violence, adolescent health and development, sexual and reproductive health, HIV and AIDS, gender relations, and human rights.

Siyanda, http://www.siyanda.org

Siyanda is a constantly growing database that holds a variety of resources on many development gender-related topics, including gender-based violence. Each resource has a short summary to help assist the individual to quickly determine its relevance to their own work, along with a link to the full text. Users can source consultants within specific fields of work, and can contribute their own details or suggest documents to be added to the site. An extremely useful resource for researchers and practitioners alike.

Special Rapporteur on violence against women, its causes and consequences,
United Nations Commission on Human Rights,
http://www.ohchr.org/english/issues/women/rapporteur/

The website for the *Special Rapporteur on violence against women* includes an introduction to the Rapporteur's mandate, annual reports, country visits, links to international standards, and a complaints form used to document cases of violence against women. Also available is access to all documents relating to the work of the Rapporteur, many in Arabic, Chinese, English, French, Spanish, and Russian languages.

Strengthening Woman's Rights, Ending Violence against Women and Girls, Protecting Human Rights: Good Practices for Development Cooperation (2005), Deutsche Gesellschaft für Technische Zusammenarbeit (GTZ), http://www2.gtz.de/dokumente/bib/05-1048.pdf

This report describes the international and regional human-rights framework related to gender-based violence and demonstrates the disastrous impact of violence against women and girls on human development, and how this directly relates to most of the Millennium Development Goals. It then illustrates practical experiences in addressing violence against women and girls in Latin America, Africa, and Asia. Included are a number of case studies covering interventions at the local, regional, national, and international levels, across various sectors, including education, justice, and the media, and involving governments, NGOs, and religious and traditional authorities.

UN Secretary-General's in-depth study on all forms of violence against women (2006), UNDAW, http://daccessdds.un.org/doc/UNDOC/GEN/N06/419/74/PDF/N0641974.pdf?OpenElement

This comprehensive review aims to highlight the persistence and unacceptability of all forms of violence against women in all parts of the world. It also seeks to strengthen the political commitment and joint efforts of all stakeholders to prevent and eliminate violence against women, and identify ways and means to ensure more sustained and effective implementation of state obligations to address all forms of violence against women, and to increase state accountability. The study is available in Arabic, Chinese, English, French, Spanish, and Russian.

UN Women Watch Violence Against Women, http://www.un.org/womenwatch/asp/user/list.asp?ParentID=3004

This directory of the UN's resources on gender and women's issues includes a section on violence against women. The website includes links to other UN resources on this issue.

Organisations

16 Days of Activism Against Gender Violence, Center for Women's Global Leadership, 160 Ryders Lane, New Brunswick, NJ 08901, tel: +1 732 932 8782, email: cwgl@igc.org, website: http://www.cwgl.rutgers.edu

Based at the Center for Women's Global Leadership, the 16 Days campaign is an annual international event, from 25 November, International Day for the Elimination of Violence Against Women, to 10 December, International Human Rights Day. The goals of the campaign include: raising awareness about VAW as a human-rights issue at the local, national, regional, and international level, and providing a forum in which organisers can develop and share new and effective strategies. Each year's campaign includes an action kit, usually available in several languages, including Arabic, French, Spanish, Russian, and English.

Amnesty International Stop Violence against Women, http://web.amnesty.org/actforwomen/index-eng

Amnesty International runs an international campaign to end trafficking and violence against women, with the website and many resources available in Arabic, French, Spanish, and English.

Anti Trafficking Center – ATC, Resavska 1/ 4, 11000 Belgrade, Serbia & Montenegro, Tel: +381 11 32 39 002, email: atc@atc.org.yu, website: http://www.atc.org.yu/Home/index.html

ATC attempts, through its programmes, to eradicate trafficking in human beings, with a special emphasis on the causes of the problem of trafficking, such as gender-based violence, poverty, unemployment, and the lack of suitable opportunities. The website, available in English and Serbian, has a range of resources on themes including trafficking, gender, violence against women, and prostitution and sex work.

Coalition Against Trafficking in Women (CATW), email: info@catwinternational.org, website: http://www.catwinternational.org/

CATW is a non-government organisation that promotes women's human rights by working internationally to combat sexual exploitation in all its forms, and especially focusing on the sex trafficking of women and girls. CATW supports anti-trafficking projects in areas that few programmes address: the links between prostitution and trafficking; challenging the demand for prostitution that promotes sex trafficking; and protecting the women and children who are its victims by working to curb legal acceptance and tolerance of the sex industry. CATW has regional networks in Asia, Latin America, Europe, Africa, and Australia.

End Child Prostitution, Child Pornography and Trafficking of Children for Sexual Purposes (ECPAT), http://www.ecpat.net/eng/index.asp

ECPAT is a network of organisations and individuals working to eliminate the commercial sexual exploitation of children. It seeks to encourage the world community to ensure that children everywhere enjoy their fundamental rights free from all forms of commercial sexual exploitation. ECPAT carry out research and develop research methodologies, explore good models for prevention work, develop learning tools, and provide advice and information to groups who are trying to make a national plan for their country. Their website includes a full online resource centre.

Equality Now, Kenya: Africa Regional Office, PO Box 2018 KNH, 00202, Nairobi, email: equalitynow@kenyaweb.com, UK: PO Box 48822, London WC2N 6ZW, email: ukinfo@equalitynow.org, USA: PO Box 20646, Columbus Circle Station, New York, NY 10023, email: info@equalitynow.org, website: http://www.equalitynow.org

Equality Now, with offices in Kenya, the UK, and the USA, documents violence and discrimination against women and girls around the world, and mobilises international action to support their efforts to stop these human-rights abuses. Through a network of concerned groups and individuals around the world, Equality Now distributes information, brings public attention to human-rights violations against women, and takes action to protest against these violations.

FGM Network
http://www.fgmnetwork.org/index.php

The purpose of the FGM Education and Networking Project is the dissemination online and offline of material related to female genital mutilation, otherwise known as female circumcision. The Project seeks to form an online clearinghouse and a community for researchers, activists, attorneys, and health-care practitioners to obtain information and network with others involved in similar projects.

GBV Prevention Network, PO Box 6770, Kampala, Uganda, tel: +256 41 531 186, email: inquiries@preventgbvafrica.org, website: http://www.preventgbvafrica.org

This pan-African website is the virtual community or meeting place for network members and other colleagues and friends interested in violence prevention on the continent. It includes often hard-to-source regional and international resources (publications, toolkits, and fact sheets) about GBV prevention, and links to many organisations working on this issue.

Global Alliance Against Traffic in Women (GAATW), 191/41 Sivalai Condominium, Soi 33,Itsaraphap Rd, Bangkok-yai, Bangkok 10600, Thailand, Tel: +66 2 864 1427/8, email: gaatw@gaatw.org, website: http://www.gaatw.net/

The Alliance is a network of non-government organisations from all regions of the world. It is committed to work for changes in the political, economic, social, and legal systems and structures which contribute to the persistence of trafficking. GAATW supports sharing of knowledge, working experiences, and working methodologies amongst its members, in order to enhance the effectiveness of collective anti-trafficking activities. The website includes information in French, Portuguese, Japanese, English, Chinese, Spanish, Russian, and Italian.

'Honour' Crimes Project, CIMEL, School of Oriental and African Studies, Thornhaugh Street, Russell Square, London WC1H 0XG UK, tel: +44 (0)20 7898 4683, email: cimel@soas.ac.uk, or INTERIGHTS, Lancaster House, 33 Islington High Street, London N1 9LH UK, tel: + 44 (0) 20 7278 3230, email: hcp@interights.org, website: http://www.soas.ac.uk/honourcrimes

The 'Honour Crimes' Project is jointly co-ordinated by CIMEL (Centre of Islamic and Middle Eastern Laws) at the School of Oriental and African Studies, London University and INTERIGHTS (International Centre for the Legal Protection of Human Rights). The project seeks to facilitate co-operation among activists, lawyers, academics, and others worldwide, and to develop and deepen understanding of 'honour' crimes, and to challenge the climate of support for the practice amongst state institutions.

Human Rights Watch, 2nd Floor, 2–12 Pentonville Road, London N1 9HF, UK, tel: +44 (0)20 7713 1995, email: hrwuk@hrw.org, website: http://hrw.org/

Human Rights Watch (HRW) advocates protecting the human rights of people around the world. Among its aims, HRW exposes human-rights violations and violence against lesbians, gays, bisexuals, transgenders, children, and women. Its website, and many of its publications, are available in English, Russian, Spanish, and French.

Institute Promundo, Rua México 31/1502, Centro, Rio de Janeiro – RJ, 20031-144, Brazil, tel: +55 (21) 2544 3114, email: promundo@promundo.org.br, website: http://www.promundo.org.br

Promundo carries out research, implements community interventions, and actively participates in networks and strategic alliances in Brazil and around the world. It works on issues to do with children, family and community, gender, and youth. Promundo places a strong emphasis on engaging young men in violence prevention and questioning traditional 'norms' associated with masculinity through 'Program H', as well as working to reduce violence related to homophobia. The website (accessible in Portuguese, Spanish, and English) offers free access to training materials and other resources.

International Gay and Lesbian Human Rights Commission (IGLHRC), 80 Maiden Lane, Suite 1505, New York, NY 10038 USA, tel: + 212 268 8040, email: iglhrc@iglhrc.org, or Buenos Aires Office for Latin America and the Caribbean, Cavia 3583, Hurlingham 1686, Buenos Aires, Argentina, tel: +54 11 4961 3531, website: http://www.iglhrc.org/site/iglhrc

As well as working on gender-based violence against lesbian and bisexual women, IGLHRC aims to secure the full enjoyment of the human rights of all people and communities subject to discrimination or abuse on the basis of sexual orientation or expression, gender identity or expression, and/or HIV status. IGLHRC undertakes advocacy, documentation, coalition building, and public education work, and its website is in both English and Spanish.

Men to Men Project, FEMNET, Off Westlands Road, P. O. Box 54562, 00200 Nairobi, Kenya, tel: +254 20 374 1301, email: admin@femnet.or.ke, website: http://www.femnet.or.ke

The recently formed Men to Men Project aims to create a core of male supporters to eliminate gender-based violence in Africa. The project is developing a long-term programme for male advocacy for gender equality and creating men who support the empowerment of women, the principles of gender equality, and who work to end gender-based violence. A regional network of men against gender-based violence is being developed with partners in Ethiopia, Kenya, Malawi, Namibia, Zambia, and South Africa.

OMCT Violence against Women Programme, OMCT International Secretariat, PO Box 21, 8 rue du Vieux-Billard, CH-1211 Geneva 8, Switzerland, tel: + 41 22 809 4939, email: omct@omct.org, website: http://www.omct.org/base.cfm?cfid=4197470&cftoken=37352841 &page=women&consol=open

The aim of this programme is to raise awareness of the problem of violence against women among the members of the SOS-Torture network and the United Nations bodies, and to take action on behalf of the victims of this form of violence. The website is in English, French, and Spanish, and contains links to reports, publications, events, and urgent appeals.

RAINBO, Suite 5A, Queens Studios, 121 Salisbury Road, London NW6 6RG, UK, tel: +44 (0)20 7625 3400, email: info@rainbo.org, website: http://www.rainbo.org

RAINBO is an African-led international non-government organisation working on issues of women's empowerment, gender, reproductive health, sexual autonomy, and freedom from violence as central components of the African development agenda. RAINBO specifically works to eliminate the practice of female circumcision/female genital mutilation through facilitating women's self-empowerment and accelerating social change.

Reproductive Health Response in Conflict Consortium (RHRC), email: info@rhrc.org, website: http://www.rhrc.org/resources/index.cfm? sector=gbv

RHRC, a seven-member consortium, aims to increase access to a range of quality, voluntary reproductive health services for refugees and displaced persons around the world. Included on its website is a section devoted to GBV resources, such as training manuals for multi-agency responses to GBV, newsletters, reports, and guidelines. There are links to RHRC projects such as the Gender-Based Violence Initiative, the Gender-Based Violence Global Technical Support Project, and a gender-based violence bibliography.

Stop Violence Against Women (STOPVAW), Minnesota Advocates for Human Rights, 650 Third Avenue South, Suite 550, Minneapolis, MN 55402-1940, USA, tel: +1 (612) 341-3302, email: stopvaw@mnadvocates.org, website: http://www.stopvaw.org

The website, set up by the Minnesota Advocates for Human Rights, and with material in English and Russian, is a forum for information, advocacy, and change, promoting women's human rights in the countries of Central and Eastern Europe and the Commonwealth of Independent States (CIS), Mongolia, and the UN Protectorate of Kosovo. Information includes research and reports, law and policy material, and training manuals, covering the issues of domestic violence, trafficking, sexual violence, and sexual harassment. It also has links to country-specific pages from the region.

United Nations Development Fund for Women (UNIFEM), 304 East 45th Street, 15th floor, New York, NY 10017 USA, tel: +1 212 906 6400, website: http://www.unifem.org/gender_issues/violence_against_women

With material available in English, French, and Spanish, UNIFEM's Violence Against Women web portal is a useful starting point for undertaking research into this issue. Materials available include facts and figures, resources, and a link to UNIFEM's Trust Fund to Eliminate VAW (the only multilateral grant-making mechanism that supports local, national, and regional efforts to combat violence).

UNESCAP Violence Against Women, Gender and Development Section, United Nations Economic and Social Commission for Asia and the Pacific, 6th Floor, Block A, United Nations Building, Rajdamnern Nok Avenue, Bangkok 10200, Thailand, tel: 662 288 1572, email: gad@un.org, website: http://www.unescap.org/esid/GAD/Issues/Violence/index.asp

The Gender and Development Section at UNESCAP works towards gender equality and women's empowerment in the Asia Pacific region. This section of the website contains resources such as statistics, publications, and reports on violence against women in the region.

'We Can' South Asia Regional Campaign, c/o Oxfam (India) Trust, C 28-29 Qutub Institutional Area, New Delhi 110 016, India, email: endvaw@gmail.com, website: http://www.wecanendvaw.org/index.htm

'We Can' is a growing coalition of civil-society groups, organisations, and individuals who have joined efforts to end violence against women in six countries of South Asia. In Bangladesh, Sri Lanka, India, Nepal, and Afghanistan the focus on the campaign is on domestic violence, while in Pakistan the emphasis is on honour killing. Through community mobilisation programmes, the campaign seeks to achieve: a fundamental shift in attitudes and beliefs that support violence against women; a collective and visible stand against violence against women; and a range of local, national, and regional alliances to address the issue of violence against women.

White Ribbon Campaign, 365 Bloor Street East, Toronto, Ontario, Canada M4W 3L4, tel: (416) 920-6684, email: info@whiteribbon.ca, website: http://www.whiteribbon.ca

The White Ribbon Campaign is an educational organisation that aims to encourage reflection and discussion that leads to personal and collective action among men to speak out against violence against women.

Index

men and boys
  income-generation opportunities 51
  neglected by relief agencies 50−1
  WOMANKIND work with 4−5
men, working with on GBV in El Salvador
  87−9
  the Masculinities Programme 90−1
  masculinities workshops 91−4
  risk analysis 94−5
Mexico, femicide 32, 35
Middle East, backlash to 'war on terror'
  154
migration, exposes women to violence 30
Millennium Development Goals (MDGs)
  22, 123, 156
  omission of VAW from 11
  threatened by GBV xvii, 1
Minimum Standards for Education in
  Emergencies 123−4, 125, 130, 161
  Guidance Note on 'Assessment Code
    of Ethics' 124
  recommendation for code of conduct
    for teachers 124
'missing women', South Asia 97, 155

Namibia, issue of male violence 116−17
Nepal
  Bimla's case 138
  Change Makers 99, 104
  Niru, a trafficked woman 134−5
  Oxfam's anti-trafficking work 137−9
  rescue of women gives cause for
    concern 135−6
Nicaragua, femicides 26, 28, 29
Nkyinkyim project, Ghana, and
  COMBATS 6

Oath of Malicounda-Bambara 75, 76
organisations, resources 182−7
Oxfam GB
  anti-trafficking work in Nepal 137−9
  focus on five key aims 133
  poverty, rights and trafficking
    women 133−6
  research, 'The Cost of Survival' 136
  support for Naripokkho 137
  working against trafficking of
    women 136−7

Pakistan, *Apna Faisla*, video song, 'We Can'
  campaign 103
parabolic solar cookers 46, 156
Paris Declaration of Aid Effectiveness
  (2005) 156
patriarchal legislation and controls 143−4

ostensibly to protect women 143
patriarchal societies 32−3
  imposing cycles of GBV 29
Peru 10
  DEMUS xxii, 7, 8
polygamy, in Cambodian society 58
power, gender inequality and violence
  against women 102
Program H, Latin America and India 114
Project Against Domestic Violence
  (PADV), Cambodia 56, 64−6
  appropriate interventions 61−2
  awareness-raising campaigns 64−5
  domestic violence as a public issue
    64−5
  a human rights issue 65−6
property grabbing xiii, xv
property grabbing, in Africa 14−23
  community sensitisation needed 22
  empirical evidence 18−20
  form of gender-based violence
    14−15, 22
  and HIV and AIDS 15−16
  responses to 20−1, 22
property rights, women's, erosion of
  customary norms and practice 16−17
public education campaigns 158

rape 8, 45, 154−5, 161
  part of war and conflict xvi, 43−4
  strategy for genocide/ethnic
    cleansing 44
  under the Rome Statute xviii
Red Feminista 35, 36, 41n, 42n, 160
Refugees International, 'culture of
  silence' in peacekeepers deplored 161
refugees, prevented from working outside
  the camps 48
religious fundamentalism, opposes
  efforts to tackle GBV 154−5
repatriation and return
  finding market needs of destination
    community 49−50
  and income-generating activities 52
  many returnees unaccompanied
    women with children 50
rescue and rehabilitation 143−4, 146
research and advocacy, Central America
  36
research methodology, resources 174−5
Rwandan genocide, systematic rape 44

schools
  advantage for girls in conflict
    situations 122

may create risks for girls 121
seed capital and microcredit 73
Senegal xx
  the Tostan programme 71–7
service providers, facilitate impunity
  33–4
sex industry, lacks labour/trade rights 147
sex work, different realities of trafficked
  women 144–9
  Farzana's story 144–7
  Monica's story 147–9
  Sofia's story, dealing with HIV 147
sex workers' organisation and action 151–3
  challenges 151–2
  NGOs vs. sex workers' interventions
    152
  self regulatory boards 152–3
sexual harassment xiv, 106, 122
  of girls in sub-Saharan schools 107
sexual minorities, resources 175–6
sexual violence xv
  in conflict 43–4
  during fuel/firewood collection 44–6
  and exploitation of girls at school,
    worldwide phenomenon 121
  in post-conflict settings 43
Shakti Shamuha, Nepal 134–5, 140n
Sierra Leone
  Classroom Assistant interviews
    128–9
  IRC supports education for Liberian
    refugees 125–6
  success of Classroom Assistant
    programme 127
16 days of Activism campaign 9, 10, 160
South Africa
  Gender Advocacy Programme (GAP)
    6, 9
  Opening Our Eyes, training manual
    for teachers 115
South Asia xvii
  gender realities 101–2
  'Let's Talk Men' project 114
  'missing women' 97, 155
  trafficking of women xiv, xix,
    xxii–xxiii
  transforming power in relationships
    97–104
  withdrawal of girls from school 109
  see also Bangladesh; India; Nepal
Sri Lanka xvi
  work of Geetha and the Affected
    Woman's Forum 103–4
state impunity, challenged at international
  level 34, 37

states, lobbied by WK and partners to
  fulfil promises 10–11
Stern Review (UK), impacts of climate
  change on vulnerable women 156
Sudan 79, 83
  FGC committees set up 78
  male facilitators encouraged women
    to speak out 82
  women aware of other practices and
    options 84
Swaziland Positive Living (SWAPOL) 21

Tanzania, rape in refugee camps 45
teachers
  attitudes to women in schools 128
  projects to raise awareness of gender
    violence in schools 114–15
  usually local community members
    122–3
  violence by 115
technologies, new, affecting GBV 155
Thailand
  Karen refugees 52
  restriction on refugees' freedom of
    movement 48
  traffickers and Burmese refugees 51
Tostan experience 71–7, 83
  confronting FGC 74
  follow-up provisions 73–4
  indigenous strategy for political
    change 77
  national debate and grassroots
    dissemination 76–7
  participatory orientation 72
  the turning point 74–6
trafficking xix
  all situations time-bound 146
  becomes redundant in new scenario
    143
  definitions 141–2
  realities of anti-trafficking work
    144–9
  resources 176–7
  should process or outcome be
    addressed 148
trafficking of women xxi–xxii
  anti-trafficking work in Nepal 137–9
  Oxfam GB working against 136–7
  poverty and rights 133–6
  in South Asia xiv, xix, xxii–xxiii
'transactional' sexual relationships 51,
  109, 126